FAST AND FABULOUS
COOKBOOK

NEW ENGLISH LIBRARY

For information about the Weight Watchers Classroom Programme, contact: Weight Watchers U.K. Limited, 11–12 Fairacres, Dedworth Road, Windsor, Berkshire SL4 4UY. Telephone: Windsor (95) 856751.

First published in the USA in 1983 by New American Library.

First published in Great Britain in 1984 by New English Library.

This paperback edition first published in 1986 by New English Library.

NEL Books are published by
New English Library,
Mill Road, Dunton Green,
Sevenoaks, Kent.
Editorial office: 47 Bedford Square, London WC1B 3DP.

Jacket photograph by Barry Bullough

Colour section photographs by David Rudkin

Typeset by South Bucks Photosetters Limited

Printed in Great Britain by
Richard Clay (The Chaucer Press) Ltd,
Bungay, Suffolk

British Library C.I.P.

ISBN 0 450 38986 1

CONTENTS

A NOTE FROM JEAN NIDETCH

Dear Reader,

I often think the most appropriate logo for our times would be the face of a clock, for these days most people lead frantically busy lives. The daily juggling acts of home/family/job/school are placing more pressure on us than ever. Of course, this affects the amount of time and effort you can afford to put into the challenges of meal preparation. That's true not only for women, but also for men who help more and more at home these days. Even youngsters want to know how to cook easy meals, as they often prepare their own meals either at home or when living on their own.

To help the busy cook prepare first-rate meals, recipes need to offer two main ingredients: ease of preparation and a relatively short cooking time. Of course, the third essential 'ingredient' is help in making only a moderate addition to the total calorie count of each day's food.

All of these factors have been blended into the recipes in our Fast and Fabulous Cookbook. We have heard your requests for help and here is our answer: a cookbook that suggests dishes which are not only figure conscious, but time conscious too. These dishes can be prepared in a minimum of time – so easily that even a novice can toss them off – and with such bewitching results that family and friends will be convinced you are a kitchen magician.

You will find simple but tasty recipes for almost any occasion, recipes that not only call for simple cookery, but, in some cases, for no cookery at all and recipes to use for hosting without hassle, even at the last minute. Whether you live alone or with your family, we believe you owe it to yourself to be free of unnecessary – and unnecessarily tempting – time in the kitchen.

For more than two decades, the Weight Watchers Organisation has been dedicated to the belief that every human being has the right to a truly rewarding lifestyle, and that weight control is an important factor in being able to feel good about yourself. That is the philosophy which underlies our famous Food Plan, our self-management plan, and the group support offered in all our meetings around the world. And that dedication is a major ingredient in every one of our best-selling cookbooks.

We are confident that this book will be another valuable friend in your kitchen and that these dishes will add to your enjoyment of life.

Jean Nidetch

Jean Nidetch

Founder
Weight Watchers International

INTRODUCTION

There are many reasons for wanting to lose weight. Some people wish to improve their appearance, while others may be trying to improve their health. But we are united in that most of us have little time for shopping and preparing food, and very often little inclination.

The problem with slimming is that it can easily turn into a vicious circle of starvation, followed by periods of eating quickly prepared and highly calorific convenience foods, simply because we know no better. This book was created to prove that there is another way of eating tasty food without piling on the pounds!

The Weight Watchers Organisation has long advocated that weight control should be a question of balance and attitude to food rather than of deprivation, and in this book we show you that you can eat well, control your weight and avoid slaving over a hot stove for hours on end!

Whether you are on your own, cooking for your family or entertaining guests, the secret lies in carefully planned advance preparation (see our Cooking for the Freezer section), resulting in the minimum of work before mealtimes.

The Weight Watchers Food Plan, on which the recipes in this book are based, is designed to combine a low calorie intake with all the necessary protein, vitamins, minerals and dietary fibre (roughage) required for good health. What's more, it's constantly being updated to take into account the very latest developments in the field of nutrition. Our recipes are perfect examples of modern cooking at its best: unfussy, well-balanced, nutritious and tasty.

The record of Weight Watchers in helping hundreds of thousands of people to lose weight and maintain their weight loss is unparalleled. A worldwide organisation, we have some 2000 weekly classes in the United Kingdom alone. Our qualified lecturers have themselves been successful members of Weight Watchers, so they know exactly how their members feel.

If you are counting calories in order to maintain your ideal weight, remember that you should aim for approximately 1500 a day if you are a woman and 1800 if you are a man or a teenager. If you wish to lose weight, you should reduce your intake to between 1000 and 1200 calories a day; 1500 if you are a man or teenager.

If you have any doubts at all about your health, you should consult your doctor before embarking on a 1000 calorie a day regime. Aim for a loss of a maximum of 2 pounds a week. It is far better to lose a small amount happily and steadily than to aim for more and end up feeling unwell, possibly returning to your former eating habits for comfort!

Finally, remember to spread your food allowance over three meals a day and always maintain a balanced and varied diet. Try to keep in mind these two important points and, with the help of this book, you'll soon find that you're losing weight in the nicest way possible. Our guess is that you will soon learn to use the time saved in the kitchen for far more exciting pursuits!

5

GENERAL INFORMATION

We include small amounts of sugar and honey in many of our recipes, but if you prefer you may use artificial sweeteners.

———— ☆ ☆ ————

Use lean meat without fat. Roast and grill on a rack and discard the juices that drain off. Skin on poultry is a source of concentrated fat and should be removed whenever possible.

———— ☆ ☆ ————

Meat shrinks when it is cooked. As a guideline, 4oz of raw meat yields approximately 3oz when cooked.

———— ☆ ☆ ————

Non-stick cookware makes it possible to cook without fat.

———— ☆ ☆ ————

You can use micro-wave ovens for many of our recipes. As there is no one standard that applies to all makes of micro-wave ovens, you will have to experiment with your own unit and follow the manufacturer's advice for timing.

———— ☆ ☆ ————

When buying margarine or oil, choose those high in polyunsaturates.

———— ☆ ☆ ————

Fish may be fresh, frozen or canned in oil, brine or tomato sauce. Drain well before weighing.

———— ☆ ☆ ————

Buy fresh, frozen, dried or canned fruit or fruit juice, without sugar added.

———— ☆ ☆ ————

Buy fresh or frozen vegetables and cook briskly in small amounts of water, or bake wrapped in foil. Scrape root vegetables sparingly since most of the nutrients and vitamins lie just under the skin.

Carefully weigh and measure all the ingredients in these recipes. Accurate weighing leads to good weight control for yourself. Use standard measuring jugs and spoons and a good dietary scale. Teaspoon and tablespoon measurements should be level.

FAST AND FUN

You don't have to spend endless time in the kitchen to enjoy good food. Now that so many cooks also work outside the home, they find that they need ideas for dishes which can be prepared in minutes, rather than hours. Meals must be tempting and nutritious, too, and appeal to all the family. Difficult? Not if you learn the tricks of combining quickly cooked fresh foods with storecupboard ingredients and lots of fruit and vegetables. Choose the small cuts of poultry, such as chicken portions, and make the most of fish fillets, eggs and liver. Reserve cold cooked meat and poultry for our delicious hot open sandwiches (pages 20 and 23). Use the luxury canned vegetables such as asparagus spears and artichoke hearts to prepare splendid soups with very little effort.

Cooking techniques help, too, in the race against the clock. Small pieces of meat and vegetables may be quickly sauteed and then simmered for a few minutes with stock, herbs and flavourings. The grill is a good friend when time is limited, but for the quickest way to a complete meal, borrow from the Chinese and try Oriental Beef and Vegetable Stir-Fry (page 24). Delicately flavoured with ginger and sherry, no one will guess that you cooked it in less than 15 minutes!

Breakfasts

Bacon-Corn Fritters
Cheese and Tomato Toast
French Toast with
  Mushrooms

Soups and Starters

Cream of Artichoke Soup
Cream of Asparagus Soup
Creamy Tomato-Vegetable
  Soup

Mushroom Saute
Orange Rice
Sauteed Tomatoes
Shrimp and Pasta Soup
Vegetable Risotto

Main Dishes

Cheesy Vegetable Pasta
Chicken and Chick Peas
Chicken Cordon Bleu
Chicken with Hot Peanut
  Sauce

Curried Aubergine and
    Lamb Stew
Curried Livers in Wine
    Sauce
Grilled Ham and Cheese
    with Mustard Dressing
Grilled Fish with Wine
    Sauce
Hot Open Roast Beef
    Sandwich
Hot Open Turkey Sandwich
'Lemon Butter' Baked Sole
Monte Cristo Sandwich
Oriental Beef and
    Vegetable Stir-Fry
Parmesan Chicken
Potato-Carrot Fritters
Prawn Supreme
Spiced Vegetable-Egg Bake
'Waldorf' Chicken Salad

Vegetables

Bacon-Flavoured Corn
    Chowder
Braised Sweet-and-Sour
    Red Cabbage
Cauliflower Polonaise
Cauliflower and Carrot Stir-
    Fry
Courgette and Corn Saute
Courgette and Apple Saute
Oriental Vegetable Stir-Fry
Pan-Fried Marrow
Sweet-and-Sour Spinach-
    Mushroom Salad

Desserts

Crunchy Pineapple Dessert
Hot Fruit Compote with
    Coconut Topping
Marmalade-Glazed Fruit
    Kebabs

Dressings and Toppings

Bilberry Topping
Chocolate Topping
Mixed Fruit Chutney
Pepper Relish
Pineapple Topping
Spicy Tomato Sauce
Sweet-and-Sour Barbecue
    Sauce

Bacon-Corn Fritters

3 oz (90 g) drained canned sweetcorn

3 tablespoons flour

1 egg

1 tablespoon imitation bacon bits

½ teaspoon baking powder

pinch pepper

2 teaspoons vegetable oil

Combine first 6 ingredients, stirring well. Heat oil in non-stick frying pan over moderate heat until hot but not smoking. Spoon batter into pan, forming 4 equal fritters; cook until edges bubble and fritters are browned on bottom. Turn fritters over and cook until browned on other side.

Makes 1 serving   *Per serving: 350 calories.*

Cheese and Tomato Toast

1 slice (1 oz/30 g) bread

1 oz (30 g) sliced Cheddar cheese

1 medium tomato, halved

Toast bread on one side, cover untoasted side with sliced cheese, put under grill with tomato halves skin side up. Grill until cheese is golden and bubbly. Serve at once.

Makes 1 serving.   *Per serving: 191 calories.*

French Toast with Mushrooms

1 teaspoon vegetable oil

1 egg

1 slice (1 oz/30 g) bread

4-5 button mushrooms, sliced

salt and pepper to taste

Heat oil gently in small non-stick pan. Beat egg and pour into shallow dish, put bread into egg and keep turning it until all the egg is soaked up. Cook in pan, turning once, until each side is golden brown; slide onto a plate and keep warm. Add sliced mushrooms to pan, adding salt and pepper to taste; saute, stirring all the time until mushrooms are cooked. Pile onto French toast and serve at once.

Makes 1 serving.   *Per serving: 205 calories.*

Cream of Asparagus Soup

6 asparagus spears (fresh, frozen or canned) cut into pieces

6 fl oz (180 ml) chicken stock, prepared according to package directions

½ bay leaf

pinch each pepper and ground thyme

2 teaspoons low-fat spread

2 teaspoons flour

1 oz (30 g) low-fat dry milk, reconstituted with ¼ pint (150 ml) water

If using fresh asparagus, trim away woody ends. Combine asparagus, stock and seasonings in a saucepan and bring to the boil. Reduce heat to low and let simmer until asparagus is tender, 5 to 8 minutes; remove from heat and let cool. Remove and discard bay leaf and transfer asparagus and cooking liquid to food processor or blender. Puree and set aside. Wipe the saucepan clean and heat margarine over low heat until bubbly and hot; add flour and stir to combine. Gradually stir in milk and cook, stirring constantly, until mixture is smooth and thickened; stir in asparagus puree and heat (do not boil).

Makes 1 serving.   *Per serving: 189 calories.*

Sauteed Tomatoes

| 3 teaspoons flour |
| ¼ teaspoon each salt and ground celery seed |
| pinch pepper |
| 2 very ripe medium tomatoes, cut into ½-inch (1-cm) thick slices |
| 1 tablespoon margarine |
| ½ small lettuce, shredded |

Mix flour and seasonings; dredge tomato slices in flour, coating both sides of each slice. Heat margarine in a non-stick frying pan over high heat until bubbly and hot; add tomatoes and saute, turning once, until browned on both sides. Arrange lettuce on serving plate and top with sauteed tomato slices.
Makes 2 servings.   *Per serving: 148 calories.*

Creamy Tomato-Vegetable Soup

| 2 teaspoons margarine |
| 1 tablespoon each chopped onion and celery |
| 2 oz (60 g) carrot, grated |
| 2 teaspoons flour |
| 1 teaspoon beef stock powder |
| 8 fl oz (240 ml) tomato juice |
| 4 teaspoons dry sherry |
| pinch pepper |
| 1 oz (30 g) low-fat dry milk, reconstituted with ¼ pint (150 ml) water |

Heat margarine in a saucepan over moderate heat until bubbly and hot; add onion and celery and saute until onion is transparent. Stir in carrot and saute until vegetables are tender. Sprinkle vegetables with flour and stock powder and stir until coated; gradually stir in juice and sherry and, stirring occasionally, bring mixture to the boil. Reduce heat to low, add pepper and let simmer until mixture thickens slightly, 2 to 3 minutes. Remove pan from heat and gradually stir in milk; return to low heat and simmer for 2 minutes (do not boil).
Makes 2 servings.   *Per serving: 145 calories.*

Mushroom Saute

1 tablespoon margarine

12 oz (360 g) mushrooms, sliced

1 tablespoon chopped spring onion

1 tablespoon dry white wine

¼ teaspoon salt

pinch pepper

Heat margarine in a non-stick frying pan over high heat until bubbly and hot; add mushrooms and spring onions and saute, stirring occasionally, until vegetables are lightly browned and moisture has evaporated. Add wine and cook, stirring constantly, for 1 minute; sprinkle with salt and pepper.

Makes 2 servings. *Per serving: 78 calories.*

Orange Rice

1 tablespoon margarine

2 oz (60 g) chopped celery

1 tablespoon chopped onion

8 fl oz (240 ml) orange juice

1½ oz (45 g) uncooked rice

1 teaspoon grated orange peel (optional)

¼ teaspoon salt

Heat margarine in medium saucepan over moderate heat until bubbly and hot; add celery and onion and saute, stirring occasionally, until vegetables are tender. Add remaining ingredients and bring to the boil. Reduce heat, cover and let simmer until liquid is absorbed and rice is tender, 12 to 15 minutes.

Makes 2 servings. *Per serving: 235 calories.*

Shrimp and Pasta Soup

2 oz (60 g) cooked vermicelli

1¼ pints (720 ml) chicken stock, prepared according to package directions

4 oz (120 g) shelled shrimps

1 small lettuce, shredded

3 oz (90 g) drained canned sweetcorn

2 oz (60 g) mushrooms, sliced

2 tablespoons chopped spring onions

1 teaspoon cornflour, blended with 1 tablespoon water

1 teaspoon teriyaki sauce

Cut vermicelli into 1-inch (2.5-cm) pieces and set aside. Heat stock in medium saucepan; stir in vermicelli, shrimps, lettuce, corn, mushrooms and spring onions. Reduce heat and let simmer for 5 minutes; stir in dissolved cornflour and teriyaki sauce and cook, stirring constantly, until thickened.
Makes 4 servings. *Per serving: 92 calories.*

Vegetable Risotto

2 teaspoons vegetable oil

2 tablespoons chopped onion

1 clove garlic, crushed

2 oz (60 g) mushrooms, chopped

2 oz (60 g) courgettes, diced

1 medium green pepper, seeded and cut into ½-inch (1-cm) squares

1 medium tomato, blanched, peeled, seeded and chopped

1½ oz (45 g) uncooked long-grain rice

6 fl oz (180 ml) chicken stock, prepared according to package directions

Heat oil in pressure cooker. Add onion and garlic and saute until onion is softened. Add mushrooms and courgettes and toss to combine. Add green pepper and tomato and saute for 3 minutes. Stir in rice; add stock. Cover, bring to pressure and cook at 15 lbs pressure for 5 minutes. Let pressure drop of its own accord. Open cooker and let stand uncovered for 5 minutes. Using a fork, toss risotto lightly before serving.

Makes 2 servings.   *Per serving: 205 calories.*

Cream of Artichoke Soup

2 teaspoons margarine
1 tablespoon chopped onion
½ garlic clove, crushed
4 teaspoons flour
8 fl oz (240 ml) chicken stock, prepared according to package directions
6 oz (180 g) canned artichoke hearts, chopped
½ oz (15 g) low-fat dry milk, reconstituted with 2½ fl oz (75 ml) water
pinch each salt and pepper
1 teaspoon chopped parsley

Heat margarine in medium saucepan until bubbly and hot; add onion and garlic and saute over moderate heat until onion is soft. Sprinkle with flour and stir to combine. Gradually add stock, stirring well to avoid lumps. Reduce heat to low and cook, stirring occasionally, until mixture is thickened, about 5 minutes. Add artichokes and cook, stirring constantly, for 3 minutes longer. Add milk, salt and pepper and cook until heated through (do not boil). Serve each portion sprinkled with ½ teaspoon parsley.

Makes 2 servings.   *Per serving: 115 calories.*

Chicken with Hot Peanut Sauce

1 teaspoon peanut oil

1½ teaspoons each chopped garlic and chopped and peeled ginger root

2 fl oz (60 ml) chicken stock, prepared according to package directions

2 tablespoons dry sherry

4½ teaspoons smooth peanut butter

1½ teaspoons each soy sauce and wine vinegar

½ teaspoon sesame oil

pinch each ground pepper and crushed red pepper

2 oz (60 g) skinned and boned cooked chicken breast, thinly sliced

2 oz (60 g) cooked vermicelli, hot

1½ teaspoons spring onion, chopped

Heat peanut oil in a small saucepan over high heat; add garlic and ginger root and saute briefly, about 30 seconds. Add all remaining ingredients except chicken, vermicelli and spring onions and bring to the boil. Reduce heat to low and cook, stirring constantly, until sauce is smooth and thickened, about 3 minutes; add chicken and stir to combine. Serve over hot vermicelli and sprinkle with spring onions.
Makes 1 serving.   *Per serving: 305 calories.*

'Lemon Butter' Baked Sole

1 sole fillet, 5 oz (150 g)

1½ teaspoons each margarine, melted, and freshly squeezed lemon juice

4 teaspoons flour

1½ teaspoons chopped parsley

pinch each salt, pepper and paprika

lemon wedge and parsley sprigs for garnish

Preheat oven to 375°F, 190°C, Gas Mark 5. Rinse fish in cold water, pat dry with paper towel and set aside. Mix margarine and lemon juice. Mix flour, chopped parsley, salt and pepper.

Dip fish into margarine mixture, then dredge in flour mixture; transfer to non-stick baking tin and drizzle any remaining margarine mixture over fish. Sprinkle with paprika. Bake until fish is golden brown and flakes easily when tested with a fork, 15 to 20 minutes. For a crisper texture, grill baked fish for 1 minute. Serve garnished with lemon wedge and parsley sprigs.
Makes 1 serving.   *Per serving: 241 calories.*

Curried Livers in Wine Sauce

1 teaspoon peanut or vegetable oil

½ medium green pepper, seeded and cut into 1-inch (2.5-cm) pieces

1 tablespoon chopped onion

½ small garlic clove, chopped, or pinch garlic powder

5 oz (150 g) chicken livers

¼ teaspoon curry powder

2 tablespoons dry white wine

2 tablespoons chicken stock, prepared according to package directions

½ teaspoon cornflour

pinch each salt and pepper

Heat oil in a small, non-stick frying pan; add green pepper, onion and garlic and saute until vegetables are softened (if garlic powder is used, add with curry powder). Add livers and cook, turning occasionally, until livers are browned, 5 to 7 minutes. Sprinkle mixture with curry powder and garlic powder, if used, then add wine and bring to the boil. Mix stock and cornflour; add to liver mixture and cook, stirring occasionally, until sauce is slightly thickened. Season with salt and pepper and serve.
Makes 1 serving.   *Per serving: 277 calories.*

Parmesan Chicken

2 tablespoons natural yogurt
½ oz (15 g) grated Parmesan cheese
4 oz (120 g) skinned and boned chicken breast, pounded to about ¼-inch (5-mm) thickness
1 teaspoon flour
pinch salt
pinch each garlic powder, onion powder and pepper
3 tablespoons plain dried breadcrumbs
2 teaspoons vegetable oil

Mix yogurt and cheese. Sprinkle chicken with flour and seasonings, then dip into yogurt mixture, coating both sides and using all the mixture. Dip chicken into breadcrumbs, turning to coat both sides with crumbs. Heat oil in a small non-stick frying pan; add chicken and cook, turning once, until browned on both sides.

Makes 1 serving. *Per serving: 402 calories.*

Chicken Cordon Bleu

1 teaspoon margarine
1 skinned and boned chicken breast, 4 oz (120 g), pounded to ⅛-inch (3-mm) thickness
1 slice boiled ham and 1 slice Emmental cheese (½ oz (15 g) each)
2 teaspoons plain dried breadcrumbs

Heat half the margarine in a small frying pan over moderate heat until bubbly and hot; add chicken and cook briefly on each side (just until no longer pink). Remove from the pan and top with ham, then cheese; starting from narrow end, roll chicken to enclose filling. Secure with toothpick and transfer to shallow individual flameproof dish; set aside. In same frying pan, heat remaining margarine over low heat until bubbly and hot; add crumbs and stir to combine. Sprinkle crumb mixture evenly over chicken roll and grill until cheese is melted, remove toothpick and serve.

Makes 1 serving. *Per serving: 288 calories.*

'Waldorf' Chicken Salad

4 oz (120 g) skinned and boned cooked chicken, cut into cubes

1 tablespoon diced celery

½ medium red eating apple, cored and cut into cubes

1½ oz (45 g) seedless green grapes, cut lengthwise into halves

2 tablespoons natural yogurt

1½ teaspoons mayonnaise

½ teaspoon chicken stock powder

1 teaspoon sunflower seeds

Place first 4 ingredients in a salad bowl. Mix yogurt, mayonnaise and stock powder well together; pour over salad and toss to coat. Sprinkle salad with sunflower seeds.
Makes 1 serving.   *Per serving: 297 calories.*

Curried Aubergine and Lamb Stew

½ teaspoon olive or vegetable oil

1 tablespoon chopped onion

½ garlic clove, chopped

3 oz (90 g) aubergine, cubed and peeled

3 oz (90 g) drained canned tomatoes, chopped

¼ teaspoon curry powder

pinch dried oregano

pinch salt

4 oz (120 g) boned cooked lamb, cut into 1-inch (2.5-cm) cubes

1 teaspoon chopped parsley

Heat oil in a medium saucepan; add onion and garlic and saute until softened. Add aubergine and saute for 2 minutes; add tomatoes, curry powder, oregano and salt and bring to the boil. Reduce heat, cover and let simmer for 15 minutes. Add lamb, cover and let simmer until thoroughly heated, about 10 minutes longer. Serve sprinkled with parsley.
Makes 1 serving.   *Per serving: 268 calories.*

Hot Open Roast Beef Sandwich

1 teaspoon margarine

2 tablespoons chopped onion

1 teaspoon flour

3 fl oz (90 ml) beef stock, prepared according to package directions

4 oz (120 g) sliced roast beef

1 slice (1 oz/30 g) rye bread, toasted

2 tomato slices

2 lettuce leaves

1 teaspoon horseradish relish

Heat margarine in small saucepan over moderate heat until bubbly and hot; add onion and saute until transparent. Sprinkle flour over mixture and stir to combine; gradually stir in stock. Cook, stirring constantly, until mixture thickens. Reduce heat to low, add roast beef and let simmer until meat is thoroughly heated. Arrange meat slices on toast. Pour gravy over meat and garnish with tomato and lettuce. Serve with horseradish.

Makes 1 serving. *Per serving: 350 calories.*

Spiced Vegetable-Egg Bake

1 teaspoon margarine

½ garlic clove, crushed

3 oz (90 g) well-drained cooked chopped broccoli (fresh or frozen)

1 teaspoon flour

4 fl oz (120 ml) skim milk

1 oz (30 g) Emmental cheese, grated

pinch salt

pinch each pepper and ground nutmeg

1 large egg

Preheat oven to 350°F, 180°C, Gas Mark 4. Heat margarine in a small non-stick frying pan until bubbly and hot; add garlic and saute for 1 minute. Remove and discard garlic clove. Add broccoli to pan and cook over medium heat, stirring constantly, for 1 to 2 minutes; sprinkle with flour and stir to combine. Stirring constantly, gradually add milk and continue cooking until mixture thickens. Remove pan from heat; add cheese, salt, pepper and nutmeg and stir until thoroughly combined. Spoon mixture into individual non-stick baking tin. Break egg into small bowl. Make a depression in the centre of the broccoli mixture and carefully slide in the egg. Bake 10 to 12 minutes or until egg is done to taste.

Makes 1 serving. *Per serving: 322 calories.*

Chicken and Chick Peas

2 teaspoons flour
pinch each salt and pepper
5 oz (150 g) skinned and boned chicken breasts, cut into 3 x 1-inch (2.5-cm) pieces
1 teaspoon each margarine and olive or vegetable oil
2 oz (60 g) green pepper, chopped
1½ oz (45 g) onion, chopped
2 medium tomatoes, blanched, peeled and chopped
9 oz (270 g) drained canned chick peas
1 teaspoon chicken stock powder

Mix flour, salt and pepper in a plastic bag; add chicken and shake until pieces are coated. Mix margarine and oil in a non-stick frying pan and heat until margarine is bubbly and hot; add chicken and saute over fairly high heat until lightly browned on all sides. Remove chicken from pan and set aside. Reduce heat to medium; add green pepper and onion to pan and cook, stirring occasionally, until vegetables are tender, 1 to 2 minutes. Add tomatoes, chick peas and stock powder and stir to combine; return chicken to pan. Reduce heat to low, cover pan and let simmer until tomatoes are reduced to a puree, 10 to 15 minutes.

Makes 2 servings. *Per serving: 275 calories.*

Potato-Carrot Fritters

4½ oz (135 g) potato, peeled and grated

2 oz (60 g) carrot, grated

1 egg, lightly beaten

3 tablespoons flour

2 tablespoons buttermilk

1½ tablespoons chopped spring onion

¼ teaspoon salt

pinch garlic powder

pinch each baking powder and pepper

2 teaspoons vegetable oil

Combine all ingredients except oil. Heat oil in a non-stick frying pan over high heat until hot but not smoking. Drop potato mixture into pan by heaping tablespoons, forming 4 equal fritters; using the back of spoon, press top of each fritter to flatten slightly. Reduce heat to medium and cook until fritters are browned on bottom; turn fritters over and cook until browned on other side.

Makes 1 serving.   *Per serving: 456 calories.*

Prawn Supreme

¾ teaspoon each margarine, melted, and olive oil

½ garlic clove, chopped

pinch each salt and pepper

5 oz (150 g) shelled prawns

1½ teaspoons chopped parsley

2 lemon wedges for garnish

Preheat grill. Combine margarine, oil, garlic, salt and pepper in shallow individual flameproof baking dish; add prawns and toss to coat. Spread prawns in single layer and grill for 3 to 4 minutes; turn prawns over and grill until firm and lightly browned, 3 to 4 minutes longer. Sprinkle with parsley and garnish with lemon wedges.

Makes 1 serving.   *Per serving: 216 calories.*

Grilled Ham and Cheese with Mustard Dressing

1 slice (1 oz/30 g) rye bread, lightly toasted

2 oz (60 g) sliced boiled ham

1 oz (30 g) Emmental cheese, sliced

½ medium tomato, thinly sliced

2 teaspoons Parmesan cheese

1½ teaspoons natural yogurt

1 teaspoon French mustard

½ teaspoon chopped chives

Heat grill. Place toast in grill pan; top toast with ham, then cheese, then tomato slices. Stir together remaining ingredients; spoon dressing over tomato slices and grill until dressing bubbles and cheese is melted.
Makes 1 serving. *Per serving: 304 calories.*

Hot Open Turkey Sandwich

1 teaspoon margarine

2 tablespoons sliced mushrooms

1 teaspoon flour

3 fl oz (90 ml) chicken stock, prepared according to package directions

4 oz (120 g) sliced skinned cooked turkey

1 slice (1 oz/30 g) pumpernickel or rye bread, toasted

2 tomato slices

2 lettuce leaves

Heat margarine in small saucepan over moderate heat until hot and bubbly; add mushrooms and saute until browned. Sprinkle flour over mixture and stir to combine; gradually stir in stock. Cook, stirring constantly, until mixture thickens. Reduce heat to low, add turkey and let simmer until turkey is thoroughly heated. Arrange turkey slices on toast. Pour gravy over turkey and garnish with tomato and lettuce.
Makes 1 serving. *Per serving: 292 calories.*

Oriental Beef and Vegetable Stir-Fry

10 oz (300 g) minced beef

1 tablespoon teriyaki sauce

½ teaspoon each chopped and peeled ginger root and chopped garlic

3 oz (90 g) frozen petit pois

4 tablespoons dry sherry

6 fl oz (180 ml) beef stock, prepared according to package directions

2 teaspoons each soy sauce and cornflour

4 oz (120 g) cooked vermicelli, hot

3 oz (90 g) spring onions, chopped

Combine beef, teriyaki sauce, ginger and garlic; form into large patty and grill on rack in grill pan, turning once, until browned on both sides, about 5 minutes. Let cool slightly, then crumble. Combine beef, peas and sherry in a medium non-stick frying pan; cook, stirring constantly, for about 2 minutes. Stir in stock. Mix soy sauce and cornflour, add to beef mixture and cook, stirring constantly, until thickened. Add cooked vermicelli and toss to combine; serve sprinkled with spring onions.

Makes 2 servings. *Per serving: 453 calories.*

Monte Cristo Sandwich

1 large egg, beaten

2 fl oz (60 ml) skim milk

1 teaspoon grated Parmesan cheese

pinch freshly ground pepper

1 slice boiled ham and 1 slice Emmental cheese (1 oz (30 g) each)

2 slices (2 oz/60 g) white bread

1 teaspoon margarine

sliced pickled cucumbers for garnish

Mix egg, milk, Parmesan cheese and pepper in a shallow bowl and set aside. Place ham, then Emmental cheese on 1 slice of bread; top with remaining slice of bread. Dip sandwich into egg mixture, turning several times until as much liquid as possible has been absorbed. Heat margarine in a small non-stick frying pan until bubbly and hot; add sandwich, pouring any remaining egg mixture over bread. Cook over low heat, turning once, until brown and crisp on both sides; garnish with sliced pickled cucumbers and serve immediately

Makes 1 serving.   *Per serving: 455 calories.*

Grilled Fish with Wine Sauce

1 teaspoon margarine
1 tablespoon chopped shallots or onion
10 oz (300 g) fish fillets such as cod or haddock
pinch each salt and white pepper
1 tablespoon mayonnaise
½ teaspoon prepared mustard
2 tablespoons lemon juice
4 tablespoons dry white wine
1 tablespoon chopped parsley

Heat margarine in a small frying pan until bubbly and hot; add shallots or onion and saute briefly (do not brown). Spread shallot/onion mixture over bottom of shallow flameproof dish large enough to hold fish in single layer. Sprinkle fish with salt and pepper and place over vegetable mixture. Combine mayonnaise and mustard; spread mixture evenly over fillets, then drizzle with lemon juice. Grill 3 inches (8 cm) from heat until fish flakes easily at the touch of a fork, 8 to 10 minutes depending on thickness of the fish. Transfer fish to serving dish and keep hot. Transfer pan juices and vegetables to small pan; add wine and cook over high heat until liquid is reduced, about 3 minutes. Pour sauce over fillets; sprinkle with parsley.

Makes 2 servings.   *Per serving: 205 calories.*

Cheesy Vegetable Pasta

2 servings frozen Bechamel (white sauce) (see page 178), thawed

2 oz (60 g) Parmesan cheese, grated

½ teaspoon dried oregano

pinch garlic powder

8 oz (240 g) each broccoli and cauliflower florets, cooked

4 oz (120 g) spiral or small macaroni, cooked

Combine Bechamel, cheese, oregano and garlic powder in a medium non-stick saucepan; cook over low heat, stirring constantly until cheese is melted and mixture is thoroughly blended. Add vegetables and pasta and cook, stirring gently, until vegetables and macaroni are coated with sauce and heated through.

Makes 2 servings. *Per serving: 357 calories.*

Sweet-and-Sour Spinach-Mushroom Salad

4 oz (120 g) fresh spinach

1 teaspoon vegetable oil

1½ teaspoons each red wine vinegar and lemon juice

¾ teaspoon sugar

pinch each salt and pepper

½ teaspoon imitation bacon bits, crushed (optional)

2 oz (60 g) mushrooms, thinly sliced

1 tablespoon thinly sliced onion

Rinse spinach several times in cold water to remove all sand and grit. Trim off stems and tear leaves into uniform bite-size pieces; place on paper towels and set aside to dry. Heat oil in a small non-stick saucepan over low heat; add vinegar, lemon juice, sugar, salt and pepper and let simmer, stirring occasionally for 1 minute. Remove from heat and stir in crushed bacon bits. Transfer torn spinach to salad bowl; add mushrooms and onions and toss gently to combine. Serve with hot dressing.

Makes 2 servings. *Per serving: 48 calories.*

Courgette and Corn Saute

4 teaspoons olive oil
2 oz (60 g) onion, chopped
1 garlic clove, chopped, or ¼ teaspoon garlic powder
9 oz (270 g) courgettes, diced
9 oz (270 g) canned tomatoes
½ teaspoon each salt and basil
¼ teaspoon oregano
pinch freshly ground pepper
6 oz (180 g) drained canned sweetcorn

Heat oil in a frying pan over medium heat; add onion and garlic (or garlic powder) and saute until onion is soft. Stir in courgettes, tomatoes and seasonings, crushing tomatoes with a wooden spoon; cover and cook until courgettes are tender, about 5 minutes. Stir in corn and cook briefly until heated through.

Makes 2 servings.   *Per serving: 240 calories.*

Cauliflower Polonaise

1 small head cauliflower
8 fl oz (240 ml) water
½ teaspoon salt
1 tablespoon margarine
3 tablespoons seasoned dried breadcrumbs
1 egg, hard-boiled and chopped

Break cauliflower into florets. Bring water to the boil in a medium saucepan and add salt. Add cauliflower and return water to the boil. Reduce heat, cover and let simmer until tender-crisp, about 10 minutes; drain, transfer to a serving dish and keep hot. Melt margarine in a small non-stick frying pan; add breadcrumbs and stir until margarine has been absorbed. Sprinkle crumb mixture and chopped egg over cauliflower and toss lightly.

Makes 2 servings.   *Per serving: 179 calories.*

Pan-Fried Marrow

1½ teaspoons margarine

1 tablespoon chopped onion

9 oz (270 g) cooked marrow

pinch each salt and pepper

Heat margarine in a small non-stick frying pan until bubbly and hot; add onion and saute until golden brown. Add marrow, spreading over surface of pan; sprinkle with salt and pepper and cook, turning with a spatula, until browned on both sides.

Makes 1 serving.   *Per serving: 81 calories.*

Bacon-Flavoured Corn Chowder

2 teaspoons margarine

2 oz (60 g) celery, diced

3 oz (90 g) onion, chopped

4 teaspoons flour

12 fl oz (360 ml) skim milk

3 oz (90 g) drained canned sweetcorn

1 teaspoon imitation bacon bits, crushed

pinch each salt and powdered mustard

pinch white pepper

ground nutmeg for garnish

Heat margarine in medium saucepan over moderate heat until bubbly and hot; stir in onion and celery. Cover pan and cook until vegetables are soft, 2 to 3 minutes. Add flour and cook, stirring constantly, for 1 minute longer. Continuing to stir, gradually add milk and bring to the boil. Reduce heat and cook, stirring constantly, until mixture is smooth and thickened, 2 to 3 minutes. Add all remaining ingredients except nutmeg and continue stirring and cooking until ingredients are thoroughly combined and mixture is hot. Pour into soup bowls and garnish each portion with a pinch of nutmeg.

Makes 2 servings.   *Per serving: 204 calories.*

Cauliflower and Carrot Stir-Fry

1½ teaspoons peanut or vegetable oil

½ teaspoon sesame oil

2 oz (60 g) carrot, diagonally sliced (⅛-inch (3-mm) thick slices), blanched

½ garlic clove, chopped or pinch garlic powder

pinch ground ginger

6 oz (180 g) cauliflower florets, blanched

Heat the oils in a small non-stick frying pan over moderate heat. Add carrot, garlic (or garlic powder) and ginger and stir-fry briefly, about 1 minute. Reduce heat, cover and cook for about 3 minutes (carrot slices should still be crisp). Add cauliflower and stir-fry until tender-crisp, about 5 minutes longer.

Makes 2 servings.   *Per serving: 63 calories.*

Braised Sweet-and-Sour Red Cabbage

4 teaspoons low-fat spread

1 medium eating apple, peeled, cored and chopped

1 tablespoon chopped onion

6 oz (180 g) shredded red cabbage

4 tablespoons red wine

1 oz (30 g) sultanas

2 teaspoons white vinegar

1 teaspoon brown sugar, firmly packed

¼ teaspoon salt

Heat half the margarine in a non-stick frying pan over moderate heat until bubbly and hot; add apple and onion and saute, stirring occasionally, until onion is transparent, 1 to 2 minutes. Stir in all remaining ingredients except margarine. Reduce heat; cover and let simmer, stirring occasionally, for 15 to 20 minutes or until cabbage is done to taste (if mixture becomes too dry, add 1-2 tablespoons water). Transfer to a serving dish and stir in remaining margarine.

Makes 2 servings.   *Per serving: 148 calories.*

Oriental Vegetable Stir-Fry

1½ teaspoons peanut oil

1 tablespoon spring onion, diagonally sliced

½ garlic clove, crushed

4 oz (120 g) celery, diagonally sliced (thin slices)

3 oz (90 g) mange-tout (stem ends and strings removed)

2 oz (60 g) red pepper, diced

3 fl oz (90 ml) water

2 teaspoons soy sauce

1 teaspoon cornflour

pinch ground ginger

pinch each salt and pepper

Heat oil over high heat in a frying pan or wok; add spring onions and garlic and stir-fry for 1 minute. Add remaining vegetables and cook, stirring quickly and frequently, for 2 minutes. Mix water, soy sauce and cornflour; pour mixture over vegetables. Add seasonings and cook, stirring constantly, until peas are tender-crisp and sauce thickens.
Makes 2 servings.   *Per serving: 59 calories.*

Courgette and Apple Saute

4 teaspoons margarine

12 oz (360 g) courgettes, sliced

2 oz (60 g) onion, thinly sliced

2 medium apples, peeled, cored and thinly sliced

¼ teaspoon salt

pinch each ground cinnamon and freshly ground pepper

Heat margarine in a frying pan over medium heat until bubbly and hot; add courgettes and onion and saute until tender-crisp, about 4 minutes. Add remaining ingredients, cover and cook just until apples soften slightly, about 5 minutes.
Makes 2 servings.   *Per serving: 167 calories.*

Hot Fruit Compote with Coconut Topping
Fruit Mixture

1 oz (30 g) dried apricots

1 large stoned prune, cut in half

½ oz (15 g) sultanas

1 tablespoon lemon juice

1 teaspoon brown sugar, firmly packed

pinch ground allspice

½ medium eating apple, cored, peeled and chopped

1½-2 teaspoons water (optional)

Topping

4 digestive biscuits, made into fine crumbs

2 teaspoons margarine, softened

1 teaspoon desiccated coconut

To Prepare Fruit Mixture: Combine first 5 ingredients in small non-stick pan; cook over low heat until sugar melts and fruit is plumped. Add apple. Add water if necessary; cover and let simmer until apple is tender. Divide mixture between 2 individual ovenproof dishes.

To Prepare Topping: Mix all ingredients for topping. Sprinkle an equal amount of crumb mixture over each portion of fruit mixture and grill until topping is browned, about 2 to 3 minutes.

Makes 2 servings.   *Per serving: 270 calories.*

Crunchy Pineapple Dessert

4 oz (120 g) canned pineapple chunks

2 fl oz (60 ml) natural yogurt

½ teaspoon each vanilla flavouring and brown sugar

Preheat grill. Puree pineapple in blender until smooth; pour into a small flameproof dish. Mix yogurt and flavouring, spoon mixture over fruit. Sprinkle yogurt mixture with sugar and grill until sugar is melted, bubbly and slightly crisp, about 3 minutes; serve immediately.
Makes 1 serving.   *Per serving: 80 calories.*

Marmalade-Glazed Fruit Kebabs

4 oz (120 g) canned pineapple chunks; drain and reserve juice

1½ oz (45 g) seedless green grapes

1½ teaspoons low-calorie orange marmalade

1 teaspoon desiccated coconut

On to each of two 12-inch (30-cm) kebab skewers, thread half the pineapple chunks and half the grapes, alternating ingredients; transfer kebabs to flameproof dish just large enough to hold them in one layer. Mix reserved juice with marmalade and heat until marmalade is melted; spoon mixture evenly over fruit. Sprinkle fruit on each skewer with ½ teaspoon coconut and grill until coconut is browned, 1 to 2 minutes.
Makes 1 serving.   *Per serving: 111 calories.*

Bilberry Topping

4 oz (120 g) fresh or frozen bilberries

1 tablespoon water

1 teaspoon sugar

¼ teaspoon cornflour mixed with 1½ teaspoons water

Mix bilberries, water and sugar in a small pan and bring to the boil. Stir in mixed cornflour and cook, stirring constantly, until mixture thickens, about 2 minutes. Pour into small bowl and let cool. Serve at room temperature or cover and refrigerate until chilled.

Makes 1 serving.   *Per serving: 88 calories.*

Chocolate Topping

1 teaspoon each cocoa and sugar

½ teaspoon cornflour

½ oz (15 g) low-fat dry milk, reconstituted with 2½ fl oz (75 ml) water

3-4 drops vanilla flavouring

Mix cocoa, sugar and cornflour in a small saucepan. Gradually stir in milk. Stirring constantly, bring mixture to the boil and continue cooking until thickened, about 2 minutes; stir in vanilla. Pour into a small bowl and cover with plastic wrap to prevent skin forming. Let cool and serve at room temperature or refrigerate and serve chilled.

Makes 1 serving.   *Per serving: 95 calories.*

Pineapple Topping

2 oz (60 g) canned crushed pineapple

¼ teaspoon cornflour

1½ teaspoons water

½ teaspoon sugar

Heat the pineapple gently in a small saucepan. Mix cornflour with water and sugar. Add to the pineapple, bring to the boil and cook, stirring until thickened, about 2 minutes. Pour into a small bowl and let cool. Serve at room temperature or cover and refrigerate until chilled.

Makes 1 serving.   *Per serving: 34 calories.*

Mixed Fruit Chutney

1 oz (30 g) dried apricots, diced

1 oz (30 g) sultanas

2 tablespoons each chopped onions and water

1½ teaspoons firmly packed brown sugar

1 teaspoon cider vinegar

¼ teaspoon ground cinnamon

pinch salt

Combine all ingredients in a small saucepan and bring to the boil. Reduce heat, cover and let simmer until apricots are tender and mixture thickens, 15 to 20 minutes. Serve immediately or let cool, transfer to a container, cover and refrigerate until ready to serve.

Makes 2 servings.   *Per serving: 79 calories.*

Pepper Relish

2 oz (60 g) each red and green peppers, diced

1 tablespoon chopped onion

1 teaspoon cider vinegar

½ teaspoon granulated sugar

½ bay leaf

¼ teaspoon salt

pinch pepper

Combine all ingredients in a small saucepan and bring to a slow boil over moderate heat. Reduce heat to low, cover and let simmer, stirring occasionally, until peppers are soft, about 15 minutes. Remove from heat and let cool. Transfer relish to container, cover and refrigerate. Remove bay leaf before serving.

Makes 2 servings.   *Per serving: 12 calories.*

Spicy Tomato Sauce

1 teaspoon vegetable oil

2 tablespoons each chopped onion and green pepper

9 oz (270 g) canned tomatoes, crushed

½ small chilli pepper, finely chopped

pinch garlic powder

pinch salt

1-2 drops hot pepper sauce

Heat oil in a small saucepan over moderate heat. Add onion and pepper and saute until onion is transparent. Reduce heat, add remaining ingredients and let simmer until sauce thickens slightly, 5 to 6 minutes. Use immediately or let cool, transfer to container, cover and refrigerate until ready to use.

Makes 1 serving.   *Per serving: 81 calories.*

Sweet-and-Sour Barbecue Sauce

4 oz (120 g) canned sliced peaches

1 tablespoon wine vinegar

2 teaspoons apricot jam

1½ teaspoons teriyaki or soy sauce

½ teaspoon firmly packed brown sugar

pinch garlic powder

Combine all ingredients in a blender and puree until smooth. Pour mixture into a small non-stick saucepan and bring to the boil. Reduce heat and cook, stirring occasionally, until thickened, about 5 minutes. Use immediately or let cool slightly, then transfer to a container, cover and refrigerate for future use.

Makes 2 servings.   *Per serving: 53 calories.*

COOKING ON A SHOESTRING

The days of really cheap food have gone for ever, but skilful cooks are able to produce delicious, imaginative meals *and* stay within their budget! Careful shopping is half the battle. Some inexpensive items are good value, but others – such as meat with a lot of fat which you have to cut away – turn out to be false economies. Lean lamb and stewing steak are usually reliable, and liver and hearts, with very little waste, are good buys. Do try Spanish-Style Tripe (page 66), a new look for an old favourite.

Bulk buying is often recommended as a way of keeping costs down, but you have to be sure that you're getting something you really can use up. If not, you can share bulk purchases with a friend!

Frozen foods have given us such year-round variety that we sometimes overlook the sound money-saving principle of buying fruit and vegetables in season. It always pays to haunt the greengrocer's during the summer when there may be a glut of soft fruit, tomatoes and courgettes. Perfect for making lots of desserts, soups and sauces at bargain prices. Or, be your own frozen foods specialist and fill up the freezer for the winter!

Breakfasts

Banana-Honey Breakfast
   Drink
Hot Cereal
Savoury Grill

Soups and Starters

Beetroot and Orange Soup
Carrots Au Gratin
Cauliflower and Tomato
   Soup
Cream of Celery Soup
Creamy Cauliflower Soup
Easy Vegetable-Barley
   Soup
Onion Popovers
Potato Soup
Smoky Mac Pate
Soft 'Cream Cheese' with
   Herbs and Garlic
Tomato, Cauliflower and
   Tarragon Soup

Main Dishes

All-in-One Fish Dish
Bacon-Liver Burgers
Bacon-Stuffed Hearts
Baked Kipper Loaf
Barbecued Butter Beans
Beef Risotto
Beef Sausage Rissoles
Calico Beans
Carrot Pudding
Cheese and Vegetable
  Pudding
Cheese, Onion and Potato
  Layer
Cheesy Fish Pie
Cheesy Pasta
Chicken Liver Croustades
  with Caper Sauce
Chicken with Buckwheat
Chilli-Cheese Corn Fritters
Chilli Con Carne
Creamy Pasta with Broccoli
Crispy Cauliflower
Curried Cheese Crunch
Curried Chicken
Danish Haddock
Fruity Lamb Curry
Fruity Lamb Pilaf
Greek-Style Lamb
Grilled White Fish with
  Tomato and Mushroom
  Sauce
Hawaiian Liver
Khitchari (Bean Kedgeree)
Lentil Curry
Liver Baked in Foil
Liver-Stuffed Marrow
Main-Meal Kidney-Bean
  and Ham Soup

Main-Meal Lamb and Split
  Pea Soup
Main-Meal Minestrone
Marrow Hot Pot
Mexican Liver
Mild Curried Chicken with
  Banana Rice
Mustard Cod
Norfolk Cheese Dumplings
  in Tomato Soup
Onion and Cheese
  Scramble
Orange Chicken with
  Rosemary
Pan-Fried Liver with
  Vegetables
Peppered Chicken
Potato-Cheese Pie
Potato Souffle
Quick Liver, Tomato and
  Onion Saute
Rich Cheese Sauce and
  Spaghetti
Sausages with Barbecued
  Beans
Savoury Stuffed Heart
Shoulder of Lamb with
  Redcurrant Sauce
Shoulder of Lamb with
  Savoury Apricot Bake
Spanish-Style Tripe
Spiced Meatballs
Spring Hot Pot
Toad in the Hole
Traditional Tripe and
  Onions with Mashed
  Potatoes
Vegetable-Pasta Medley in
  Onion-Cheddar Sauce
Whitebait Minceur
West Indian Lamb
Yogurt-Topped Beef Pie

Vegetables and Salads

Broccoli-Stuffed Potato
Hot Potato Salad
Italian-Style Scalloped
   Potatoes
Parmesan-Topped Stuffed
   Potato

Desserts

Apricot Surprise
Blackberry Cheesecake
Bread Pudding
Brown Sugar Custard
Orange Spanish 'Cream'
Raisin-Bread Pudding
Spicy Apple Crumble
Yogurt 'Cream' Ice with
   Orange

Banana-Honey Breakfast Drink

1 egg
8 fl oz (240 ml) chilled skim milk
1 tablespoon bran
1 teaspoon wheatgerm
1 teaspoon honey
½ medium banana, chopped

Place all ingredients in blender container and liquidise.
Makes 1 serving.   *Per serving: 250 calories.*

Savoury Grill

1 slice (1 oz/30 g) bread
1½ teaspoons yeast extract
2½ oz (75 g) cottage cheese
1 tomato, sliced

Toast bread and spread with yeast extract. Top with cottage
cheese and sliced tomato. Place under medium grill for 4 to 5
minutes or until cheese mixture is heated through.
Makes 1 serving.   *Per serving: 253 calories.*

Cauliflower and Tomato Soup

18 oz (540 g) cauliflower, chopped

4 tablespoons tomato puree

6 fl oz (180 ml) water

¾ pint (450 ml) chicken stock, prepared according to package directions

salt and pepper to taste

3 oz (90 g) button mushrooms, chopped

1 teaspoon basil

1 tablespoon chopped parsley

Place all ingredients in a large saucepan. Bring to the boil, cover pan and cook for 15 to 20 minutes or until vegetables are tender. Drain, reserve liquid; put liquid and 2 tablespoons of cooked vegetables in blender and puree until smooth. Return to saucepan with rest of vegetables and reheat before serving.
Makes 4 servings.   *Per serving: 38 calories.*

Tomato, Cauliflower and Tarragon Soup

3 oz (90 g) onion, chopped

¾ pint (450 ml) water

8 oz (240 g) cauliflower florets

7 oz (210 g) canned tomatoes

8 teaspoons white wine

1 teaspoon dried tarragon

1 tablespoon sugar

salt and pepper to taste

Blanch onion in a little water for 2 to 3 minutes. Add all remaining ingredients. Bring to the boil and simmer for 45 minutes. Rub through a sieve or puree in blender. Adjust seasoning.
Makes 2 servings.   *Per serving: 82 calories.*

Hot Cereal

¾ oz (20 g) instant oat cereal

1 tablespoon bran

2 teaspoons brown sugar

1 oz (30 g) raisins

¼ pint (150 ml) skim milk

Mix dry ingredients together in cereal bowl. Heat milk to just below boiling, add to bowl and stir well.
Makes 1 serving.   *Per serving: 253 calories.*

Smoky Mac Pate

4 oz (120 g) smoked mackerel fillet

5 oz (150 g) low-fat soft cheese

2 tablespoons lemon juice

2 tablespoons finely chopped onion

black pepper to taste

4 slices (4 oz/120 g) bread, toasted

Skin mackerel and flake; add cheese, lemon juice, onion and pepper. Blend all ingredients together until they form a smooth paste, spoon into individual dishes. Chill thoroughly and serve with slices of toast cut into fingers.
Makes 4 servings.   *Per serving: 463 calories.*

Carrots au Gratin

4 teaspoons margarine

3 teaspoons flour

6 fl oz (180 ml) skim milk

12 oz (360 g) cooked fresh or frozen carrots, sliced

2 oz (60 g) Cheddar cheese, grated

2 tablespoons plain dried breadcrumbs

Heat half the margarine in a saucepan until bubbly and hot; add flour and stir to combine. Gradually stir in milk and bring to the boil. Reduce heat and cook, stirring constantly, until mixture is smooth and thickened. Add carrots and cheese and cook, stirring constantly, until cheese is melted. Remove from heat. Preheat oven to 375°F, 190°C, Gas Mark 5. Divide carrot mixture between 2 individual ovenproof dishes. Melt remaining margarine in a small non-stick frying pan. Add breadcrumbs and stir until thoroughly combined. Sprinkle over the carrot mixture, dividing evenly, and bake until topping is browned, 20 to 25 minutes.

Makes 4 servings. *Per serving: 242 calories.*

Easy Vegetable-Barley Soup

3 oz (90 g) green cabbage, coarsely chopped
2 oz (60 g) onion, coarsely chopped
2 oz (60 g) each sliced celery, carrot and courgettes
2 oz (60 g) cut green beans
4 oz (120 g) canned tomatoes
4 teaspoons margarine
2 oz (60 g) mushrooms, sliced
18 fl oz (540 ml) beef stock, prepared according to package directions
8 oz (240 g) cooked medium barley
1 small bay leaf
pinch each thyme, salt and freshly ground pepper

Chop cabbage finely in a food processor or vegetable mill. Transfer to a large bowl. Repeat with onion, celery, carrot, courgettes, green beans and tomatoes, chopping or shredding each vegetable separately. Heat margarine in a large saucepan until bubbly and hot; add chopped vegetables and mushrooms and cook, stirring occasionally, until cabbage begins to wilt, about 10 minutes. Add remaining ingredients and bring to the boil. Reduce heat, cover and let simmer for 30 minutes, stirring occasionally. Remove and discard bay leaf before serving.

Makes 4 servings. *Per serving: 135 calories.*

Cream of Celery Soup

2 teaspoons margarine

8 oz (240 g) celery, chopped

2 oz (60 g) onion, chopped

1 teaspoon chicken stock powder

4 teaspoons flour

8 fl oz (240 ml) skim milk

pinch white pepper

Melt margarine in non-stick saucepan, add celery, onion and stock powder and stir until combined. Cover and let simmer until vegetables are tender, 10 to 15 minutes. Sprinkle flour over vegetable mixture and cook, stirring constantly, for 1 minute; gradually stir in milk and continue to cook, stirring constantly, until mixture thickens (do not boil). Remove from heat and let cool slightly. Pour half the soup into a blender and puree on low speed until smooth; return pureed mixture to saucepan and cook, stirring, until thoroughly combined and heated through.

Makes 2 servings.   *Per serving: 135 calories.*

Onion Popovers

3 fl oz (90 ml) skim milk

1 egg

2 teaspoons finely chopped onion

1 teaspoon vegetable oil

pinch salt

2 oz (60 g) self-raising flour

Preheat oven to 400°F, 200°C, Gas Mark 6. Mix all ingredients except flour; add flour and, using electric mixer, beat until blended. Divide mixture between 4 small deep non-stick bun tins. Place on baking sheet and bake until firm and golden brown, 20 to 25 minutes. Serve warm.

Variation – Cheese Popovers: Omit onion. Add 1 teaspoon grated Parmesan cheese with the flour and proceed as directed.

Makes 2 servings.   *Per serving: 183 calories.*

Cheese Popovers per serving: 192 calories.

Soft 'Cream Cheese' with Herbs and Garlic

10 oz (300 g) cottage cheese

mixed fresh herbs as available, e.g. thyme, tarragon, chervil, chives, parsley

1 or 2 cloves garlic

3 tablespoons single cream

salt and pepper to taste

Sieve the cottage cheese. Roughly chop enough herbs to give about 1 tablespoon, then chop very finely with the garlic. Mix into the cheese, together with the cream. Add seasonings to taste. Pack into 4 small dishes; cover and leave for a few hours or overnight for the flavour to develop.

Makes 4 servings.   *Per serving: 90 calories.*

Beetroot and Orange Soup

1 lb 2 oz (540 g) cooked beetroot

9 oz (270 g) cucumber

2 tablespoons chopped spring onions

grated peel of 1 orange

4 fl oz (120 ml) orange juice

1 tablespoon chopped parsley

2 pints (1 litre 200 ml) vegetable stock, prepared according to package directions

salt and pepper to taste

8 fl oz (240 ml) natural yogurt

Peel and chop the beetroot. Peel and halve the cucumber, then scoop out the seeds and chop the flesh. Place all the vegetables in a saucepan with the finely grated orange peel and the juice, parsley, stock and seasoning. Bring to the boil and simmer for about 20 minutes. Puree in blender, adjust seasoning and chill. Mix in the yogurt, reserving 1 tablespoon, and pour soup into a tureen. Swirl remaining yogurt into the centre before serving.

Makes 6 servings.   *Per serving: 72 calories.*

Potato Soup

12 oz (360 g) potatoes, peeled and diced

8 oz (240 g) leeks, sliced in rings

approximately 1 ¼ pints (720 ml) water (enough to keep vegetables covered)

½ pint (300 ml) skim milk

1 chicken stock cube

2 tablespoons chopped fresh dill

salt and pepper to taste

2 tablespoons low-fat spread

chopped chives, parsley or dill for garnish (optional)

Cook vegetables in water until tender. Add milk, stock cube, dill, salt and pepper. Simmer for 15 to 20 minutes or until soup begins to thicken and the potatoes begin to break up. Stir in low-fat spread. Serve immediately. Garnish with chives, parsley or dill if desired.

Makes 4 servings.   *Per serving: 140 calories.*

Creamy Cauliflower Soup

8 oz (240 g) cauliflower florets, fresh or frozen

2 tablespoons onion, chopped

½ pint (300 ml) water

2 teaspoons each margarine and flour

1 teaspoon chicken stock powder

pinch ground celery seed

pinch white pepper

2 teaspoons chopped parsley to garnish

Boil 4 fl oz (120 ml) water in a saucepan and add cauliflower and onion. Return water to the boil. Reduce heat, cover and let simmer until florets are tender, about 5 to 10 minutes. Remove from heat and let cool slightly. Pour vegetables and liquid into blender or food processor and puree until smooth; set aside. Heat margarine in the same saucepan until bubbly and hot; add flour and cook, stirring constantly, for 1 minute. Stir in stock powder and remaining water and bring to the boil. Reduce heat and cook, stirring constantly, until mixture is smooth and thickened. Add pureed vegetables and seasonings to saucepan; cook over low heat, stirring constantly, until thoroughly combined and heated. Pour into soup bowls and sprinkle each portion with 1 teaspoon parsley.

Makes 2 servings. *Per serving: 80 calories.*

Norfolk Cheese Dumplings in Tomato Soup
Soup

8 oz (240 g) canned tomatoes with juice
8 fl oz (240 ml) chicken stock, prepared according to package directions
salt and pepper to taste

Dumplings

5 teaspoons self-raising flour
1 slice (1 oz/30 g) bread, made into crumbs
1 oz (30 g) Cheddar cheese, finely grated
salt and pepper to taste
pinch mixed herbs (optional)
1 egg, beaten

Place tomatoes and stock in blender container and blend until smooth. Pour into saucepan, add salt and pepper to taste, bring to boil and simmer gently. Meanwhile, prepare dumplings. Mix together flour, crumbs and ¾ oz (20 g) cheese. Add salt, pepper and herbs. Mix well and bind with egg. Shape into 4 small dumplings and add to the soup. Replace lid and simmer for 10 minutes. Sprinkle with remaining cheese before serving.

Makes 2 servings. *Per serving: 389 calories.*

Bacon-Liver Burgers

5 oz (150 g) chicken livers

1 tablespoon each chopped onion and celery

3 oz (90 g) peeled cooked potato, mashed

1½ teaspoons imitation bacon bits, crushed

pinch each salt and pepper

2 teaspoons seasoned dried breadcrumbs

1 teaspoon margarine

2 teaspoons tomato ketchup

Cook livers in a non-stick frying pan over high heat just until they lose red colour, 2 to 3 minutes; transfer to bowl and mash with a fork. Combine onion and celery in same pan; cover and cook over low heat until vegetables are soft. Add cooked vegetables, potato, bacon bits, salt and pepper to mashed livers and mix until thoroughly combined; shape mixture into two equal patties. Press patties into breadcrumbs, turning to coat both sides. Heat margarine in clean frying pan over moderate heat until bubbly and hot; add patties and cook until browned on all sides, 2 to 4 minutes. Serve with ketchup.
Makes 1 serving.   *Per serving: 354 calories.*

Curried Cheese Crunch

5 oz (150 g) cottage cheese

1 teaspoon curry powder

4 teaspoons salad cream

1 oz (30 g) sultanas

1 tablespoon finely chopped onion

1 stick celery, chopped; retain leaves

4 radishes, chopped

2-inch (5-cm) chunk cucumber, sliced

1 teaspoon toasted sesame seeds

Combine first 8 ingredients. Top with chopped celery leaves and toasted sesame seeds.
Makes 1 serving.   *Per serving: 291 calories.*

Mexican Liver

2 teaspoons flour

1 teaspoon chilli powder

5 oz (150 g) sliced beef liver, cut into 2-inch (5-cm) long strips

1 teaspoon vegetable oil

2 tablespoons chopped onion

2 oz (60 g) canned tomatoes, chopped

1½ oz (45 g) drained canned sweetcorn

¼ teaspoon salt

pinch pepper

Mix flour and chilli powder; dredge liver strips in mixture to coat, being sure to use all the mixture. Heat oil in a small non-stick frying pan over high heat; add onion and saute until transparent, about 3 minutes. Reduce heat to moderate, add liver and cook, turning once, until lightly browned on all sides; stir in tomatoes, corn, salt and pepper. Reduce heat to low, cover pan and let simmer for 10 minutes.
Makes 1 serving.   *Per serving: 375 calories.*

Cheese, Onion and Potato Layer

12 oz (360 g) potato, peeled and thinly sliced

8 oz (240 g) onion, thinly sliced

10 oz (300 g) low-fat soft cheese mixed with ¼ pint (150 ml) skim milk

salt and pepper to taste

4 teaspoons grated Parmesan cheese

4 teaspoons low-fat spread

Layer potato and onion and cheese mixture alternately in ovenproof casserole, seasoning each layer with salt and pepper and finishing with potato. Sprinkle top with Parmesan cheese. Dot with low-fat spread, bake for 1¼ to 1½ hours at 350°F, 180°C, Gas Mark 4.
Makes 2 servings.   *Per serving: 465 calories.*

Shoulder of Lamb with Savoury Apricot Bake

1 shoulder of lamb, 3 lb 8 oz to 4 lb (1 kg 680 g – 1 kg 920 g)
6 oz (180 g) dried apricot halves, soaked and chopped
12 oz (360 g) bean sprouts
4 oz (120 g) onion, sliced in rings
12 oz (360 g) cooked brown rice
8 fl oz (240 ml) chicken stock, prepared according to package directions
salt and pepper to taste

Trim lamb of excess fat. Place on rack in a baking tin, pour a little water into base of pan. Sprinkle meat with salt and pepper, cover with foil and bake in moderate oven, 350°F, 180°C, Gas Mark 4, allowing 20 minutes to the pound plus 20 minutes longer. Meanwhile mix together the apricots, bean sprouts, onion rings and rice and put into an ovenproof dish. Pour over the stock and season with salt and pepper. Cover with foil and cook alongside the lamb for the last 45 minutes of cooking time. When the lamb is cooked, lift from the oven and rest for 10 minutes before carving it into 6 lean 4-oz (120-g) servings. Serve each with a portion of the savoury apricot bake.

Makes 6 servings. *Per serving: 341 calories.*

Grilled White Fish with Tomato and Mushroom Sauce

2 teaspoons vegetable oil
2 oz (60 g) onion, finely chopped
4 oz (120 g) mushrooms, finely chopped
6 oz (180 g) tomatoes, skinned and chopped
¼ teaspoon garlic salt
pepper to taste
10 oz (300 g) fillet of white fish, skinned and boned

Heat oil in non-stick frying pan. Add onions and mushrooms and saute without browning for 2 to 3 minutes. Add tomatoes, garlic, salt and pepper and saute for a further 2 to 3 minutes. Meanwhile grill fish on rack under hot grill, turning once. Cook until fish flakes easily with a fork, approximately 10 minutes. Arrange fish on serving dish and spoon over vegetable mixture. Serve at once.

Makes 2 servings.   *Per serving: 173 calories.*

Fruity Lamb Pilaf

8 teaspoons olive oil
6 oz (180 g) Patna rice
½ pint (300 ml) chicken stock, prepared according to package directions
1 lb (480 g) cooked lean lamb, cut into small cubes
2 onions, chopped
1 clove garlic, crushed
7-8 oz (210-240 g) canned tomatoes, with juice
1 oz (30 g) currants
1 oz (30 g) sultanas
salt and pepper to taste
pinch each dried rosemary and thyme
5 fl oz (150 ml) natural yogurt

Heat 4 teaspoons oil in a heavy pan and saute rice gently until transparent. Add stock. Cover pan and cook over low heat until liquid is absorbed, about 20 minutes. Keep hot. In the meantime saute the chopped onions and crushed garlic in the remaining oil in a non-stick pan. When golden brown, add the tomatoes with juice, currants, sultanas, seasonings and herbs and simmer gently for 5 minutes. Add lamb and cook for 10 minutes, adding hot rice for last 5 minutes of cooking time. Stir in yogurt and serve at once.

Makes 4 servings.   *Per serving: 546 calories.*

Spring Hot Pot

1 lb 4 oz (600 g) stewing veal
6 oz (180 g) carrots, thinly sliced
4 oz (120 g) onion, finely chopped
2 sticks celery, thinly sliced
4 oz (120 g) mushrooms, sliced
1 tablespoon chopped parsley
1 teaspoon each chopped thyme and sage
salt and pepper
½ pint (300 ml) chicken stock, prepared according to package directions
¼ pint (150 ml) skim milk
2 teaspoons cornflour
chopped parsley to garnish

Trim the veal of any visible fat and cut into cubes. Put first nine ingredients into a pressure cooker, stir well. Close the cooker, bring to high pressure and cook for 10 minutes. Reduce pressure quickly, lift out the meat and vegetables and keep hot. Bring liquid to the boil. Add the cornflour, blended with milk and stir over low heat until thickened. Return the meat and vegetables to the sauce, heat through and check seasoning. Garnish with a little chopped parsley.

Makes 4 servings.   *Per serving: 198 calories.*

Carrot Pudding

1 lb (480 g) carrots, diced
12 oz (360 g) potatoes, peeled and diced
salt to taste
¼ pint (150 ml) skim milk
1 tablespoon finely grated onion
4 teaspoons margarine
8 oz (240 g) Cheddar cheese, grated

Place carrots and potatoes in a large saucepan; cover with water, add salt to taste, bring to the boil and cook for 8 to 10

minutes, or until vegetables are tender. Drain and mash well.
Add milk, grated onion and margarine; beat until thick and
creamy. Add half the cheese and beat again. Turn into a
flameproof dish, cover with remaining cheese and place under
a hot grill until bubbly and golden.

Makes 4 servings.   *Per serving: 365 calories.*

Chilli Con Carne

12 oz (360 g) minced beef
1 pint 4 fl oz (720 ml) water
12 oz (360 g) green pepper, seeded and chopped
4 oz (120 g) onions, chopped
2 oz (60 g) celery, chopped
1 oz (30 g) chilli pepper, seeded and chopped
½ garlic clove, crushed
8 oz (240 g) canned tomatoes, chopped with liquid
4 tablespoons tomato puree
1 tablespoon chilli powder or to taste
½ teaspoon black pepper
¼-½ teaspoon cayenne pepper or a few drops hot pepper sauce, or to taste
pinch cumin
2 cloves
1 bay leaf
salt to taste
12 oz (360 g) drained canned red kidney beans

Combine beef and 1 pint (600 ml) water in saucepan, simmer
for 15 minutes or until beef loses its red colour. Strain and
refrigerate liquid until fat congeals on top; remove fat and
discard. Set aside 6 fl oz (180 ml) liquid. Freeze remaining
liquid for later use. Combine the next 6 ingredients in
saucepan. Cook for 5 minutes. Add tomato puree, 4 fl oz (120
ml) water, seasonings, beans, reserved 6 fl oz (180 ml) liquid
and beef. Simmer for 30 minutes.

Makes 4 servings.   *Per serving: 291 calories.*

All-in-One Fish Dish

4 teaspoons vegetable oil

6 oz (180 g) onion, finely chopped

2 oz (60 g) green pepper, finely chopped

4 oz (120 g) mushrooms, sliced

15 oz canned tomatoes, chopped

1 teaspoon dill

2 tablespoons lemon juice

4 tablespoons white wine

4 x 5-oz (150-g) frozen cod steaks

12 oz (360 g) potatoes, peeled and cut into bite-size pieces

salt and pepper to taste

12 oz (360 g) cooked broccoli

Heat oil in large, deep frying pan with lid. Saute onions and peppers gently for a few minutes until onion is transparent. Add mushrooms, chopped tomatoes, dill, lemon juice and wine and simmer for 10 minutes. Add cod steaks, chopped potatoes and a little water if needed to cover the fish. Cover pan and allow to cook gently for 20 minutes. Add salt and pepper to taste. Serve with broccoli.

Makes 4 servings. *Per serving: 269 calories.*

Quick Liver, Tomato and Onion Saute

2 teaspoons margarine

2 oz (60 g) sliced onion, separated into rings

1 medium tomato, cut into 5 slices

¼ teaspoon marjoram

4 teaspoons flour

¼ teaspoon salt

pinch freshly ground pepper

5 oz (150 g) calf liver, thinly sliced

parsley sprigs for garnish

Heat half the margarine in a frying pan; add onion rings in a

single layer and saute until lightly browned and tender (not soft). Remove from pan and keep hot. In the same pan arrange tomato slices in a single layer and cook each side briefly; gently remove from pan and set aside with onions. Sprinkle vegetables with marjoram and keep hot. Mix flour, salt and pepper; dredge liver in seasoned flour, turning slices to coat all sides. In same pan heat remaining margarine until bubbly and hot; add liver and saute, turning once, until done to taste (do not overcook); remove to serving plate and top with onion rings and tomato slices. Serve garnished with parsley sprigs.
Makes 1 serving.   *Per serving: 385 calories.*

West Indian Lamb

8 x 4-oz (120-g) lean lamb chops
4 oz (120 g) onion, chopped
1 teaspoon ground cumin
½ teaspoon ground ginger
½ teaspoon ground coriander
¼ teaspoon chilli powder
2 oz (60 g) sultanas
½ pint (300 ml) vegetable stock, prepared according to package directions
2 teaspoons flour
4 tablespoons toasted coconut

Trim the lamb chops of all visible fat. Place the chops under a hot grill and cook for 3 minutes each side. Transfer chops to the pressure cooker with all remaining ingredients except the flour and coconut. Stir well. Close cooker, bring to high pressure and cook for 15 minutes. Reduce pressure quickly. Remove chops and keep hot. Blend the flour with a little cold water and stir into the sauce. Replace cooker over low heat and stir until the sauce has thickened. Pour over the chops and garnish with the toasted coconut.
Makes 4 servings.   *Per serving: 375 calories.*

Rich Cheese Sauce and Spaghetti

2 tablespoons margarine

2½ fl oz (75 ml) natural yogurt

2 oz (60 g) grated Parmesan cheese

12 oz (360 g) cooked spaghetti

salt and freshly ground pepper to taste

pimento strips to garnish

Melt margarine in small non-stick saucepan. Add yogurt and cheese. Cook gently until cheese melts; add spaghetti. Mix well and season. Serve hot. Garnish with pimento strips.
Makes 4 servings.   *Per serving: 220 calories.*

Lentil Curry

8 oz (240 g) onion, chopped

6 oz (180 g) carrot, diced

2 sticks celery, diced

4 cloves garlic, finely chopped

4 teaspoons curry powder

8 teaspoons low-fat spread

4 teaspoons flour

12 oz (360 g) tomatoes, skinned and chopped

1½ lb (720 g) cooked lentils

4 teaspoons lemon juice

salt and pepper to taste

8 oz (240 g) hot, cooked long grain rice (3 oz/90 g uncooked)

Saute onion, carrot, celery and garlic in low-fat spread until tender. Add curry and flour and cook, stirring, for 2 minutes. Add tomatoes, lentils, lemon juice, salt and pepper. Bring gently to the boil and simmer for 10 minutes. Serve at once with hot rice.
Makes 4 servings.   *Per serving: 320 calories.*

Orange Chicken with Rosemary

5-oz (150-g) chicken breast, cubed

1 teaspoon vegetable oil

1 ½ oz (45 g) spring onions, chopped

½ pint (300 ml) chicken stock, prepared according to package directions

1 medium orange, peeled and thinly sliced

½ teaspoon dried rosemary

salt and pepper to taste

Place chicken on rack in grill pan and cook, approximately 5 minutes. Heat oil in non-stick frying pan and saute spring onions until lightly browned. Add chicken and all remaining ingredients and stir to combine. Cover and cook for 10 to 15 minutes or until chicken is tender. Serve at once.
Makes 1 serving. *Per serving: 275 calories.*

Beef Sausage Rissoles

1 lb 4 oz (600 g) beef sausages

2 slices (2 oz/60 g) brown bread, made into crumbs

3 tablespoons finely chopped onion

2 tablespoons tomato ketchup

2 teaspoons yeast extract

dash Worcestershire sauce

pinch mixed herbs

salt and pepper to taste

Rinse sausages in cold water. Slit and peel off skins. Place sausage meat in a large basin and mix with remaining ingredients. Wet hands and shape mixture into 8 flat cakes of equal size. Grill on a rack under moderate heat, turning once, until golden on each side. Serve hot or cold.
Makes 4 servings, 2 rissoles each. *Per serving: 382 calories.*

Shoulder of Lamb with Redcurrant Sauce

1 shoulder of lamb (approximately 3 lb 8 oz / 1 kg 680 g)

1 tablespoon rosemary

garlic salt

Sauce

4 tablespoons redcurrant jelly

2 tablespoons lemon juice

2 tablespoons water

salt and pepper to taste

Sprinkle lamb with rosemary and garlic salt. Roast on a rack in a moderate oven 350°F, 180°C, Gas Mark 4, for 30 minutes per pound. Combine sauce ingredients in a saucepan and heat until jelly is dissolved. Serve an equal portion over each 4 oz (120 g) serving of lamb.

Makes 6 servings.   *Per serving: 258 calories.*

Potato-Cheese Pie

4 large eggs

12 oz (360 g) peeled potatoes, grated

10 oz (300 g) cottage cheese

1 tablespoon chopped green pepper

2 tablespoons chopped onion

2 teaspoons salt

pinch pepper

Preheat oven to 375°F, 190°C, Gas Mark 5. Beat eggs well in a large bowl; add remaining ingredients and stir to combine. Divide potato mixture into 4 individual non-stick baking tins and bake until top of each pie is golden brown and mixture is set, about 45 minutes. To serve, invert pies on to serving dish.

Makes 4 servings.   *Per serving: 234 calories.*

Greek-Style Lamb

1 lb (480 g) aubergines, thinly sliced
salt and pepper to taste
4 teaspoons vegetable oil
2 medium onions, chopped
12 oz (360 g) cooked lean lamb, minced
3 tablespoons tomato puree
4 fl oz (120 ml) white wine
8 oz (240 g) canned tomatoes with juice
½ teaspoon oregano
½ teaspoon basil
¾ oz (20 g) flour
3 slices (3 oz/90 g) bread, made into crumbs
4 teaspoons margarine
½ pint (300 ml) skim milk
3 oz (90 g) Cheddar cheese, grated
1 egg, lightly beaten

Sprinkle the aubergines with salt. Leave in a colander to drain for 30 minutes. In a saucepan heat 2 teaspoons oil; add onion and saute until transparent. Stir in the minced lamb, tomato puree, wine, tomatoes and herbs with one third of the flour. Bring to the boil, cover and simmer for 30 minutes. Season. Rinse aubergines, squeeze and pat dry. Saute in frying pan with remaining 2 teaspoons oil. Layer the aubergines in a shallow ovenproof dish with the lamb mixture and 2 oz (60 g) of the breadcrumbs. To make the sauce, melt the margarine in a saucepan, stir in the remaining flour and cook gently for 1 minute, stirring. Remove pan from heat and gradually stir in milk. Bring to the boil and cook, stirring, until sauce thickens. Remove from heat, then stir in 2 oz (60 g) grated cheese and the beaten egg. Spoon sauce over meat and aubergine layers and sprinkle with remaining cheese and breadcrumbs. Bake in oven at 350°F, 180°C, Gas Mark 4 for 45 minutes or until golden.

Makes 4 servings.   *Per serving: 524 calories.*

Khitchari (Bean Kedgeree)

8 oz (240 g) red kidney beans, soaked overnight

3 oz (90 g) uncooked brown rice

8 oz (240 g) onion, peeled and chopped

2 medium carrots, peeled and diced

4 cloves garlic

1 teaspoon turmeric

1 teaspoon ground ginger

2 teaspoons ground cumin

½ teaspoon chilli powder

2 pints (1 litre 200 ml) chicken stock, prepared according to package directions

3 tablespoons lemon juice

salt and pepper to taste

mixed green salad, e.g. lettuce, cucumber and watercress

Put soaked beans in a saucepan with next 9 ingredients. Bring to the boil, stirring from time to time; cover pan and simmer, 45 to 60 minutes or until contents are tender. Stir occasionally during cooking. Add lemon juice, salt and pepper and serve at once with a mixed green salad.

Makes 4 servings.   *Per serving: 266 calories.*

Potato Souffle

4 teaspoons margarine

2 oz (60 g) each finely chopped onions or spring onions and grated carrot

3 tablespoons flour

2 oz (60 g) low-fat dry milk, reconstituted with 8 fl oz (240 ml) water

3 oz (90 g) peeled cooked potato, mashed

2 large eggs, separated

½ teaspoon salt

pinch each white pepper and cream of tartar

Preheat oven to 350°F, 180°C, Gas Mark 4. Heat margarine in

medium saucepan until bubbly and hot; add onions and carrot and saute until onions soften, about 2 minutes (do not brown). Add flour and stir quickly to combine. Remove pan from heat and add milk, stirring until well combined. Cook over low heat, stirring constantly, until thickened; add mashed potato and mix well. Remove pan from heat and quickly stir in egg yolks; season with salt and pepper and set aside. Using electric mixer at high speed, beat egg whites until foamy; add cream of tartar and beat until stiff peaks form. Gently fold egg whites into potato mixture. Turn potato mixture into a non-stick ovenproof casserole and bake for 30 minutes or until puffed and golden brown. Serve immediately.

Makes 2 servings.   *Per serving: 395 calories.*

Crispy Cauliflower

8 oz (240 g) mushrooms, sliced
1 medium-sized cauliflower
16 fl oz (480 ml) skim milk
3 tablespoons flour
4 teaspoons margarine
salt and pepper to taste
2 oz (60 g) lean back bacon, grilled and chopped
8 oz (240 g) Cheddar cheese, grated
2 slices (2 oz/60 g) bread, made into crumbs
parsley for garnish

Poach sliced mushrooms in 2 fl oz (60 ml) skim milk for 1 to 2 minutes or until tender. Cook cauliflower in boiling salted water, drain, break into florets and transfer to flameproof dish. Melt margarine in saucepan over low heat, stir in flour and mix well. Gradually add milk, stirring constantly until thickened. Stir in pepper, salt, bacon, mushrooms and cooking liquid and 6 oz (180 g) cheese, stirring until all the cheese has melted. Pour over cauliflower, making sure to coat evenly. Mix remaining cheese with breadcrumbs, sprinkle evenly over top of cauliflower and place under hot grill until golden brown. Garnish with parsley.

Makes 4 servings.   *Per serving: 430 calories.*

Whitebait Minceur

6 oz (180 g) fresh or frozen whitebait

1 tablespoon oil

4 teaspoons wholemeal flour

salt and pepper to taste

lemon slices for garnish

Prepare whitebait. Heat the oil in a heavy frying pan and add the whitebait. Saute lightly for about 10 minutes and then stir in the flour, making sure all the fish are covered. Season with salt and pepper. Continue cooking for another 5 minutes, until flour darkens. Garnish with lemon slices and serve with green vegetables.

Makes 1 serving.   *Per serving: 395 calories.*

Pan-Fried Liver with Vegetables

1 lb 4 oz (600 g) pigs liver, sliced

2 tablespoons flour

1 tablespoon oil

2 tablespoons margarine

1 garlic clove, crushed

3 oz (90 g) red pepper, seeded and sliced

4 oz (120 g) mushrooms, sliced

12 oz (360 g) tomatoes, skinned and chopped

4 teaspoons brown sugar

2 teaspoons lemon juice

1 teaspoon basil

2 teaspoons steak sauce

salt to taste

8 oz (240 g) hot cooked pasta

parsley for garnish

Toss the liver in the flour. Heat oil and margarine in large non-stick frying pan; add garlic, pepper and mushrooms and saute for 2 minutes. Add the liver and brown on both sides.

Stir in the next 6 ingredients. Cover the pan and simmer gently for 10 to 15 minutes. Divide evenly and serve with hot pasta. Garnish with parsley.

Makes 4 servings. *Per serving: 433 calories.*

Sausages with Barbecued Beans

10 oz (300 g) beef chipolata sausages
4 teaspoons vegetable oil
2 tablespoons chopped onion
2 tablespoons chopped green pepper
2 medium apples, peeled, cored and chopped
18 oz (540 g) canned baked beans
2 oz (60 g) sultanas
2 teaspoons mild curry powder
4 teaspoons brown sugar
1 tablespoon tomato puree
1 teaspoon Worcestershire sauce
1 teaspoon French mustard

Grill sausages on a rack under moderate heat, turning once, until cooked and golden brown. Keep hot. Pour oil into a large non-stick pan and gently saute onion, pepper and apples for 2 to 3 minutes. Add baked beans and remaining ingredients and cook over moderate heat until mixture is hot. Add sausages to the pan and heat through thoroughly.

Makes 4 servings. *Per serving: 395 calories.*

Calico Beans

3 oz (90 g) canned red kidney beans, rinsed
3 oz (90 g) canned butter beans, rinsed
6 oz (180 g) baked beans in tomato sauce
3 oz (90 g) finely chopped onion
2 tablespoons tomato ketchup
1 tablespoon brown sugar
1 tablespoon chopped mint
¼ teaspoon dry mustard powder
1 teaspoon vinegar
salt to taste

Gently mix beans with the chopped onion. Mix together
ketchup, sugar, chopped mint, vinegar, mustard powder and
salt. Pour over bean mixture and gently fold in. Transfer to a
baking dish and bake for 1 hour covered and 30 minutes
uncovered at 300°F, 150°C, Gas Mark 2. Serve hot or cold with
mixed salad.

Makes 2 servings. *Per serving: 190 calories.*

Liver Baked in Foil

5 oz (150 g) lambs liver, thinly sliced
3 oz (90 g) onion, thinly sliced
3 oz (90 g) tomatoes, skinned and sliced
3 oz (90 g) potatoes, peeled and thinly sliced
salt and pepper to taste
2 tablespoons finely chopped parsley
2 teaspoons low-fat spread

Take a sheet of foil measuring 10 x 10 inches (25 x 25 cm).
Arrange on the foil alternate layers of liver, onion, tomato and
potato. Sprinkle each layer with parsley and seasonings. Dot
top layer with low-fat spread. Fold edges of foil together to
make a parcel, keeping it loose. Cook in a moderately hot oven
375°F, 190°C, Gas Mark 5, for 30 to 40 minutes.

Makes 1 serving. *Per serving: 401 calories.*

Cheesy Pasta

8 teaspoons margarine
2 tablespoons flour
½ pint (300 ml) skim milk
10 oz (300 g) low-fat soft cheese
4 oz (120 g) Cheddar cheese, grated
1 teaspoon grated nutmeg
4 oz (120 g) lean back bacon
1 lb (480 g) cooked ribbon noodles
8 teaspoons grated Parmesan cheese

Melt margarine in saucepan. Stir in flour and cook gently for 1 minute. Gradually add skim milk, stirring until thickened. Add low-fat soft cheese, grated Cheddar cheese and nutmeg. Stir to combine. Keep hot. Meanwhile grill bacon until crisp. Remove any visible fat and chop finely. Add bacon and freshly cooked noodles to sauce. Divide evenly into 4 portions and sprinkle each with 2 teaspoons grated Parmesan cheese.
Makes 4 servings.   *Per serving: 586 calories.*

Hawaiian Liver

1 teaspoon vegetable oil
6 oz (180 g) lambs liver, sliced
2 spring onions, finely sliced
1 teaspoon sage
salt and pepper to taste
4 fl oz (120 ml) cider
¼ medium-sized pineapple or 2 rings canned pineapple
4 oz (120 g) hot cooked rice

Heat oil in non-stick frying pan and brown liver quickly on both sides with the finely sliced onions. Add sage, seasoning and cider. Cut skin from pineapple, chop flesh and add to pan. Bring to the boil, cover and simmer for 5 minutes. Serve at once with hot rice.
Makes 1 serving.   *Per serving: 579 calories.*

Main-Meal Minestrone

2 teaspoons olive oil

4 oz (120 g) cooked ham, diced

2 garlic cloves, chopped

3 oz (90 g) each chopped onion, celery, carrot and courgettes

½ pint (300 ml) water

8 fl oz (240 ml) tomato juice

6 oz (180 g) drained canned red kidney beans

2 tablespoons chopped fresh basil or 1 teaspoon dried

1 beef stock cube

pinch each oregano and pepper

4 oz (120 g) cooked small macaroni

2 tablespoons chopped parsley

Heat oil in medium saucepan; add ham and garlic and saute briefly (do not brown garlic). Add onion, celery, carrot and courgettes and cook, stirring occasionally, until vegetables are tender, about 5 minutes; add all remaining ingredients except macaroni and parsley and bring to the boil. Reduce heat and let simmer, stirring occasionally, for about 15 minutes; add macaroni and parsley and let simmer until heated.
Makes 2 servings.   *Per serving: 297 calories.*

Creamy Pasta with Broccoli

4½ oz (135 g) uncooked pasta

4 teaspoons olive oil

1 garlic clove, chopped

10 oz (300 g) low-fat soft cheese

8 oz (240 g) cooked broccoli florets; reserve 4 fl oz (120 ml) cooking liquid

½ teaspoon salt

¼ teaspoon freshly ground pepper

4 teaspoons Parmesan cheese

Cook pasta in boiling water in a large saucepan to cover,

according to package directions. While pasta is cooking, heat oil in a non-stick frying pan; add garlic and saute until golden. Add low-fat soft cheese and cook, stirring occasionally, until cheese begins to melt and bubbles appear. Add reserved cooking liquid, salt and pepper and stir to combine. Drain pasta well and return to saucepan; add cheese mixture and broccoli and toss lightly to combine. Serve each portion sprinkled with 1 teaspoon Parmesan cheese.

Makes 4 servings.   *Per serving: 298 calories.*

Yogurt-Topped Beef Pie

1 medium onion, peeled and chopped

4 teaspoons margarine

8 oz (240 g) cooked lean beef, minced

pinch mixed herbs

2 tablespoons tomato puree

1 teaspoon Worcestershire sauce

salt and pepper to taste

6 oz (180 g) potatoes, peeled and sliced

8 oz (240 g) tomatoes, skinned and sliced

1 egg, beaten

¾ oz (20 g) flour

5 fl oz (150 ml) natural yogurt

paprika for garnish

Preheat oven to 375°F, 190°C, Gas Mark 5. In a non-stick saucepan gently saute onion in the margarine until transparent. Add the minced meat, mixed herbs, tomato puree and Worcestershire sauce. Season to taste. Heat mixture through gently, stirring frequently to avoid burning. Meanwhile, cook potato slices until just tender, but not soft. Layer the meat mixture and tomato slices in a casserole. Top with a layer of potatoes. Cover and bake for 30 minutes. Blend the egg with the flour and yogurt. Season to taste and pour over the pie. Return casserole to the oven and cook for a further 30 minutes. Sprinkle with paprika before serving.

Makes 2 servings.   *Per serving: 528 calories.*

Peppered Chicken

4 x 8-oz (240-g) chicken joints

salt and pepper to taste

2 teaspoons paprika

6 oz (180 g) shallots

1 clove garlic

3 oz (90 g) red pepper, seeded

¾ pint (450 ml) chicken stock, prepared according to package directions

15 oz (450 g) canned tomatoes with juice

5 fl oz (150 ml) natural yogurt

8 oz (240 g) cooked noodles

Skin chicken joints, season and place on rack in the grill pan. Sprinkle with paprika. Grill on each side for approximately 10 minutes or until golden brown and cooked through. Put chicken in a large saucepan with peeled shallots. Crush garlic and add to pan with thinly sliced red pepper, stock and canned tomatoes with juice. Bring to the boil, cover and simmer for 25 minutes. Remove from the heat, cool slightly and stir yogurt into pan. Serve with cooked noodles.

Makes 4 servings.   *Per serving: 303 calories.*

Spanish-Style Tripe

1 lb 4 oz (600 g) dressed tripe

2 tablespoons margarine

4 oz (120 g) onion, finely sliced

12 oz (360 g) tomatoes, chopped

1 clove garlic, crushed

2 tablespoons chopped parsley

¼ teaspoon ground mace

salt and pepper to taste

4 fl oz (120 ml) vegetable stock, prepared according to package directions

Cook the tripe until tender, then cut into fine strips. Melt the margarine, add the onion and saute until soft. Add the tripe, tomatoes, garlic, parsley, mace, salt and pepper. Saute for 5 minutes. Add the stock and cook until all ingredients are tender, approximately 20 minutes.

Makes 4 servings.   *Per serving: 155 calories.*

Savoury Stuffed Heart

1 x 6-oz (180-g) pigs heart

Stuffing

1 slice (1 oz/30 g) bread, made into crumbs

1 tablespoon chopped parsley

1 stick celery, finely chopped

1 teaspoon grated lemon rind

1 tablespoon lemon juice

salt and pepper to taste

8 fl oz (240 ml) beef stock, prepared according to package directions

2 teaspoons flour

Wash and trim fat from heart. Place heart in a basin of salted water. Meanwhile, combine breadcrumbs, parsley, celery, lemon rind and lemon juice in a basin. Add salt and pepper to taste; mix thoroughly. Drain heart and fill cavity with stuffing mix. Close top with wooden cocktail stick and place in a small ovenproof casserole with lid. Mix stock with flour; pour over heart, cover with lid or foil and bake in a moderate oven, 325°F, 160°C, Gas Mark 3, for 1½ to 2 hours or until heart is tender.

Makes 1 serving.   *Per serving: 266 calories.*

Mustard Cod

2½ fl oz (75 ml) natural yogurt

1 teaspoon dry English mustard

1 teaspoon vegetable oil

5 oz (150 g) cod fillets, skinned and boned

paprika and salt to taste

Mix together yogurt and mustard. Heat oil in non-stick frying pan and saute fish until it flakes. Spoon over the yogurt and mustard mixture and heat through. Sprinkle with paprika and salt. Serve with a hot vegetable of your choice.

Makes 1 serving. *Per serving: 152 calories.*

Curried Chicken

1 teaspoon vegetable oil

2 oz (60 g) onion, chopped

½-1 teaspoon curry powder

salt to taste

2 teaspoons lemon juice

1 tablespoon tomato puree

3 tablespoons water

4 oz (120 g) lean cooked chicken, diced

½ oz (15 g) sultanas

2 oz (60 g) hot cooked rice

1 teaspoon desiccated coconut

1 teaspoon chopped parsley

Heat oil in non-stick frying pan. Add onion and saute gently until transparent, approximately 2 minutes. Add curry powder and salt to taste, then lemon juice, tomato puree and water. Stir to combine and allow to simmer for 1 to 2 minutes; add diced chicken and sultanas and bring to the boil. Cover and simmer for 10 minutes. Serve at once with rice and sprinkle with desiccated coconut and chopped parsley.

Makes 1 serving. *Per serving: 383 calories.*

Bacon-Stuffed Hearts

4 x 6-oz (180-g) lamb hearts

½ pint (300 ml) beef stock, prepared according to package directions

Stuffing

4 x 1-oz (30-g) slices lean back bacon, grilled until crisp, then diced

4 slices (4 oz/120 g) white bread, made into crumbs

1 tablespoon chopped parsley

pinch each sage, rosemary and thyme

2 fl oz (60 ml) skim milk

juice of half a lemon

Wash the hearts well in cold water. Remove skin and membrane. Cut the dividing wall to make one cavity. Soak for one hour in cold salted water, rinse and drain. Mix the dry stuffing ingredients together and bind with skim milk and lemon juice. Pack into hearts. Put into a casserole, add the stock and cover tightly. Bake at 370°F, 190°C, Gas Mark 5 for 1 to 1½ hours.

Makes 4 servings. *Per serving: 353 calories.*

Barbecued Butter Beans

6 oz (180 g) canned, drained butter beans

2 oz (60 g) onion, sliced

4 tablespoons tomato puree

4 fl oz (120 ml) chicken stock, prepared according to package directions

1 teaspoon Worcestershire sauce

pinch chilli powder or to taste

dash hot pepper sauce

½ teaspoon sugar

Preheat oven to 350°F, 180°C, Gas Mark 4. Layer beans and onions in a casserole. Combine remaining ingredients, mix well and pour over bean mixture. Bake for 30 to 40 minutes.

Makes 1 serving. *Per serving: 252 calories.*

Beef Risotto

3 oz (90 g) onion

4 teaspoons vegetable oil

3 oz (90 g) long grain rice

½ pint (300 ml) beef stock, prepared according to package directions

dash Worcestershire sauce

4 medium tomatoes, skinned

4 oz (120 g) peas

12 oz (360 g) cooked minced beef

Peel and finely chop onion. Heat oil in non-stick frying pan. Saute onion over gentle heat for about 10 minutes or until brown. Add rice and saute a further 2 minutes until rice becomes transparent. Stir stock and Worcestershire sauce into rice, bring to the boil, cover and simmer gently for 10 minutes. Chop tomatoes and add to frying pan with peas and minced beef. Continue to heat for a further 10 minutes until rice and vegetables are cooked.

Makes 4 servings. *Per serving: 351 calories.*

Cheesy Fish Pie

6 teaspoons low-fat spread

1½ oz (45 g) flour

¾ pint (450 ml) skim milk

10 oz (300 g) low-fat soft cheese

4 fl oz (120 ml) white wine

12 oz (360 g) cooked white fish, flaked

2 oz (60 g) chopped onion

salt and pepper to taste

9 oz (270 g) cooked potato, mashed

Melt fat, stir in flour, add milk and bring to the boil, stirring, until thickened. Cook for 2 minutes. Add soft cheese and wine. Cook sauce for a further 2 minutes. Add flaked fish and onion. Season to taste and spoon into ovenproof dish. Spread

mashed potato over top and brown under grill. Serve at once.
Makes 4 servings.   *Per serving: 315 calories.*

Toad in the Hole

1 lb 2 oz (540 g) beef chipolata sausages
4½ oz (135 g) plain flour
pinch salt
2 eggs
½ pint (300 ml) skim milk
2 tablespoons vegetable oil

Preheat oven to 425°F, 220°C, Gas Mark 7. Grill sausages on a rack under medium heat until fat and juices cease to run, turning once. Sausages should be lightly browned. Sift flour and salt into a bowl. Add eggs and a little milk. Beat together, gradually adding the rest of the milk, to make a smooth batter. Pour oil into an 8 x 6-inch (20 x 15-cm) non-stick baking tin and place in oven until very hot. Remove from oven and pour in batter. Place equal portions of sausages in each quarter section of tin. Bake for 15 minutes, then reduce heat to 375°F, 190°C, Gas Mark 5 and bake for a further 10 minutes or until batter is well-risen and brown.
Makes 4 servings.   *Per serving: 520 calories.*

Chilli-Cheese Corn Fritters

3 oz (90 g) Cheddar cheese, grated

3 oz (90 g) drained canned sweetcorn

1 egg

3 tablespoons plain dried breadcrumbs

pinch each garlic powder, onion powder, chilli powder and baking powder

pinch each salt and ground red pepper

1 tablespoon vegetable oil

Combine all ingredients except oil; let stand a few minutes for flavours to blend. Heat oil in non-stick frying pan over moderate heat until hot but not smoking; spoon corn mixture into pan, forming 6 equal fritters. Using the back of a spoon, press top of each fritter to flatten slightly; cook until browned on bottom. Turn fritters over and cook until browned on other side.

Makes 2 servings.   *Per serving: 397 calories.*

Main-Meal Lamb and Split Pea Soup

12 oz (360 g) lean lamb, chopped

8 oz (240 g) onions, chopped

2 tablespoons margarine

2 pints (1 litre 200 ml) vegetable stock, prepared according to package directions

4 oz (120 g) green split peas, pre-soaked according to package directions

12 oz (360 g) potato, peeled and diced

1 teaspoon oregano

salt and freshly ground black pepper

1 tablespoon chopped parsley

Cook lamb on rack under hot grill until rare, about 8 minutes, turning once. Saute onions in the margarine in a large non-stick saucepan for 5 minutes. Add lamb, pour in the stock, add the soaked split peas, potato and oregano and season well with salt and pepper. Bring to the boil and simmer gently for 1½ to

2 hours. Stir in the chopped parsley and serve immediately.
Makes 4 servings.   *Per serving: 373 calories.*

Fruity Lamb Curry

2 oz (60 g) onion, chopped
6 oz (180 g) carrots, sliced
6 oz (180 g) peas
12 fl oz (360 ml) chicken stock, prepared according to package directions
2 tablespoons lemon juice
2 teaspoons curry powder
pinch ground bay leaves
8 oz (240 g) cooked lean lamb, cubed
8 oz (240 g) canned crushed pineapple with juice
2 oz (60 g) sultanas
4 teaspoons cornflour mixed with water to a thin paste
salt and pepper to taste
4 oz (120 g) hot cooked rice

Combine onion, carrots, peas, stock, lemon juice, curry powder and ground bay leaves in a saucepan and cook until vegetables are tender-crisp. Add cooked lamb, crushed pineapple with juice and sultanas; bring to the boil, lower heat and cook for further 10 minutes. Thicken mixture with cornflour paste and cook for a further 5 to 10 minutes, stirring occasionally. Season with salt and pepper to taste. Serve with rice.
Makes 2 servings.   *Per serving: 513 calories.*

Liver-Stuffed Marrow

2 rings cut from the middle of a medium-sized marrow (approximately 6-8 oz (180-240 g))
5 oz (150 g) lambs liver
1 slice (1 oz/30 g) bread, made into crumbs
1 tablespoon finely chopped onion
1 tablespoon tomato puree
1 teaspoon yeast extract
pinch oregano
salt and pepper to taste
1 medium tomato
2 teaspoons low-fat spread

Peel marrow and remove pith carefully without breaking rings. Blanch liver in boiling water for 2 minutes, drain and cool, then mince. Mix liver, breadcrumbs, onion, tomato puree, yeast extract and seasonings. Place marrow rings on a large sheet of foil on a baking tray. Divide filling between rings, packing well down. Top each ring with 1 tomato half, cut side down. Dot each ring with 1 teaspoon low-fat spread. Fold edges of foil together to form a parcel, pinching edges to seal. Bake in a moderate oven, 350°F, 180°C, Gas Mark 4 for 25 to 30 minutes or until marrow is tender.
Makes 1 serving.   *Per serving: 417 calories.*

Onion and Cheese Scramble

4 eggs
4 fl oz (120 ml) skim milk
4 teaspoons margarine
4 oz (120 g) Cheshire cheese, grated
2 tablespoons finely chopped onion
salt and pepper to taste
4 slices (4 oz/120 g) bread, toasted
1 green pepper, seeded and sliced

Beat the eggs well. Add the skim milk and mix thoroughly.

Melt margarine in fairly large non-stick saucepan, add egg mixture and cook, stirring all the time until the mixture thickens. Add the cheese, onion, salt and pepper and stir until the cheese has just melted. Serve immediately on toast, garnished with slices of green pepper.

Makes 4 servings.　　　　　　　　　　　*Per serving: 327 calories.*

Chicken Liver Croustades with Caper Sauce

2 slices (2 oz/60 g) white bread
10 oz (300 g) chicken livers, cut into halves
2 teaspoons flour
4 fl oz (120 ml) natural yogurt
2 teaspoons each French mustard and margarine
3 oz (90 g) onion, chopped
4 teaspoons white wine
2 teaspoons chopped capers
½ teaspoon Worcestershire sauce
pinch each salt and pepper
2 teaspoons chopped parsley

Preheat oven to 400°F, 200°C, Gas Mark 6. Flatten each slice of bread with a rolling pin. Press each slice into an individual ovenproof bowl, forming bread into bowl shape, and bake until lightly browned, about 7 minutes. Sprinkle livers with half the flour and set aside. Mix yogurt, mustard and remaining flour and set aside. Heat margarine in a frying pan until bubbly and hot; add onion and saute until soft, about 2 minutes. Add livers and saute until browned, about 3 minutes; stir in wine and bring to the boil. Add yogurt mixture, stirring to combine; add capers, Worcestershire sauce, salt and pepper and cook, stirring constantly, until thickened. Stir in parsley. Fill each croustade with an equal amount of liver mixture.

Makes 2 servings.　　　　　　　　　　　*Per serving: 367 calories.*

Baked Kipper Loaf

| 8 oz (240 g) canned kippers, drained |
| 2 slices (2 oz/60 g) bread, made into crumbs |
| lemon juice to taste |
| ¼ pint (150 ml) skim milk |
| 2-3 gherkins, coarsely chopped |
| 2 eggs, beaten |
| 4 teaspoons low-fat spread, melted |
| pepper to taste |
| 2 teaspoons finely chopped onion |
| 2 hard-boiled eggs, sliced, for garnish |
| cress or parsley for garnish |

Preheat oven to 350°F, 180°C, Gas Mark 4. Mix together all ingredients except hard-boiled eggs and cress or parsley. Pack well into a greased 6-inch (15-cm) souffle dish or mould. Stand dish in a baking dish half filled with water and bake for 40 minutes or until firm to touch. Turn out and garnish with boiled eggs and cress or parsley. May be served hot or cold.
Makes 4 servings.   *Per serving: 269 calories.*

Danish Haddock

| 4 oz (120 g) lean back bacon |
| 12 oz (360 g) button mushrooms, sliced |
| 12 oz (360 g) peas |
| 4 x 6-oz (180-g) haddock fillets, skinned and boned |
| 4 teaspoons low-fat spread |
| salt and pepper to taste |

Grill bacon until crisp; chop into small pieces. Arrange sliced mushrooms and peas over base of casserole; lay fish fillets over vegetables, dot with low-fat spread and sprinkle with chopped bacon, salt and pepper. Cover with foil and bake at 350°F, 180°C, Gas Mark 4 for 20 minutes. Remove foil and bake for a further 5 minutes. Serve at once.
Makes 4 servings.   *Per serving: 271 calories.*

Marrow Hot Pot

12 oz (360 g) marrow, peeled and sliced

6 oz (180 g) tomatoes, skinned and sliced

8 oz (240 g) onion, peeled and sliced

3 tablespoons chicken stock, prepared according to package directions

12 oz (360 g) potatoes, peeled

8 oz (240 g) Cheddar cheese, grated

salt and freshly ground black pepper

Preheat oven to 350°F, 180°C, Gas Mark 4. Cook marrow, tomatoes and onions in a non-stick pan with the stock for 5 to 10 minutes, stirring constantly. Parboil potatoes in boiling, salted water for 10 minutes. Drain, cut into ¼-inch (5-mm) slices. Arrange layers of vegetables in an ovenproof dish. Sprinkle cheese and seasoning between each layer. Finish with layer of potatoes and cheese. Bake in oven for 45 minutes and brown under grill before serving.

Makes 4 servings. *Per serving: 327 calories.*

Main-Meal Kidney Bean and Ham Soup

2 teaspoons margarine

1 tablespoon each chopped onion, celery and carrot

½ teaspoon chicken stock powder

¼ teaspoon oregano

4 oz (120 g) boiled ham, diced

8 oz (240 g) canned tomatoes, chopped

6 oz (180 g) drained canned red kidney beans

2-4 tablespoons water

Heat margarine in a saucepan until bubbly and hot; add onion, celery, carrot, stock powder and oregano and stir to combine. Cover and simmer over moderate heat until vegetables are tender. Stir in remaining ingredients, adding water gradually until soup reaches desired consistency. Cover and let simmer until piping hot.

Makes 2 servings. *Per serving: 211 calories.*

Cheese and Vegetable Pudding

¼ pint (150 ml) skim milk

3 oz (90 g) carrots, thinly sliced

2 oz (60 g) onion, thinly sliced

1 slice (1 oz/30 g) bread, made into crumbs

1 oz (30 g) Cheddar cheese, grated

salt and cayenne pepper

pinch dry mustard

1 egg

3 oz (90 g) tomato for garnish

Preheat oven to 400°F, 200°C, Gas Mark 6. Pour milk into saucepan, add carrots and half the onion, simmer for a few minutes, stir in breadcrumbs and most of the cheese. Season with salt, cayenne pepper and mustard powder. Lightly beat egg and stir into milk mixture. Pour into a small ovenproof dish, top with remaining onion slices and cheese. Bake until golden and well risen, approximately 30 minutes. Garnish with tomato.

Makes 1 serving.   *Per serving: 359 calories.*

Mild Curried Chicken with Banana Rice

2 teaspoons vegetable oil

4 oz (120 g) onion, chopped

1-2 teaspoons curry powder

pinch salt

2 tablespoons lemon juice

2 tablespoons mango chutney

2 tablespoons dried red and green peppers

6 tablespoons water

8 oz (240 g) cooked lean chicken, diced

1 medium banana

4 oz (120 g) hot cooked rice

Heat oil in non-stick frying pan. Add onion and saute until

transparent. Add curry powder and salt to taste, then add 1 tablespoon lemon juice, chutney, dried peppers and water. Stir to combine and simmer for 1 to 2 minutes. Add diced chicken and bring to the boil. Cover with lid and simmer for 10 minutes. Meanwhile peel banana and slice into rings. Sprinkle banana with lemon juice and combine with hot cooked rice. Divide rice and banana mixture evenly and top each portion with half curried chicken mixture.

Makes 2 servings.   *Per serving: 370 calories.*

Vegetable-Pasta Medley in Onion-Cheddar Sauce

2 teaspoons margarine

1 tablespoon chopped onion

4 teaspoons flour

8 fl oz (240 ml) skim milk

2 oz (60 g) strong Cheddar cheese, grated

¼ teaspoon Worcestershire sauce

pinch each salt and pepper

4 oz (120 g) each cooked broccoli florets and diagonally sliced carrots (¼-inch (5-mm) thick slices)

4 oz (120 g) cooked small macaroni or shell pasta

Heat margarine in non-stick saucepan until bubbly and hot; add onion and cook until transparent, about 2 minutes. Add flour and stir until well mixed; continue cooking and stirring for 1 minute longer. Remove pan from heat and gradually stir in milk; return to moderate heat and cook, stirring constantly, until mixture is smooth and thickened. Reduce heat to low and add cheese and seasonings; cook, stirring constantly, until cheese is melted and mixture is well blended. Add vegetables and macaroni and cook, stirring gently, until macaroni and vegetables are heated through and coated with sauce.

Makes 2 servings.   *Per serving: 319 calories.*

Spiced Meatballs

4 oz (120 g) onion, finely chopped

6 oz (180 g) mushrooms, finely chopped

1 lb 4 oz (600 g) minced beef

salt to taste

1 tablespoon paprika

Sauce

1 tablespoon lemon juice

1 beef stock cube

2 teaspoons brown sugar

15 oz (450 g) canned tomatoes with juice

1 lb (480 g) hot cooked noodles

Mix the finely chopped onion and mushrooms with the minced beef; season with salt and paprika. Knead the mixture together and divide into 12 equal parts. Roll into balls. Grill the meatballs on a rack until well browned. Lift out and place on a heatproof dish. Place sauce ingredients in blender container and puree until smooth. Pour sauce over meatballs. Bake at 350°F, 180°C, Gas Mark 4, for 30 to 35 minutes. Serve with hot cooked noodles.
Makes 4 servings.   *Per serving: 420 calories.*

Chicken with Buckwheat

2 oz (60 g) uncooked buckwheat groats (kasha)

1 egg, lightly beaten

1 tablespoon each chopped onion and red pepper

1 teaspoon margarine

6 fl oz (180 ml) chicken stock, prepared according to package directions

6 oz (180 g) skinned and boned cooked chicken, diced

½ medium tomato, chopped

Mix buckwheat and egg. Heat non-stick frying pan over high heat; add buckwheat mixture and cook, stirring constantly, until buckwheat is dry and grains are separated (be careful not to burn). Reduce heat to low and add onion, red peppers and margarine, stirring to combine; add stock. Cover pan and let mixture simmer until all liquid has been absorbed, 8 to 10 minutes. Add chicken and tomato and continue cooking over low heat, stirring occasionally, until chicken is thoroughly heated through.

Makes 2 servings.   *Per serving: 296 calories.*

Traditional Tripe and Onions with Mashed Potatoes

1 lb 4 oz (600 g) dressed tripe
1 pint (600 ml) skim milk
1 lb (480 g) onions, chopped
salt and pepper to taste
2 tablespoons margarine
1 lb 4 oz (600 g) peeled and diced potatoes
2 fl oz (60 ml) skim milk
2 tablespoons margarine
salt and pepper to taste
1½ oz (45 g) flour

Put tripe, 1 pint (600 ml) skim milk, chopped onions, salt and pepper and margarine in a large non-stick saucepan. Bring to the boil, lower heat and cover. Simmer until tripe is tender; approximately 1 hour. Meanwhile cook potatoes until tender; drain and mash with rest of milk and margarine, adding salt and pepper to taste. Beat until creamy and keep hot. Five minutes before end of cooking time of tripe, mix flour to a paste with water and stir into tripe. Continue to cook until thickened. Serve at once with mashed potatoes.

Makes 4 servings.   *Per serving: 434 calories.*

Italian-Style Scalloped Potatoes

1 tablespoon olive oil

3 oz (90 g) onion, chopped

2 garlic cloves, chopped

8 oz (240 g) canned tomatoes, crushed

1 tablespoon chopped fresh basil or ½ teaspoon dried

2 anchovy fillets, mashed

6 oz (180 g) peeled potatoes, thinly sliced

1 oz (30 g) grated Parmesan cheese

Heat oil in non-stick frying pan; add onion and garlic and saute until onion is lightly browned. Add tomatoes, basil and anchovies and cook, stirring occasionally, until mixture thickens slightly. Preheat oven to 425°F, 210°C, Gas Mark 7. Spread half the tomato mixture in a shallow medium casserole; arrange potato slices evenly over sauce and spoon remaining sauce over potatoes. Sprinkle evenly with cheese and bake until potatoes are cooked and cheese has melted and formed a crust, 30 to 35 minutes.

Makes 2 servings.   *Per serving: 230 calories.*

Parmesan-Topped Stuffed Potato

2 teaspoons margarine

2 tablespoons chopped shallots or onion

1 baked potato (9 oz/270 g), cut in half lengthwise

3 oz (90 g) cooked fresh or frozen broccoli, pureed

2 fl oz (60 ml) natural yogurt

pinch each salt and pepper

2 teaspoons grated Parmesan cheese

Heat margarine in small non-stick frying pan until bubbly and hot; add shallots or onion and saute briefly, about 1 minute. Remove from heat and set aside. Preheat oven to 400°F, 200°C, Gas Mark 6. Scoop pulp from potato halves into a small bowl, reserving shells; add sauteed shallots or onions, broccoli, yogurt, salt and pepper and mash until thoroughly blended. Divide mixture into reserved shells and sprinkle each with 1 teaspoon cheese; bake until lightly browned, 20 to 25 minutes.

Makes 2 servings. *Per serving: 196 calories.*

Hot Potato Salad

2 teaspoons vegetable oil

2 oz (60 g) each diced onion and green pepper

1 teaspoon flour

6 fl oz (180 ml) chicken stock, prepared according to package directions

2 teaspoons cider vinegar

½ teaspoon caster sugar

pinch pepper

9 oz (270 g) peeled cooked potatoes, thinly sliced

Heat oil in non-stick frying pan; add onion and green pepper and cook, stirring occasionally, until vegetables are tender. Sprinkle flour over mixture and cook, stirring constantly, for 1 minute; gradually stir in stock and bring to the boil. Reduce heat and let simmer until mixture thickens; stir in vinegar, sugar and pepper. Add potato slices and cook until thoroughly heated, 2 to 3 minutes longer.

Makes 2 servings. *Per serving: 182 calories.*

Broccoli-Stuffed Potato

2 teaspoons margarine

2 tablespoons chopped shallots or onion

3 oz (90 g) cooked, chopped fresh or frozen broccoli, pureed

2 fl oz (60 ml) chicken stock, prepared according to package directions

1 baked potato (9 oz/270 g), cut in half lengthwise

2 oz (60 g) Cheddar cheese, grated

pinch each salt, pepper and paprika

Heat margarine in small non-stick frying pan until bubbly and hot. Add shallots or onion and saute briefly, about 1 minute. Add broccoli and stock and stir to combine. Remove from heat and set aside. Preheat oven to 400°F, 200°C, Gas Mark 6. Scoop pulp from potato halves into a small bowl, reserving shells. Add broccoli mixture, cheese and seasonings to bowl and mash until thoroughly blended. Divide mixture into reserved shells and bake until lightly browned, 20 to 25 minutes.

Makes 2 servings. *Per serving: 280 calories.*

Brown Sugar Custard

8 fl oz (240 ml) skim milk

1 tablespoon firmly packed light brown sugar

1 large egg, lightly beaten

1 teaspoon vanilla flavouring

8 fl oz (240 ml) water

Mix milk and sugar in a small saucepan and heat to just below boiling; let cool. Add egg and vanilla and stir well to combine. Divide mixture evenly between 2 small individual heatproof bowls. Cover each tightly with foil. Pour water into pressure cooker; place rack in cooker and set bowls on the rack. Close cover securely; bring to pressure and cook at 15 lbs pressure for 4 minutes. Immediately hold cooker under running cold water to bring pressure down. Serve custard at room temperature or refrigerate until chilled.

Makes 2 servings. *Per serving: 115 calories.*

Yogurt 'Cream' Ice with Orange

2 fl oz (60 ml) thawed frozen concentrated orange juice

10 fl oz (300 ml) natural yogurt

4 teaspoons caster sugar

1 teaspoon finely grated orange peel

1 egg white

1 medium orange, peeled and sliced

In a bowl, whip the concentrated orange juice with the natural yogurt, sugar and grated orange peel. Transfer to freezer tray and freeze to a soft mush. Return to bowl and beat. Whisk egg white until stiff peaks form and fold into orange yogurt mixture. Re-freeze until consistency of sorbet. Serve in a glass and top with orange slices.

Makes 2 servings. *Per serving: 170 calories.*

Bread Pudding

4 slices (4 oz/120 g) wholemeal bread

1½ oz (45 g) self-raising flour

1½ oz (45 g) bran flakes

2 fl oz (60 ml) skim milk

4 tablespoons low-fat spread

2 teaspoons ground allspice

1 teaspoon grated orange peel

1 teaspoon grated lemon peel

3 tablespoons marmalade

2 oz (60 g) sultanas

2 oz (60 g) raisins

2½ teaspoons caster sugar

Preheat oven to 325°F, 160°C, Gas Mark 3. Soak the bread in water, drain and gently squeeze out excess water. Put into a large bowl, add flour and bran flakes. Mix together. Warm milk in small saucepan. Add low-fat spread, allspice and grated peels. Stir until fat is melted then pour onto bread mixture, adding marmalade, sultanas and raisins. Mix together thoroughly to a dropping consistency – if too stiff add more skim milk. Spoon into an 8 x 6-inch (20 x 15-cm) non-stick baking tin. Sprinkle top with sugar. Bake for 1 to 1½ hours or until firm to the touch. Leave to cool in the tin.
Makes 4 or 8 servings.   *Per serving: 162 or 324 calories.*

Raisin-Bread Pudding

4 teaspoons margarine

2 teaspoons sugar

1 large egg, separated

2 fl oz (60 ml) each skim milk and orange juice

½ teaspoon grated orange peel

2 slices currant bread (2 oz/60 g), cut into ½-inch (1-cm) cubes

Using electric mixer on medium speed, beat together 3 teaspoons margarine and 1 teaspoon sugar until combined;

add egg yolk and beat until fluffy. Add milk, juice and peel and beat at low speed until combined (mixture will appear grainy). Stir in bread cubes and let stand for 15 minutes, then stir again. Preheat oven to 350°F, 180°C, Gas Mark 4. Grease 2 individual ovenproof bowls with ½ teaspoon margarine each and set aside. In a separate mixing bowl, using clean beaters, beat egg white at high speed until soft peaks form; add remaining sugar and continue beating until stiff peaks form. Gently fold beaten egg white into bread mixture. Turn bread mixture into greased bowls and bake for 30 minutes (until pudding is puffed and browned). Let stand for 5 minutes before serving.

Makes 2 servings.   *Per serving: 226 calories.*

Orange Spanish 'Cream'

2 teaspoons unflavoured gelatine

8 fl oz (240 ml) skim milk

1 large egg, separated

4 teaspoons sugar

2 tablespoons thawed frozen concentrated orange juice

½ teaspoon grated orange peel

1 medium orange, peeled and sectioned

In blender container, sprinkle gelatine over 2 fl oz (60 ml) milk and let stand to soften, about 5 minutes. Bring remaining milk to the boil in a small saucepan. Add to softened gelatine and blend at low speed until gelatine is dissolved. Add egg yolk and 2 teaspoons sugar and blend until well mixed; add juice and orange peel and blend for 1 minute longer. Pour into a bowl, cover and chill until mixture mounds slightly when dropped from a spoon, 20 to 30 minutes. Beat egg white in a separate bowl, using an electric mixer, until soft peaks form. Add remaining sugar and continue beating until stiff but not dry. Fold beaten white into chilled gelatine mixture; turn into a glass serving bowl or divide into 4 dessert dishes. Cover and chill until set, 2 to 3 hours. Serve each portion garnished with a quarter of the orange sections.

Makes 4 servings.   *Per serving: 86 calories.*

Apricot Surprise

4 teaspoons margarine
8 slices (8 oz/240 g) wholemeal bread
4 oz (120 g) sultanas
1 lb (480 g) canned apricot halves, sliced
4 eggs
2 pints (1 litre 200 ml) skim milk
3 tablespoons sugar
1 teaspoon mixed spice

Spread margarine on bread. Cut into small squares. Arrange in overlapping layers in large ovenproof dish. Sprinkle with sultanas and sliced apricots. Whisk eggs with milk and sugar and pour over bread and fruit. Sprinkle with mixed spice and bake in fairly hot oven, 400°F, 200°C, Gas Mark 6, for 35 minutes, or until set and brown on top.

Makes 8 servings. *Per serving: 258 calories.*

Blackberry Cheesecake

8 digestive biscuits, crushed
4 tablespoons low-fat spread
6 tablespoons sugar
4 teaspoons unflavoured gelatine
2 fl oz (60 ml) hot water
10 oz (300 g) low-fat soft cheese
¼ pint (300 ml) skim milk
1 tablespoon lemon juice
1 lb 4 oz (600 g) prepared ripe blackberries (reserve some for garnish)
1 egg white

Mix the biscuit crumbs with low-fat spread and half the sugar. Use to line the bottom of a 7½-inch (19-cm) cake tin with removable base. Dissolve the gelatine in hot water. Combine the remaining sugar, low-fat soft cheese, skim milk, lemon juice and gelatine mixture in a basin and beat thoroughly. Fold blackberries into the mixture. Beat egg white until stiff peaks are formed and gently fold into mixture in basin. Pour onto crumb base. Smooth the top and decorate with reserved berries. Chill for 1 to 2 hours. Carefully remove the cake on the base of the tin, transfer to a plate and serve.

Makes 8 servings.   *Per serving: 268 calories.*

Spicy Apple Crumble

3 medium cooking apples
1 tablespoon water
1 oz (30 g) raisins
2 tablespoons brown sugar
3 oz (90 g) plain flour
4 tablespoons low-fat spread
1 tablespoon shredded coconut
3 oz (90 g) porridge oats
pinch each cinnamon and ground cloves

Peel and core apples, place in saucepan with 1 tablespoon water and cook over gentle heat until soft and fluffy. Stir in raisins and 2 teaspoons of brown sugar. Place in large ovenproof dish. Rub fat into flour. Mix together with coconut, porridge oats, remaining sugar and spices. Sprinkle mixture over stewed apple and bake in oven at 350°F, 180°C, Gas Mark 4, for 20 minutes or until golden brown.

Makes 4 servings.   *Per serving: 303 calories.*

NON-COOK CREATIONS

Non-cooked meals aren't just for lazy summer days. There are lots of occasions all year round when it's nice to put a tasty dish together without a mountain of pots and pans to wash afterwards.

Apart from making toast or dissolving gelatine, you can take a rest from the cooker altogether while making recipes from this section! The secret of success lies in using a really wide variety of ingredients. Salads don't have to be just green leaves and tomatoes. For instance, try Fruited Coleslaw (page 101) with grapes, orange and apple, or Honeyed Fruit and Carrot Salad (page 103), a delicious mixture of carrots, prunes and apple. We've included some hearty main-dish salads, too, and dips and dressings with herbs, cheese and yogurt. No need to be bored when there's such a choice!

There are easy 'sweet treats', too – gorgeous cheesecakes with a biscuit crumb base or ice cream dressed up in tempting new ways.

You'll even find ideas for breakfast, the meal which can so easily be lacking in imagination. Try Apricot Muesli or Banana and Peanut Breakfast (page 92) when you want to start the day right – without cooking.

Breakfasts

Apricot Muesli
Banana and Peanut
    Breakfast
Banana Split Breakfast
Coconut-Bilberry Parfait

Starters and Dips

Cucumber-Yogurt Dip
'Creamy' Cucumber and
    Lime Starter

Honeydew Refresher
Melon Melange
Sardine Dip
Smoked Salmon Pate
Smoked Salmon and
    Horseradish Relish
    Appetizer
Tangy Cheese Dip
Zippy Parsley Dip

Salads and Side Dishes

Asparagus Vinaigrette

Fruited Coleslaw
Honeyed Fruit and Carrot
   Salad
Jellied Beetroot Salad
Macaroni-Cheddar Salad
Melon and Strawberry
   Salad
Mixed Green Salad with
   Dressing
Mushroom Salad
Oriental Ginger Slaw
Oriental Salad
Spiced Orange Salad
Tabbouleh
Tomato-Cucumber Salad
   with Parsley Dressing

Main Dishes

Banana and Soft Cheese
   Quickie
Beef and Tomato Special
Cheese Salad with
   'Creamy' Dressing
Cottage Tomato
Lamb and Bean Salad with
   Vinaigrette Dressing
Liver Sausage Open
   Sandwich
Ploughman's Lunch
Salad Nicoise
Salmon Pate

Desserts and Snacks

Blackcurrant Cheesecake
Calypso 'Cream'
Chocolate Truffles
Ginger Ice Cream
Mixed Fruit Ambrosia
Peach Cheesecake
Peanut Butter Bonbons
Peanut Fudge Sundae

Dressings

Anchovy-Garlic Dressing
Buttermilk-Herb Dressing
Cranberry-Orange Relish
Spicy Blue Cheese
   Dressing
Sweet Herb Vinaigrette
   Dressing

Drinks

Fruit Flip
Fruity Milk Shake
Strawberry Fizz
Strawberry Milk Shake

Coconut-Bilberry Parfait
Special treat for breakfast.

*2½ oz (75 g) bilberries

2½ fl oz (75 ml) natural yogurt

½ teaspoon each sugar, vanilla flavouring and lemon juice

¾ oz (20 g) bran buds

1 teaspoon desiccated coconut

Set aside 1 bilberry for garnish and spoon remaining berries into a sundae glass. Combine yogurt, sugar, vanilla and lemon juice, mixing well; spoon over berries, reserving 1 tablespoon yogurt mixture for garnish. Combine cereal and coconut; sprinkle over yogurt mixture and top with remaining yogurt mixture and reserved bilberry.
*Any berry can be used as an alternative.
Makes 1 serving.   *Per serving: 180 calories.*

Banana Split Breakfast

½ medium banana, peeled and cut in half lengthwise

½ teaspoon lemon juice

2½ oz (75 g) cottage cheese

2 teaspoons strawberry jam, melted

½ teaspoon sunflower seeds

Arrange banana quarters on small plate and brush each with ¼ teaspoon lemon juice; spoon cheese into hollow between banana quarters. Pour melted jam over cheese and sprinkle with sunflower seeds.
Makes 1 serving.   *Per serving: 156 calories.*

Apricot Muesli
When using this recipe, remember to soak the apricots the night before.

1½ oz (45 g) muesli

1 oz (30 g) dried apricots, presoaked and chopped

5 fl oz (150 ml) natural yogurt

Combine all ingredients in a dessert bowl and serve at once.
Makes 1 serving.   *Per serving: 285 calories.*

Banana and Peanut Breakfast

1 slice (1 oz/30 g) wholemeal bread
1 tablespoon crunchy peanut butter
½ medium banana

Toast wholemeal bread and spread with peanut butter while
still warm. Slice banana and arrange over peanut butter. Serve
immediately.
Makes 1 serving.   *Per serving: 196 calories.*

Smoked Salmon and Horseradish Relish Appetizer

1 tablespoon horseradish relish
2 tablespoons natural yogurt
lettuce leaves
2 oz (60 g) smoked salmon, thinly sliced
2 teaspoons chopped red onion
2 stoned black olives, sliced
2 each radish roses, lemon wedges, and dill or parsley sprigs for garnish

Mix horseradish relish and yogurt. Cover and refrigerate until
ready to serve. Line each of 2 salad plates with 2 lettuce leaves;
top each portion of lettuce with 1 oz (30 g) smoked salmon, 1
teaspoon onion and 1 sliced olive. Garnish each serving with a
radish rose, lemon wedge, and dill or parsley sprig. Cover with
plastic wrap and refrigerate until ready to serve. Just before
serving, top each portion of smoked salmon with an equal
amount of horseradish relish.
Makes 2 servings.   *Per serving: 60 calories.*

'Creamy' Cucumber and Lime Starter

1 lime-flavoured jelly
12 fl oz (360 ml) hot water
5 oz (150 g) low-fat soft cheese
2 tablespoons mayonnaise
½ medium cucumber, peeled and cubed
1 stick celery, finely chopped
1 lime, cut into quarters
shredded lettuce

Dissolve jelly in hot water and transfer to blender with low-fat soft cheese and mayonnaise; puree until smooth. Pour into a basin and stir in cucumber cubes and chopped celery. Spoon mixture into 4 individual jelly moulds, or 1 large mould. Chill in refrigerator until firm. To unmould, dip in hot water for a few seconds and turn out on a bed of lettuce, garnish with lime and serve at once.

Makes 4 servings.   *Per serving: 175 calories.*

Tangy Cheese Dip

5 oz (150 g) low-fat soft cheese
2 tablespoons natural yogurt
1 tablespoon horseradish relish
salt and black pepper to taste
1 medium carrot cut into strips
chunk of cucumber cut into strips
1 medium green pepper, seeded and cut into strips
2 slices (2 oz/60 g) bread, toasted and cut in fingers

Combine first 4 ingredients and beat until smooth. Spoon into a small bowl. Set bowl on a large serving dish and surround with vegetables and toast fingers.

Makes 4 servings.   *Per serving: 100 calories.*

Cucumber-Yogurt Dip

1 medium cucumber, peeled, seeded and coarsely grated

1 teaspoon chopped spring onions

½ garlic clove, crushed

1 teaspoon salt

pinch ground cumin

pinch white pepper

2½ fl oz (75 ml) natural yogurt

Squeeze and discard liquid from cucumber. Mix cucumber, spring onions and seasonings; add yogurt and stir to combine. Serve at room temperature or chilled.
Makes 2 servings.   *Per serving: 32 calories.*

Honeydew Refresher

5 oz (150 g) very ripe honeydew melon, cut into chunks

4 fl oz (120 ml) chilled orange juice

2 slices lemon

Chill two champagne glasses. In blender or processor combine melon and orange juice. Blend until smooth; divide mixture into chilled glasses and garnish each with a lemon slice. Serve immediately.
Makes 2 servings.   *Per serving: 34 calories.*

Melon Melange

5 oz (150 g) each watermelon and cantaloupe melon chunks

6 oz (180 g) small seedless green grapes

2 fl oz (60 ml) dry white wine

2 teaspoons clear honey

mint sprigs for garnish

Combine all ingredients except garnish in small serving bowl; cover and refrigerate for at least 2 hours. Serve garnished with mint sprigs.
Makes 2 servings.   *Per serving: 120 calories.*

Sardine Dip

10 oz (300 g) low-fat soft French cheese

8 oz (240 g) canned sardines

1 tablespoon horseradish relish

½ teaspoon Worcestershire sauce

4 tablespoons mayonnaise

2 sticks celery, cut in short lengths

1 medium carrot, cut into strips

Place all ingredients except celery and carrot in blender container and puree for 30 seconds. Chill well before serving. Serve as a dip with the raw vegetables.

Makes 4 servings.   *Per serving: 330 calories.*

Zippy Parsley Dip

½ oz (15 g) parsley sprigs, rinsed and thoroughly dried with paper towels

2 tablespoons chopped onion

2 teaspoons mayonnaise

1 anchovy fillet

½ garlic clove

pinch pepper

2½ oz (75 g) cottage cheese

Combine all ingredients except cheese in blender and blend until pureed, scraping down sides of container as necessary; add cheese, blend just until smooth (do not puree or mixture will be too thin). Refrigerate, covered, until chilled (chilling will thicken mixture slightly). Serve as a dip for raw vegetables or as a salad dressing.

Makes 2 servings.   *Per serving: 80 calories.*

Smoked Salmon Pate

3 oz (90 g) smoked salmon pieces

2½ fl oz (75 ml) natural yogurt

1 tablespoon olive oil

1 teaspoon lemon juice

1 slice (1 oz/30 g) white bread, made into crumbs

black pepper to taste

2 slices (2 oz/60 g) wholemeal bread, toasted and cut into fingers

lettuce and tomato slices for garnish

Put smoked salmon, yogurt, oil and lemon juice in blender and puree until smooth. Add breadcrumbs and puree for a few seconds. Spoon into a dish, adding black pepper to taste. Chill in refrigerator until needed. Garnish with lettuce and tomato slices and serve with toast fingers.

Makes 2 servings.   *Per serving: 254 calories.*

Asparagus Vinaigrette

2 tablespoons wine vinegar

1 tablespoon each lemon juice, olive oil and water

¼ teaspoon each powdered mustard and grated lemon rind

pinch each salt and white pepper

24 asparagus spears, cooked and chilled

2 tablespoons chopped pimento

Combine all ingredients, except vegetables, in jar with tight-fitting lid; cover and shake well. Arrange asparagus spears in shallow dish; add dressing and gently turn spears in dressing to coat. Sprinkle with pimento.

Makes 2 servings.   *Per serving: 95 calories.*

Mixed Green Salad with Dressing

1 medium sized lettuce

1 medium head chicory (optional)

1 bunch watercress

1 small cucumber

1 small green pepper (optional)

3-4 spring onions

1 punnet cress

2-3 sticks celery

chopped herbs such as parsley, basil, mint, lovage, chives, etc.

1 clove garlic, peeled

Dressing

4 tablespoons olive oil

pinch each salt, pepper, sugar and dry mustard

2 tablespoons wine vinegar

Prepare salad greens by washing lettuce and tearing into small pieces. Slice chicory or keep leaves intact. Remove leaves and stalks from watercress; chop. Skin and slice or dice cucumber. Remove seeds and membranes from pepper and slice in rings or chop. Chop onions or cut dark green tops into 'brushes'. Rub salad bowl with garlic clove. Arrange salad greens in the bowl. Combine dressing ingredients in a small jar with tight-fitting lid and shake vigorously. Just before serving, pour dressing over salad and toss well to coat.

Makes 6-8 servings.   *Per serving: 77 or 102 calories.*

Melon and Strawberry Salad

1 small cantaloupe melon, cut in half and seeded
5 oz (150 g) strawberries, hulled
2 tablespoons freshly squeezed lime or lemon juice
2 teaspoons vegetable oil
1 teaspoon grated lime or lemon peel
¼ teaspoon salt
pinch pepper
4 lettuce leaves
2 lime or lemon slices

Using melon-baller, scoop pulp from cantaloupe shells, reserving shells (or scoop out pulp with spoon, then cut pulp into bite-size chunks). Place melon and strawberries in bowl and set aside. Combine all remaining ingredients except lettuce and lime or lemon slices; pour mixture over fruit and toss well to coat. Line 2 salad plates with 2 lettuce leaves each and top with a melon shell; divide fruit mixture into shells and garnish each portion with a lime or lemon slice, twisted to butterfly shape.

Makes 2 servings.   *Per serving: 101 calories.*

Jellied Beetroot Salad

1 blackcurrant-flavoured jelly
¼ pint (150 ml) hot water
½ pint (300 ml) cold water
12 oz (360 g) cooked beetroot, diced
2 tablespoons finely chopped red onion
2 tablespoons finely chopped celery
lettuce leaves for garnish

Break jelly into pieces and dissolve in hot water. Add cold water and leave until syrupy. Add beetroot, onion and celery; pour into a wetted mould and chill until set. To serve, unmould jelly onto serving dish lined with lettuce leaves.

Makes 6 servings.   *Per serving: 71 calories.*

Macaroni-Cheddar Salad

6 oz (180 g) cooked elbow macaroni

2 oz (60 g) celery, diagonally sliced (¼-inch/5-mm slices)

2 oz (60 g) Cheddar cheese, grated

2 tablespoons chopped onion

¼ teaspoon salt

4 pimento-stuffed green olives, sliced

1 tablespoon each mayonnaise and natural yogurt

pinch pepper

4 lettuce leaves

½ medium tomato

pinch paprika

Combine all ingredients except lettuce, tomato and paprika, tossing to mix well; cover and refrigerate until ready to serve. To serve, arrange lettuce on a serving plate and top with macaroni mixture; cut tomato into wedges and arrange round salad. Sprinkle macaroni mixture with paprika.

Makes 2 servings.   *Per serving: 291 calories.*

Oriental Ginger Slaw

4 fl oz (120 ml) tomato juice

1 teaspoon each chopped, peeled ginger root and soy sauce

½ teaspoon sugar

½ small garlic clove, crushed

1 tablespoon vegetable oil

4 oz (120 g) green cabbage, shredded

2 oz (60 g) carrot, grated

To Prepare Dressing: in blender combine juice, ginger root, soy sauce, sugar and garlic and blend until smooth. Remove centre plastic cap from blender cover and, with motor running, slowly drizzle in oil, blending until well mixed. Combine cabbage and grated carrot in bowl; add dressing and toss well. Cover and chill until ready to serve.

Makes 2 servings.   *Per serving: 100 calories.*

Fruited Coleslaw

2 tablespoons natural yogurt

2 teaspoons mayonnaise

1 teaspoon each sugar and lemon juice

pinch salt

1 medium orange, peeled and segmented

6 oz (180 g) green cabbage, shredded

1 medium red apple, cored and chopped

6 oz (180 g) seedless green grapes, cut into halves

4 lettuce leaves

Combine yogurt, mayonnaise, sugar, lemon juice and salt, mixing well. Cut orange segments into halves, removing as much pith as possible. Combine orange with cabbage, apple, and grapes; pour mayonnaise mixture over fruit mixture and toss until well coated. Serve on bed of lettuce leaves.

Makes 2 servings.　　　　　　　　　　　　*Per serving: 169 calories.*

Tomato-Cucumber Salad with Parsley Dressing

1 medium tomato, thinly sliced

½ medium cucumber, scored and thinly sliced

1 tablespoon chopped parsley

2 teaspoons vegetable oil

2 teaspoons each lemon juice and wine vinegar

¼ teaspoon each salt, powdered mustard and paprika

pinch pepper

Arrange tomato and cucumber slices in overlapping circles on large circular dish. Combine remaining ingredients, stirring well to blend; pour over salad. Cover with plastic wrap and refrigerate lightly before serving.

Makes 2 servings.　　　　　　　　　　　　*Per serving: 58 calories.*

Tabbouleh

1½ oz (45 g) uncooked cracked wheat (bulgur)

3 fl oz (90 ml) water

2 fl oz (60 ml) lemon juice

2 medium tomatoes, chopped

2 oz (60 g) each spring onions and green pepper, chopped

1 tablespoon chopped parsley

1 tablespoon olive oil

½ teaspoon salt

1 teaspoon chopped mint

pinch each ground cumin and ground coriander

8 lettuce leaves

mint sprigs and ½ lemon slice for garnish

Combine cracked wheat, water and lemon juice in large bowl; cover and refrigerate until all liquid is absorbed, about 1 hour. Add all remaining ingredients, except lettuce, to cracked wheat mixture and stir to combine. Line serving dish with lettuce leaves and spoon tabbouleh over lettuce. Garnish with mint sprigs and lemon slice.

Makes 2 servings. *Per serving: 181 calories.*

Spiced Orange Salad

2 medium oranges, peeled and sliced

6 thin onion rings

2 tablespoons lemon juice

1 tablespoon olive oil

1 small garlic clove, crushed

¼ teaspoon each salt and pepper

3 stoned black olives, sliced

1 tablespoon chopped parsley

Combine all ingredients except olives and parsley; toss well. Cover and refrigerate until chilled. Just before serving, toss again. Arrange orange mixture decoratively on serving plate

and garnish with olives and parsley.
Makes 2 servings.   *Per serving: 109 calories.*

Honeyed Fruit and Carrot Salad

8 oz (240 g) carrots, coarsely grated

1 medium apple, cored and chopped

1 large stoned prune, chopped

½ oz (15 g) seedless raisins, chopped

1 teaspoon chopped sunflower seeds

4 teaspoons lemon juice

½ teaspoon honey

Combine carrots, fruits and sunflower seeds in serving bowl.
Mix lemon juice with honey; pour over salad and toss well.
Makes 2 servings.   *Per serving: 86 calories.*

Oriental Salad

2 oz (60 g) cooked roast beef, pork or skinned chicken, cut into thin strips

2 oz (60 g) cooked long-grain rice

1 egg, scrambled in non-stick pan

1 stick celery, sliced diagonally

1 tablespoon chopped spring onions

1 tablespoon teriyaki sauce

2 teaspoons each dry sherry and vegetable oil

pinch garlic powder

½ teaspoon honey

pinch each powdered mustard and ground ginger

4 lettuce leaves

Combine first 5 ingredients in salad bowl and toss; cover and
refrigerate for at least 30 minutes. Combine remaining
ingredients, except lettuce, in small bowl; cover and
refrigerate until ready to serve. Stir dressing and pour over rice
mixture; toss to coat all ingredients. Serve on bed of lettuce
leaves.
Makes 1 serving.   *Per serving: 383 calories.*

Mushroom Salad

1 tablespoon olive oil	
1½ teaspoons lemon juice	
¼ teaspoon each salt and oregano	
pinch pepper	
6 oz (180 g) mushrooms, sliced	
1 tablespoon chopped spring onions	
4 lettuce leaves	

Thoroughly combine oil, lemon juice and seasonings; add mushrooms and spring onions and toss to coat. Cover bowl and refrigerate until chilled. To serve, line dish with lettuce leaves. Toss salad again and serve on lettuce.

Makes 2 servings. *Per serving: 76 calories.*

Salad Nicoise

Salad

8 oz (240 g) drained canned tuna, flaked

16 chilled iceberg lettuce leaves, torn into bite-size pieces

2 chilled medium tomatoes, each cut into 8 wedges

8 stoned black olives, sliced

4 large eggs, hard-boiled, each cut into 8 wedges

Dressing

2 tablespoons olive oil

4 teaspoons white wine vinegar

2 teaspoons chopped fresh basil

2 anchovy fillets, chopped

2 teaspoons lemon juice

1 teaspoon French mustard

To Prepare Salad: Combine first 4 ingredients and toss. In large salad bowl arrange egg wedges over tuna mixture and set aside.

To Prepare Dressing: In blender or processor combine

remaining ingredients and blend until smooth, scraping mixture down from sides of container as necessary. Pour dressing over salad and serve immediately.

Makes 4 servings.   *Per serving: 290 calories.*

Liver Sausage Open Sandwich

1 slice (1 oz/30 g) rye bread
1 teaspoon margarine
2-3 lettuce leaves
6 slices cucumber
3 oz (90 g) liver sausage, sliced
1 tablespoon cucumber relish
1 medium tomato, sliced
salt and pepper to taste

Spread rye bread with margarine. Arrange lettuce leaves, cucumber slices and liver sausage on the bread. Season with salt and pepper. Spoon over cucumber relish and top with tomato slices. Wrap in cling film until ready to serve.

Makes 1 serving.   *Per serving: 399 calories.*

Cottage Tomato

½ small green pepper, seeded and chopped
2 oz (60 g) ham, chopped
2½ oz (75 g) cottage cheese
1 beefsteak tomato
shredded lettuce
2 teaspoons chopped chives
chunk of cucumber, finely sliced
1 tablespoon mayonnaise

Mix green pepper, ham and cottage cheese. Halve tomato and scoop out pulp and seeds; add these to cheese mixture and combine. Pack into tomato halves. Arrange lettuce and cucumber on a small plate; put tomato halves in the centre and serve with mayonnaise.

Makes 1 serving.   *Per serving: 280 calories.*

Ploughman's Lunch

1 x 2-oz (60-g) crusty roll or slice French bread

2 teaspoons margarine

2 oz (60 g) Cheddar or Edam cheese

1 tablespoon chutney or pickle

2 pickled onions

1 small pickled cucumber

1 medium tomato, quartered

few sprigs watercress for garnish

½ pint (300 ml) cider or beer

Arrange bread, margarine, cheese, chutney or pickle, pickled cucumber and tomato on a large dinner plate. Garnish with watercress and serve with glass of cider or beer.
Makes 1 serving.   *Per serving: 569 calories.*

Lamb and Bean Salad with Vinaigrette Dressing

8 oz (240 g) boned cooked lamb, cut into thin strips

12 oz (360 g) drained canned small white beans

2 oz (60 g) spring onions, chopped

4 fl oz (120 ml) red wine vinegar

2 tablespoons water

4 teaspoons olive or vegetable oil

½ teaspoon pepper

¼ teaspoon each oregano and salt

2 tablespoons chopped parsley

Combine lamb, beans and spring onions in a large bowl. Combine remaining ingredients, except parsley, in jar with tight-fitting lid; cover, shake well and pour over bean mixture. Toss well, then cover and refrigerate for 2 hours; toss again after about 1 hour. Sprinkle with parsley just before serving.
Makes 4 servings.   *Per serving: 235 calories.*

Salmon Pate

12 oz (360 g) canned salmon

2 slices (2 oz/60 g) white bread, made into crumbs

2 tablespoons mayonnaise

salt and pepper to taste

2-4 teaspoons wine vinegar

Break up salmon with a fork, add remaining ingredients and mash to a fine paste. Turn into a serving dish, cover and chill lightly before serving.
Makes 4 servings.   *Per serving: 221 calories.*

Banana and Soft Cheese Quickie

1 slice (1 oz/30 g) bread, toasted

1 teaspoon margarine

2 teaspoons strawberry jam

5 oz (150 g) low-fat soft cheese

½ medium banana, sliced

Spread toast with margarine and jam; add cheese and top with banana slices. Serve at once.
Makes 1 serving.   *Per serving: 389 calories.*

Beef and Tomato Special

4 oz (120 g) corned beef, diced

4 oz (120 g) canned tomatoes with juice

salt and pepper to taste

1 tablespoon gelatine

¼ pint (150 ml) hot water

watercress for garnish

Put corned beef and tomatoes with juice in blender or processor and puree. Add seasoning to taste. Dissolve gelatine in hot water and add to beef and tomato; puree for 1 minute. Pour into a wetted mould and chill in refrigerator until firm. Unmould onto a serving dish and garnish with watercress.
Makes 1 serving.   *Per serving: 300 calories.*

Cheese Salad with 'Creamy' Dressing

Salad

6 oz (180 g) lettuce, finely shredded

2 medium tomatoes, skinned and sliced

chunk of cucumber, peeled and sliced

1 bunch radishes, trimmed and sliced

2 medium red eating apples, cored, sliced and tossed in
1 tablespoon lemon juice

2 oz (60 g) dried apricots, presoaked and chopped

2 oz (60 g) Cheddar cheese, grated

Dressing

1 hard-boiled egg

1 egg, separated

pinch salt

1 teaspoon caster sugar

1 teaspoon dry English mustard

1 tablespoon cider vinegar

1 tablespoon olive oil

Divide salad ingredients between 2 large dinner plates and
arrange attractively. To make dressing, remove yolk from
hard-boiled egg, finely chop white and set aside. Mix
uncooked egg yolk with cooked yolk and beat well together
until blended. Whisk egg white until light and foamy; add salt,
sugar, mustard, vinegar, oil and chopped egg white to yolks
and beat until well mixed. Gently fold in egg white and serve
over salad.

Makes 2 servings.   *Per serving: 415 calories.*

Blackcurrant Cheesecake

4 digestive biscuits
4 teaspoons margarine, melted
10 oz (300 g) cottage cheese
10 oz (300 g) drained, canned blackcurrants, reserve juice
1 blackcurrant-flavoured jelly

Crush biscuits and mix with melted margarine. Press mixture into a 6-7-inch (15-17.5-cm) loose bottomed cake tin. Chill in refrigerator. Put cottage cheese and blackcurrants in blender and puree until smooth. Heat reserved juice and dissolve jelly in it. Add this to the contents of the blender and puree for a further 2 to 3 seconds. Pour over biscuit base and chill in refrigerator until firm.

Makes 4 servings.   *Per serving: 284 calories.*

Calypso 'Cream'

1 oz (30 g) seedless raisins
4 drops rum flavouring
2 teaspoons caster sugar
5 fl oz (150 ml) natural yogurt
1 teaspoon instant coffee powder
1 teaspoon desiccated coconut, toasted*

Chop raisins roughly and mix well with rum flavouring and sugar. Add yogurt and coffee powder and stir thoroughly. Transfer mixture to a large wine glass and chill in refrigerator. Top with toasted coconut before serving.

*Spread coconut on foil and brown under the grill.

Makes 1 serving.   *Per serving: 216 calories.*

Chocolate Truffles

4 oz (120 g) seedless raisins

4 teaspoons honey

4 teaspoons hot water

8 teaspoons low-fat spread

4 teaspoons cocoa

2 oz (60 g) low-fat dry milk

Soak raisins in honey and hot water. Cream low-fat spread and mix with cocoa and dry milk; mix in raisins. Spoon into small foil tray, press flat and chill well in refrigerator. To serve, remove from refrigerator and cut into ½-inch (1-cm) cubes.
Makes 8 servings.   *Per serving: 101 calories.*

Peanut Butter Bonbons

¾ oz (20 g) cornflakes, crushed

1 oz (30 g) seedless raisins, finely chopped

3 tablespoons crunchy peanut butter

½ teaspoon caster sugar

Measure 1½ teaspoons crushed cornflakes into a small bowl and set aside. In another bowl combine raisins with remaining crumbs; add peanut butter and mash thoroughly with a fork. Using a heaped teaspoonful of mixture at a time, form with palms of hands into 1-inch (2.5-cm) balls (should yield 8 balls). Roll each ball in reserved cornflake crumbs, coating all sides. Arrange coated balls on a plate in a single layer; cover lightly with plastic wrap and refrigerate until chilled. Just before serving, roll each ball in sugar and place in a fluted paper sweet case.
Makes 2 servings.   *Per serving: 222 calories.*

Ginger Ice Cream

6 oz (180 g) frozen vanilla ice cream

½ teaspoon grated, peeled ginger root

In blender or processor, blend ice cream with grated ginger

until smooth. Divide mixture between 3 small dishes. Serve at
once.
Makes 3 servings.   *Per serving: 97 calories.*

Mixed Fruit Ambrosia

* ½ medium papaya, peeled, seeded and cut into ½-inch (1-cm) cubes

2 oz (60 g) canned mandarin orange segments

3 oz (90 g) seedless green grapes

4 teaspoons lemon juice

1 teaspoon sugar

¼ teaspoon rum flavouring

2 teaspoons desiccated coconut

Combine all ingredients except coconut, tossing to mix well.
Divide mixture into 2 sundae glasses and sprinkle each portion
with 1 teaspoon coconut.
*1 red eating apple, diced, may be used as an alternative.
Makes 2 servings.   *Per serving: 96 calories.*

Peach Cheesecake

8 digestive biscuits

8 teaspoons margarine, melted

1 peach-flavoured jelly

½ pint (300 ml) hot water

5 oz (150 g) low-fat soft cheese

5 fl oz (150 ml) natural yogurt

8 oz (240 g) drained, canned peach slices

Crush biscuits and add to melted margarine. Press mixture
into base of 6-7-inch (15-17.5-cm) loose bottomed cake tin.
Dissolve jelly in hot water. Put in blender with low-fat soft
cheese, yogurt and half the canned peach slices. Puree until
smooth. Pour on to biscuit crumb base and chill in refrigerator
until firm. Decorate with remaining peach slices and serve at
once.
Makes 8 servings.   *Per serving: 190 calories.*

Peanut Fudge Sundae

12 oz (360 g) canned fruit cocktail with juice

6 tablespoons crunchy peanut butter

2 tablespoons golden syrup

4 x 2-oz (60-g) slices vanilla ice cream

Drain juice from the fruit cocktail into a basin and mix well with the peanut butter and syrup. To make up sundaes, make layers of fruit, ice cream and peanut butter mixture in 4 tall glasses, dividing evenly.

Makes 4 servings.   *Per serving: 308 calories.*

Cranberry-Orange Relish

2½ oz (75 g) cranberries

1 tablespoon thawed frozen concentrated orange juice

2 teaspoons orange marmalade

1 teaspoon sugar

Combine all ingredients in blender or processor and blend until pureed, scraping down sides of container as necessary. Serve immediately or refrigerate until ready to use. Serve with turkey, chicken or ham.

Makes 2 servings.   *Per serving: 43 calories.*

Sweet Herb Vinaigrette Dressing

1 tablespoon olive oil

2 teaspoons white wine vinegar

1 teaspoon fresh basil or ¼ teaspoon dried

½ teaspoon each lemon juice and French mustard

¼ teaspoon sugar

pinch each salt, pepper, garlic powder and onion powder

In blender or processor combine all ingredients and blend until thoroughly mixed, scraping down sides of container as necessary. Transfer to jar with tight-fitting lid; cover and refrigerate until ready to use. Just before serving, shake or stir well.

Makes 2 servings.   *Per serving: 71 calories.*

Anchovy-Garlic Dressing

4 oz (120 g) drained canned anchovies

2 fl oz (60 ml) red wine vinegar

8 teaspoons vegetable oil

1 clove garlic

pinch of oregano

Combine all ingredients in blender and puree until smooth. Serve with green or mixed salad.

Makes 4 servings. *Per serving: 153 calories.*

Buttermilk-Herb Dressing

8 fl oz (240 ml) buttermilk

1 tablespoon each mayonnaise and lemon juice

½ teaspoon each salt, sugar and prepared mustard

¼ teaspoon each oregano and basil

½ garlic clove, crushed, or pinch garlic powder

pinch pepper

Combine all ingredients, stirring well to mix thoroughly. Cover and refrigerate until ready to use. Stir again just before serving. Use as salad dressing or as a dip for raw vegetables.

Makes 2 servings. *Per serving: 120 calories.*

Spicy Blue Cheese Dressing

2½ oz (75 g) cottage cheese

1 oz (30 g) Danish blue cheese

2 tablespoons natural yogurt

2 teaspoons each chopped spring onions and parsley

¼ teaspoon each horseradish relish and Worcestershire sauce

¼ teaspoon French mustard

pinch white pepper

Combine cottage and blue cheeses and sieve into a bowl; add remaining ingredients and stir until combined.

Makes 2 servings. *Per serving: 96 calories.*

Fruit Flip

20 fl oz (600 ml) natural yogurt

12 oz (360 g) canned peach slices

8 tablespoons canned juice

4-6 ice cubes

Place all ingredients in blender and puree until smooth. Divide evenly between 4 tall glasses, adding a colourful straw to each. Alternatively, place half the ingredients in blender and puree, then repeat with remaining ingredients.

Makes 4 servings.   *Per serving: 134 calories.*

Fruity Milk Shake

4 oz (120 g) canned crushed pineapple

½ medium banana, peeled and cut into chunks

1 tablespoon thawed frozen concentrated orange juice

8 fl oz (240 ml) buttermilk

1 teaspoon sugar

½ teaspoon vanilla flavouring

4 ice cubes

In blender or processor combine pineapple, banana and orange juice and blend until smooth; add milk, sugar and vanilla flavouring and blend until combined. Place 2 ice cubes in each of two large tumblers and pour an equal amount of shake into each tumbler; serve immediately.

Variation: Tutti-Frutti Fizz – Add 2 fl oz (60 ml) soda water to each portion of shake.

Makes 2 servings.   *Per serving: 87 calories.*

Strawberry Fizz

2½ oz (75 g) strawberries, reserve 1 for garnish

2 oz (60 g) strawberry or vanilla ice cream

2 fl oz (60 ml) skim milk

1 teaspoon sugar

½ teaspoon vanilla flavouring

2 fl oz (60 ml) chilled soda water

Chill a large tumbler. In blender or processor combine all ingredients except reserved strawberry and soda and blend for about 30 seconds; add soda and, using an on-off motion, blend just until combined. Pour into chilled tumbler and garnish with reserved strawberry; serve immediately.

Makes 1 serving. *Per serving: 160 calories.*

Strawberry Milk Shake

2½ oz (75 g) strawberries

4 teaspoons low-fat dry milk

2 oz (60 g) vanilla ice cream

2 fl oz (60 ml) water

1 teaspoon sugar

2 digestive biscuits

In blender or processor combine strawberries and low-fat dry milk and blend until strawberries are crushed; add remaining ingredients and blend until smooth. Serve with digestive biscuits.

Makes 1 serving. *Per serving: 280 calories.*

READY AND PREPARED

Storecupboards have existed since cooking began, but nowadays it's hard to imagine how our ancestors ever managed without a fridge! If you master the art of keeping a well-planned cupboard, plus a cleverly stocked fridge, you need never be without the ingredients for a meal. Not just a makeshift meal, either, as our recipes show.

Cheese, eggs, cooked meat or poultry may be teamed with vegetables and salads for a wide variety of imaginative dishes. Make sure your storecupboard includes tomato puree, canned corn and delicious canned fruits, and don't forget to keep a good stock of rice and pasta, those invaluable staples which provide the basis for countless meals.

Choose the greengrocer who has the freshest, most inviting vegetables and salad items, and refrigerate them as soon as you can. Wrap green vegetables in a paper towel and then in a plastic bag – the paper absorbs any condensation. Wrap cut cheese tightly in cling film. Put fresh fish in the coldest part of the fridge and use within 48 hours. Cooked meat or poultry should be cooled quickly for use in other dishes. Place in a basin and stand it in iced water, then cover and refrigerate.

Most importantly, your storecupboard should be cool and dry. Many packet foods carry a date stamp now, but it's a good idea to put the date on cans with a wax pencil and use them in rotation.

Breakfasts

Bacon Omelette
Savoury Cheese on Toast
Toasted Cheese and Apple
  Sandwich

Soups and Starters

Carrot 'Pomerance'
Carrot and Tomato Soup
Cheese-Filled Pears
Cheese and Potato Bake
Curried Cauliflower Soup
Minty Cucumber Soup
Mushrooms with Wine

Salads and Side Dishes

Piquant Stir-Fried
  Mushrooms
Courgette and Pepper
  Salad
Italian Tomato-Cheese
  Salad
Vegetable-Cheddar Salad
Confetti Rice Salad
Macaroni Salad
Hot Potato and Pepper
  Salad

Main Dishes

Baked Vegetable, Cheese
  and Egg Pie
Beef Spread
Cheesy Danish
  Mushrooms
Chicken Fricassee
Corned Beef Cottage Pie
Curried Rice Salad
Devilled Lamb
Egg and Potato Cakes
Frankfurter-Vegetable Stir-
  Fry
Grilled Mackerel and
  Cheese Open Sandwich
Hot Asparagus Sandwich
Liver Sausage Pate
Mackerel Crispies
Mexican Stir-Fry
Oven Cheese Sandwich
Pasta Salad
Pilchard Pie
Rice or Pasta with Quick
  Meat Sauce

Savoury Bean and Corned
  Beef Bake
Seasoned Bean and Egg
  Salad
Smoked Sausage Savoury
Spaghetti Carbonara
Sunny Fish Pie
Sweet-and-Sour Cabbage
  and Ham Saute
Tuna-Macaroni Salad
Turkey Pilaf
Turkey with Sweet-and-
  Sour Sauce

Desserts

Fluffy Strawberry
  Cheesecake
Lemon, Curd, Cheese
  Mousse
Nutty Chocolate Dream

Savoury Cheese on Toast

| 1 medium tomato |
| 1 tablespoon chopped onion |
| 1 slice (1 oz/30 g) wholemeal bread |
| 1 teaspoon margarine |
| 1 oz (30 g) Cheddar cheese, grated |

Pour boiling water over tomato, leave for 3 to 4 seconds, lift out, remove skin and chop tomato finely. Mix with chopped onion. Toast bread and spread with margarine, top with onion and tomato mixture, cover with grated cheese and cook under grill until golden and bubbly.

Makes 1 serving.   *Per serving: 229 calories.*

Toasted Cheese and Apple Sandwich

| 2 slices (2 oz/60 g) white bread |
| 2 teaspoons margarine |
| ½ medium apple, peeled, cored and sliced |
| 1 oz (30 g) Cheddar cheese, grated |

Spread bread with margarine, top 1 slice with the apple, cover with grated cheese and second slice of bread. Cook in sandwich toaster or under grill, turning once, until golden.

Makes 1 serving.   *Per serving: 347 calories.*

Carrot and Tomato Soup

| 8 oz (240 g) drained canned carrots |
| 16 fl oz (480 ml) tomato juice |
| ½ teaspoon garlic salt |
| 1 chicken stock cube, crumbled |
| ground black pepper to taste |
| 1 teaspoon tarragon |

Put all ingredients in blender and puree until smooth. Pour into a saucepan and bring to the boil, adding a little water if too thick. Serve at once.

Makes 4 servings.   *Per serving: 32 calories.*

Bacon Omelette

1 oz (30 g) lean back bacon

1 teaspoon vegetable oil

1 egg

salt and pepper to taste

1 slice (1 oz/30 g) brown bread, toasted

1 teaspoon margarine

Grill bacon until crisp, then cool and chop. Meanwhile, beat the egg until light and foamy and add salt and pepper to taste. Heat oil in non-stick pan and pour in egg mixture. When top of the omelette is set and the bottom browned, spoon in chopped bacon. Carefully fold in half and serve at once with toast spread with margarine.

Makes 1 serving.   *Per serving: 313 calories.*

Carrot 'Pomerance'

6 oz (180 g) carrot, finely grated

4 fl oz (120 ml) fresh or frozen orange juice

Combine in blender and puree until smooth. Pour into a tall glass and chill until required.

Makes 1 serving.   *Per serving: 64 calories.*

Cheese and Potato Bake

4 oz (120 g) Cheshire cheese, grated

12 oz (360 g) canned new potatoes, sliced

6 tablespoons single cream

salt and pepper to taste

shredded lettuce

Arrange layers of cheese and potato slices in shallow ovenproof casserole, sprinkling with salt and pepper and finishing with a layer of cheese. Spoon over cream and bake in a hot oven, 425°F, 220°C, Gas Mark 7, for 30 minutes or until hot and well browned. Serve on bed of shredded lettuce.

Makes 4 servings.   *Per serving: 207 calories.*

Mushrooms with Wine

1 clove garlic

2 teaspoons margarine

6 oz (180 g) button mushrooms

4 teaspoons white wine

4 teaspoons soy sauce

1 teaspoon chopped parsley

2 slices (2 oz/60 g) brown bread, toasted and cut into fingers

Finely chop garlic. Melt margarine in non-stick frying pan and saute garlic until golden. Add whole mushrooms and saute until lightly browned. Add wine, soy sauce and parsley and cook, stirring, for about 2 minutes. Serve with toast fingers.
Makes 2 servings.   *Per serving: 114 calories.*

Minty Cucumber Soup

1 large onion, roughly chopped

1 medium cucumber, peeled and chopped

2 tablespoons finely chopped mint

1½ pints (900 ml) chicken stock, prepared according to package directions

salt to taste

2 tablespoons arrowroot or cornflour

20 fl oz (600 ml) natural yogurt

Add onion, cucumber and mint to the chicken stock in a large saucepan; bring to the boil and simmer, covered, for about 15 minutes or until vegetables are tender. Transfer to blender and puree; return to pan. Blend arrowroot with a little water, add to the soup, bring to the boil and simmer, stirring, for 3 to 4 minutes. Pour the soup into a bowl, cool, stir in yogurt and chill well in refrigerator.
Makes 8 servings.   *Per serving: 62 calories.*

Curried Cauliflower Soup

¾ pint (450 ml) chicken stock, prepared according to package directions

6-8 oz (180-240 g) cauliflower, cooked

1 teaspoon curry powder

1 x 2-oz (60-g) brown roll

Place chicken stock, cauliflower and curry powder in blender and puree until smooth. Place in saucepan and bring to the boil; simmer for 3 to 4 minutes. Serve at once with brown roll.
Makes 1 serving.   *Per serving: 171 calories.*

Cheese-Filled Pears

2 very ripe medium pears, cut lengthwise into halves and cored

1 teaspoon lemon juice

2 oz (60 g) Gorgonzola or Danish blue cheese (at room temperature)

1 tablespoon margarine (at room temperature)

1 teaspoon sunflower seeds, toasted

mint sprigs and lemon slices for garnish

Brush cut side of each pear half with lemon juice; place halves, cut-side up, on each of two salad plates. Beat cheese and margarine together until smooth; fill an icing bag fitted with star tip with cheese mixture. Pipe out an equal amount of mixture into each pear half. Sprinkle each with a few sunflower seeds; serve immediately or cover with plastic wrap and refrigerate until ready to serve. Serve each portion garnished with mint and lemon slices.
Makes 2 servings.   *Per serving: 215 calories.*

Piquant Stir-Fried Mushrooms

3 teaspoons vegetable oil

1 clove garlic

½-inch (1-cm) piece root ginger

1 leek, halved and thinly sliced

8 oz (240 g) button mushrooms, stalks removed

large pinch salt

1½ teaspoons toasted sesame seeds

1 teaspoon soy sauce

shredded lettuce

Heat oil in wok or frying pan with garlic and ginger. Cook for 1 to 2 minutes, stirring. Remove garlic and ginger. Add leek and stir-fry for 2 minutes. Add mushrooms and stir-fry for a further 2 minutes. Add salt and half the sesame seeds. Sprinkle over soy sauce and toss all ingredients together for about 1 minute. Sprinkle over remaining sesame seeds and serve immediately on bed of shredded lettuce.

Makes 2 servings.   *Per serving: 105 calories.*

Courgette and Pepper Salad

8 oz (240 g) courgettes

pinch salt

½ medium red pepper, seeded and chopped

2 tablespoons chopped onion

½ teaspoon lemon juice

pinch pepper

2 servings Spicy Blue Cheese Dressing (see page 113)

Grate courgettes into a colander. Add salt and mix well. Place colander over a bowl and cover courgettes with a plate topped with a heavy weight. Leave for one hour. Remove weight and press courgettes to remove any remaining liquid. Mix courgettes, red pepper, onion, lemon juice and pepper in a salad bowl. Add dressing and toss to coat.

Makes 2 servings.   *Per serving: 66 calories.*

Confetti Rice Salad

1 tablespoon each diced celery and green pepper

1 tablespoon each chopped pimento and chopped parsley

2 teaspoons chopped onion

1 teaspoon each olive oil and white wine vinegar

¼ teaspoon each salt, dried oregano and dried basil

pinch pepper

4 oz (120 g) cooked long-grain rice

Combine all ingredients except rice in a salad bowl and toss until well mixed; add rice and toss to combine. Cover and refrigerate lightly before serving.
Makes 2 servings.   *Per serving: 97 calories.*

Hot Potato and Pepper Salad

1 teaspoon each vegetable oil and margarine

2 oz (60 g) diced green pepper

2 tablespoons chopped onion

9 oz (270 g) peeled cooked potatoes, cut into cubes

1 tablespoon finely chopped red pepper

¼ teaspoon salt

pinch each pepper and paprika

Combine oil and margarine in a non-stick frying pan and heat until margarine is bubbly and hot; add green pepper and onion and saute over moderate heat, stirring occasionally, until onion is transparent, about 3 minutes. Reduce heat and add remaining ingredients; cook, stirring occasionally, until potatoes are well heated through, about 5 minutes.
Makes 2 servings.   *Per serving: 153 calories.*

Italian Tomato-Cheese Salad

2 medium tomatoes, cut into wedges

1 oz (30 g) mozzarella cheese, cut into cubes

4 stoned black olives, sliced

2 teaspoons Italian salad dressing

¼ teaspoon salt

2 large lettuce leaves

Mix all ingredients except lettuce and toss lightly to coat with dressing. Cover and refrigerate until chilled. Serve on lettuce leaves.

Makes 2 servings.   *Per serving: 77 calories.*

Vegetable-Cheddar Salad

6 oz (180 g) broccoli florets, blanched

3 oz (90 g) sliced mushrooms

2 oz (60 g) strong Cheddar cheese, grated

2 teaspoons sunflower seeds

1 tablespoon each chives, lemon juice and olive oil

¼ teaspoon each garlic powder and powdered mustard

pinch each salt and pepper

Mix first 4 ingredients in a salad bowl. Mix remaining ingredients; pour over salad and toss to coat. Cover and refrigerate lightly before serving.

Makes 2 servings.   *Per serving: 216 calories.*

Macaroni Salad

2 fl oz (60 ml) buttermilk or natural yogurt
1 tablespoon mayonnaise
½ teaspoon sugar
¼ teaspoon each salt and prepared mustard
pinch each garlic powder and pepper
4 oz (120 g) cooked elbow macaroni
1 tablespoon each chopped celery and tomato
2 tablespoons each chopped red pepper and spring onions

Combine buttermilk, mayonnaise, sugar and seasonings in a salad bowl, stirring until smooth and well mixed. Add remaining ingredients and toss to coat with dressing. Cover and refrigerate until ready to serve, at least 1 hour.

Makes 2 servings.   *Per serving: 148 calories.*

Baked Vegetable, Cheese and Egg Pie

3 oz (90 g) cauliflower, cooked
4 fl oz (120 ml) beef stock, prepared according to package directions
2 tablespoons finely chopped onion
salt and pepper to taste
6 oz (180 g) spring greens, cooked and chopped
1 slice (1 oz/30 g) bread, made into crumbs
1 oz (30 g) Cheddar cheese, grated
1 egg, hard-boiled and finely chopped

Place cauliflower, stock and onion in blender. Puree until smooth, season to taste and mix with spring greens. Turn into a non-stick baking tin. Mix breadcrumbs with cheese and spread over vegetables. Bake at 375°F, 190°C, Gas Mark 5 for 20 minutes or until vegetables are heated through and cheese has melted. Remove, sprinkle with chopped egg and serve at once.

Makes 1 serving.   *Per serving: 331 calories.*

Devilled Lamb

8 oz (240 g) boned cooked lamb, cut into ¼-inch (5-mm) thick slices

4 teaspoons strong French mustard

¼ teaspoon thyme

4 teaspoons plain dried breadcrumbs

1 tablespoon vegetable oil

Spread both sides of each lamb slice with thin coating of mustard; sprinkle with thyme, then coat each slice lightly with an equal amount of crumbs, being sure to use all the crumbs. Heat oil in non-stick frying pan over moderate heat; add lamb and cook, turning once, until browned on both sides, about 4 minutes on each side.

Makes 2 servings.   *Per serving: 315 calories.*

Beef Spread

2 teaspoons low-fat spread

1 small onion, chopped

3 mushrooms, chopped

¼ teaspoon celery seeds

¼ teaspoon black pepper

salt to taste

4 oz (120 g) cooked beef, finely diced

2 water biscuits

Heat low-fat spread in non-stick frying pan and saute onions, mushrooms, celery seeds, black pepper and salt for 2 to 3 minutes. Add diced beef and saute for 10 minutes. Cool mixture, then put into blender and puree until smooth. Spoon into small dish and chill well before serving. Serve with water biscuits.

Makes 1 serving.   *Per serving: 360 calories.*

Tuna-Macaroni Salad

6 oz (180 g) broccoli florets

2 eggs

1 medium tomato

4 oz (120 g) cooked small shell macaroni

4 oz (120 g) drained canned tuna, flaked

8 thin onion rings

4 stoned black olives, cut into halves

2 servings Buttermilk-Herb Dressing (see page 113)

Cook broccoli in lightly salted boiling water until tender-crisp, about 6 to 8 minutes. If preferred, broccoli may be steamed for 8 to 10 minutes. Drain florets and transfer to container; cover and chill lightly. Hard-boil eggs (10 to 12 minutes in boiling water). Crack shells and cool eggs under running cold water. Chill lightly. To make up salad, shell the eggs and cut each into quarters. Cut tomato into 8 equal wedges. Mix broccoli, macaroni, tuna and onion rings in a large serving bowl. Arrange tomato wedges, egg quarters and olive halves over mixture. Divide dressing into 2 small individual bowls and serve with the salad.
Makes 2 servings.   *Per serving: 419 calories.*

Sunny Fish Pie

12 fish fingers

14 oz (420 g) canned tomatoes

9 oz (270 g) canned sweetcorn

chopped parsley for garnish

Grill fish fingers for 5 minutes each side. Put tomatoes and sweetcorn into an ovenproof casserole; arrange fish fingers on top. Cook at 350°F, 180°C, Gas Mark 5 for 30 minutes. Garnish with parsley.
Makes 3 servings.   *Per serving: 300 calories.*

Turkey Pilaf

4 fl oz (120 ml) tomato juice

4 oz (120 g) cooked turkey, diced

1 medium tomato, peeled and chopped

1 small onion, cooked and chopped

2 oz (60 g) cooked peas

pinch mixed herbs

2 oz (60 g) cooked rice

salt and pepper to taste

Preheat oven to 375°F, 190°C, Gas Mark 5. Heat tomato juice
gently in a saucepan, add remaining ingredients and mix well.
Turn into a casserole and bake for about 30 minutes or until
thoroughly hot.
Makes 1 serving.   *Per serving: 309 calories.*

Egg and Potato Cakes

12 oz (360 g) cooked mashed potato

1 tablespoon finely chopped onion

1 tablespoon chopped parsley

3 hard-boiled eggs

2 teaspoons French mustard

1 egg, lightly beaten

2 tablespoons flour seasoned with salt and pepper

2 tablespoons vegetable oil

4 medium tomatoes

6 oz (180 g) button mushrooms

Mix potato, onion and parsley. Mash hard-boiled eggs, using a
fork and add to potato mixture with French mustard. Beat
well. Work in beaten egg and mix well to combine. Sprinkle
board with seasoned flour, turn potato mixture on to this and
shape into 4 equal cakes. Heat oil in non-stick frying pan and
cook cakes on both sides until cooked through and golden
brown. Meanwhile, halve tomatoes and grill, seasoning with

salt and pepper. Wash and slice mushrooms and gently saute in non-stick pan, seasoning with salt and pepper. Cover pan and shake frequently to prevent mushrooms sticking. Cook for 3 to 4 minutes. Arrange egg and potato cakes on a hot dish with the mushrooms and tomatoes and serve at once.

Makes 2 servings. *Per serving: 525 calories.*

Corned Beef Cottage Pie

6 oz (180 g) potato, cooked

2 teaspoons low-fat spread

3 tablespoons skim milk

1 teaspoon vegetable oil

1 medium onion, chopped

3 oz (90 g) corned beef, cubed

2 teaspoons tomato relish

salt and pepper to taste

Mash potato with low-fat spread and milk. Heat vegetable oil in non-stick frying pan. Saute onions until transparent. Add cubed corned beef. Saute for about 5 minutes. Add relish, salt and pepper and mix together. Put in ovenproof dish; spread mashed potato over the top. Cook under grill until top is golden brown and serve at once.

Makes 1 serving. *Per serving: 497 calories.*

Liver Sausage Pate

3 oz (90 g) liver sausage

2 teaspoons each pickle relish and mayonnaise

pinch each onion powder and garlic powder

2 lettuce leaves

4 cream crackers, halved

Mash liver sausage to a smooth paste; add relish, mayonnaise and seasonings and mix well. Line a serving dish with lettuce leaves; mound pate in centre of lettuce and surround with halved cream crackers. Cover lightly and chill until ready to serve.

Makes 2 servings. *Per serving: 254 calories.*

Cheesy Danish Mushrooms

4 large flat mushrooms

2 oz (60 g) Danish blue cheese, grated

1 slice (1 oz/30 g) bread, toasted

2 tablespoons chopped parsley

large pinch onion powder

large pinch garlic powder

salt and freshly ground black pepper to taste

rind of ¼ lemon

1 tablespoon lemon juice

Wipe the mushrooms with a damp cloth. Remove stalks and place these in a blender container with the cheese, bread, parsley, seasonings, lemon rind and juice. Puree at high speed until the mixture is smooth. Divide mixture evenly between the mushroom caps. Place in an ovenproof dish and bake at 325°F, 160°C, Gas Mark 3, for 15 to 20 minutes. Serve with a mixed green salad.

Makes 1 serving.   *Per serving: 298 calories.*

Hot Asparagus Sandwich

4 slices (4 oz/120 g) bread

2 teaspoons French mustard

2 oz (60 g) Cheddar cheese, sliced

6 oz (180 g) drained canned asparagus spears

4 fl oz (120 ml) skim milk

2 eggs

pinch ground nutmeg

2 teaspoons margarine

Spread each slice of bread with ½ teaspoon mustard. Top each of 2 bread slices with half the cheese and half the asparagus spears (cut spears in half lengthwise and trim to fit if necessary). Top with remaining bread slices, mustard side down, to make sandwiches. Combine milk and eggs in a small bowl. Dip sandwiches into milk-egg mixture, turning until all liquid is absorbed. Melt margarine in a non-stick frying pan;

cook sandwiches on both sides until golden brown.
Makes 2 servings.   *Per serving: 415 calories.*

Grilled Mackerel and Cheese Open Sandwich

1 slice (1 oz/30 g) bread
2 oz (60 g) smoked mackerel
1 spring onion, finely sliced
salt and pepper to taste
1 medium tomato, sliced
1 oz (30 g) Cheshire cheese, grated
mixed green salad

Toast bread on one side. Place fish on untoasted side. Cover fish with onion and season with salt and pepper. Top with tomato and cheese. Grill slowly until cheese is melted. Serve with green salad.
Makes 1 serving.   *Per serving: 335 calories.*

Curried Rice Salad
Turn that leftover chicken into a delicious meal in minutes.

8 fl oz (240 ml) buttermilk
1 tablespoon mayonnaise
1 teaspoon sugar
½ teaspoon curry powder
¼ teaspoon salt
pinch white pepper
8 oz (240 g) skinned and boned cooked chicken, diced
4 oz (120 g) cooked long-grain rice
2 medium tomatoes, peeled, seeded and chopped
1 tablespoon chopped red pepper
1 tablespoon each chopped spring onions and chopped parsley

Combine first 6 ingredients in a salad bowl. Add remaining ingredients and toss lightly. Cover and refrigerate lightly before serving.
Makes 2 servings.   *Per serving: 347 calories.*

Spaghetti Carbonara

2 teaspoons margarine
3 oz (90 g) chopped onion
1 garlic clove, crushed
4 oz (120 g) cooked ham, diced
4 fl oz (120 g) skim milk
2 eggs
¼ teaspoon freshly ground pepper
6 oz (120 g) hot cooked spaghetti
4 teaspoons grated Parmesan cheese

Heat margarine in saucepan over moderate heat until bubbly and hot; add onion and garlic and saute until onion is transparent. Add ham and cook, stirring constantly, for about 3 minutes. Reduce heat to low. Beat eggs with the milk; very slowly pour egg mixture into saucepan, stirring constantly. Continue stirring and cook over low heat until mixture is thickened; stir in pepper. Add hot spaghetti and toss to combine; sprinkle with Parmesan cheese.

Makes 2 servings.   *Per serving: 370 calories.*

Frankfurter-Vegetable Stir-Fry

2 teaspoons vegetable oil
3 oz (90 g) each sliced onion and thinly sliced carrot and green pepper
1 small garlic clove, crushed, or ½ teaspoon garlic powder
3 oz (90 g) shredded green cabbage
6 oz (180 g) frankfurters, sliced
2 fl oz (60 ml) chicken stock, prepared according to package directions
1 teaspoon each cornflour and soy sauce

Heat oil in non-stick pan over moderate heat; add onion, carrot, pepper and garlic and saute until onion is transparent, about 5 minutes. Reduce heat to low and add cabbage; cover pan and cook, stirring occasionally, until cabbage becomes wilted, about 10 minutes. Add frankfurters and cook until well heated through. Mix stock, cornflour and soy sauce, pour over frankfurter mixture and cook, stirring constantly, until slightly thickened.

Makes 2 servings.   *Per serving: 322 calories.*

Mexican Stir-Fry

A useful recipe using storecupboard items and leftover chicken to make up this spicy dish.

1 tablespoon vegetable oil
3 oz (90 g) chopped onion
2 garlic cloves, chopped
2 oz (60 g) each diced red and green peppers
2 tablespoons chopped drained canned chilli peppers
4 oz (120 g) canned tomatoes, pureed
4 fl oz (120 ml) chicken stock, prepared according to package directions
½ teaspoon chilli powder
pinch ground cayenne pepper
3 oz (90 g) drained canned red kidney beans
4 oz (120 g) skinned and boned cooked chicken, diced
4 oz (120 g) cooked long-grain rice
4 teaspoons grated Parmesan cheese

Heat oil in a non-stick frying pan over moderate heat; add onion and garlic and saute for 3 minutes. Add red and green peppers and chilli peppers and saute until vegetables are tender-crisp, about 2 minutes longer; stir in puree, stock, chilli powder and cayenne pepper and bring to the boil. Reduce heat to low and cook for about 5 minutes to blend flavours; add beans, chicken and rice and cook until well heated through. Serve sprinkled with cheese.

Makes 2 servings.   *Per serving: 335 calories.*

Turkey with Sweet-and-Sour Sauce

¼ pint (150 ml) wine vinegar

12 oz (360 g) tomatoes, sliced

3 sticks celery, chopped

salt and pepper to taste

1 tablespoon brown sugar

½ teaspoon capers

8 oz (240 g) cooked turkey, cut into neat pieces

Put vinegar, tomatoes, celery, seasonings, sugar and capers into a saucepan. Simmer for 10 to 15 minutes; add turkey, bring back to the boil and simmer for a further 10 minutes.
Makes 2 servings. *Per serving: 214 calories.*

Smoked Sausage Savoury

2 teaspoons margarine

2 teaspoons vegetable oil

1 large onion, chopped

1 garlic clove, crushed

2 medium tomatoes, skinned and chopped

12 oz (360 g) knackwurst, sliced

12 oz (360 g) baked beans

2 teaspoons brown sugar

2 tablespoons Worcestershire sauce

1 teaspoon French mustard

2 tablespoons tomato ketchup

black pepper to taste

4 x 2-oz (60-g) crusty rolls

Heat margarine and oil in large non-stick frying pan over moderate heat; add onion and garlic and saute until transparent. Add tomatoes, knackwurst and beans and stir for 2 minutes. Add remaining ingredients and cook, stirring frequently, for 6 to 8 minutes or until well heated through. Serve each portion with a crusty roll.
Makes 4 servings. *Per serving: 495 calories.*

Seasoned Bean and Egg Salad

6 oz (180 g) drained canned white kidney beans (cannellini beans)

4 stoned black olives, sliced

1 tablespoon each chopped onion, chopped parsley and lemon juice

2 teaspoons chopped pimento

1 teaspoon olive oil

pinch each garlic powder, salt and pepper

1 teaspoon chopped mint

½ small lettuce, shredded

2 large eggs, hard-boiled

2 medium tomatoes

Mix beans, olives, onion, parsley, lemon juice, pimento, oil and seasonings in a salad bowl. Cover and chill lightly. Divide shredded lettuce between 2 salad plates and top each portion with an equal amount of bean mixture. Cut each egg into 6 wedges and the tomatoes into 12 wedges; alternate 6 egg and tomato wedges around each portion of bean mixture.
Makes 2 servings. *Per serving: 218 calories.*

Pilchard Pie

4 oz (120 g) canned pilchards, drained

3 oz (90 g) potato, cooked

2 fl oz (60 ml) skim milk

salt and pepper to taste

1 slice (1 oz/30 g) bread, made into crumbs

1 medium tomato, peeled and sliced

3 teaspoons margarine

Preheat oven to 375°F, 190°C, Gas Mark 5. Flake fish in basin, mix with potato, milk and seasonings. Transfer to shallow ovenproof dish, sprinkle with breadcrumbs and arrange tomato slices on top. Dot with margarine and bake in oven for 30 minutes or until top is golden brown.
Makes 1 serving. *Per serving: 432 calories.*

Pasta Salad

4 oz (120 g) courgettes, grated or shredded

2 oz (60 g) cooked small macaroni

4 oz (120 g) boiled ham

2 oz (60 g) Cheddar cheese, diced

2 medium tomatoes, cut into wedges

1 tablespoon chopped onion

1 tablespoon each olive oil, wine vinegar and lemon juice

½ teaspoon oregano

¼ teaspoon each salt and garlic powder

pinch pepper

8 lettuce leaves

Combine all ingredients except lettuce in a salad bowl and toss until well mixed. Cover and refrigerate lightly. Toss again just before serving on bed of lettuce leaves.
Makes 2 servings.   *Per serving: 336 calories.*

Oven Cheese Sandwich

1 slice (1 oz/30 g) bread

½ teaspoon French mustard

1 oz (30 g) Cheddar cheese, grated

1 egg

¼ pint (150 ml) skim milk

salt and pepper to taste

Cut the bread in half and make a sandwich with the prepared mustard and cheese. Place in a shallow ovenproof dish. Beat the egg with the milk, season to taste and pour over the sandwich. Cover dish with foil and bake at 350°F, 180°C, Gas Mark 4 for about 30 minutes. Serve with green vegetables.
Makes 1 serving.   *Per serving: 346 calories.*

Mackerel Crispies

6 oz (180 g) cooked mashed potato

4 oz (120 g) drained canned mackerel fillets

2 tablespoons chopped parsley

1 tablespoon lemon juice

2 eggs

2 fl oz (60 ml) skim milk

salt and pepper to taste

2 tablespoons vegetable oil

6 oz (180 g) green peas, cooked

2 medium tomatoes, halved and grilled

Beat potato and mackerel fillets together; add parsley and lemon juice and continue to beat; beat eggs with milk, adding salt and pepper to taste. Stir into potato mixture and beat well. Heat oil in large non-stick frying pan; drop tablespoonfuls of mixture in and cook over fairly high heat, turning once, until golden on both sides. Continue until all mixture is used up. Serve at once with peas and tomatoes.

Makes 2 servings.   *Per serving: 465 calories.*

Sweet-and-Sour Cabbage and Ham Saute

2 teaspoons vegetable oil

6 oz (180 g) cooked ham, cut into cubes

4 oz (120 g) sliced onions

12 oz (360 g) shredded green cabbage

4 teaspoons white vinegar

2 teaspoons brown sugar

pinch salt and pepper to taste

Heat oil in non-stick frying pan; add ham and onions and saute until browned. Add cabbage and stir until well mixed; add remaining ingredients and cook, stirring occasionally, until cabbage is tender and liquid has evaporated.

Makes 2 servings.   *Per serving: 219 calories.*

Rice or Pasta with Quick Meat Sauce

12 fl oz (360 ml) tomato juice
¼ teaspoon oregano
1 bay leaf
¼ teaspoon garlic salt
2 teaspoons brown sugar
8 oz (240 g) minced cooked beef or lamb
8 oz (240 g) hot cooked rice or pasta

Place the tomato juice in a saucepan with oregano, bay leaf, garlic salt, sugar and minced meat. Bring to the boil, cover and simmer for 20 minutes. Remove and discard bay leaf. Serve over cooked rice or pasta.

Makes 2 servings.   *Per serving: 386 calories.*

Savoury Bean and Corned Beef Bake

6 oz (180 g) baked beans
8 oz (240 g) corned beef, chopped
1 large onion, chopped and blanched in boiling water for 1-2 minutes
1 teaspoon mixed herbs
salt and pepper to taste
6 oz (180 g) sliced cooked potatoes
1 tablespoon margarine, melted

Mix beans, corned beef and onion with herbs, salt and pepper to taste. Spoon into ovenproof casserole and arrange sliced potatoes on top. Brush slices with melted margarine and bake in hot oven, 425°F, 220°C, Gas Mark 7, for 25 to 30 minutes or until top is golden.

Makes 2 servings.   *Per serving: 460 calories.*

Chicken Fricassee

1 oz (30 g) low-fat dry milk
5 oz (150 g) cottage cheese
4 oz (120 g) cooked chicken, diced
1 tablespoon chopped onion
3 oz (90 g) canned peas
salt, pepper and chicken barbecue seasoning to taste
2 slices (2 oz/60 g) bread, toasted

Make dry milk up to ¼ pint (150 ml) with water. Mix with cottage cheese and rub through sieve or puree in blender container. Place chicken in a saucepan with the cheese mixture, onion and peas. Season to taste and simmer gently for 15 minutes, stirring with a wooden spoon. Sprinkle with chicken barbecue seasoning and serve with triangles of toast.
Makes 2 servings.   *Per serving: 290 calories.*

Lemon 'Curd' Cheese Mousse

1 tablespoon unflavoured gelatine
3 fl oz (90 ml) hot water
5 oz (150 g) low-fat soft cheese
grated rind of 1 lemon
2 tablespoons lemon juice
¼ pint (150 ml) skim milk
2 tablespoons caster sugar
2-3 drops yellow food colouring, optional

Sprinkle gelatine over hot water and stir until dissolved. Put rest of ingredients in blender and puree until smooth; add dissolved gelatine and blend for a few seconds. Pour into 2 dessert bowls. Chill until firm.
Makes 2 servings.   *Per serving: 205 calories.*

Nutty Chocolate Dream

2 teaspoons chocolate syrup or sauce

2 oz (60 g) vanilla ice cream, softened

1 tablespoon crunchy peanut butter

2 tablespoons skim milk

Mix chocolate syrup or sauce into softened ice cream, put into small freezer-safe dessert dish and freeze. Meanwhile, gently heat peanut butter with skim milk and when well mixed and hot, pour over the ice cream mixture and serve at once.

Makes 1 serving. *Per serving: 240 calories.*

Fluffy Strawberry Cheesecake

8 digestive biscuits

8 teaspoons margarine, melted

10 oz (300 g) low-fat soft cheese

2 eggs, separated

5 oz (150 g) drained canned strawberries

3 tablespoons single cream

3 teaspoons gelatine

3 fl oz (90 ml) hot water

Crush biscuits and mix with melted margarine. Press mixture onto base of 6-7 inch (15-17.5-cm) loose bottomed cake tin. Put in refrigerator until firm. Put low-fat soft cheese, egg yolks, strawberries and cream in blender and puree until smooth. Dissolve gelatine in hot water, add to cheese mixture in blender and puree for a few seconds. Beat egg whites until stiff, fold into cheese mixture and pour onto biscuit base. Chill until firm.

Makes 4 servings. *Per serving: 410 calories.*

COOKING FOR THE FREEZER

Your freezer is a good friend if you really make it *work* for you! Commercial packs of meat, fish, fruit and vegetables are good to have on hand, but you can save yourself even more precious time by freezing complete dishes.

Casseroles, soups and stews freeze beautifully – anything, in fact, which has been cooked in a sauce. Pastry, baked or unbaked, can be frozen too. When you can, divide desserts, sorbets and sweet or savoury sauces into servings and freeze in individual containers.

There are, of course, some items which do not freeze well. Hard-boiled eggs tend to go rubbery. Gelatine is fine in mousses and cold soufflés, but clear jellies will go watery when thawed. If a recipe includes cream or yogurt, it is best to add this after reheating, or the mixture may separate.

Most casserole dishes, soups and sauces can be successfully reheated straight from the freezer, either in a moderate oven or over a low flame. But this process can take a long time and it's usually better to thaw the food first if possible. Bring the mixture slowly to the boil and then simmer meat or poultry for at least 10 minutes

Dedicated freezer owners like to do 'batch' cookery, but even if you can't manage this, it's well worth while to *double* your quantities when cooking. Use half and freeze half, and you'll always have a meal tucked away for an extra busy day.

Breakfasts

Freezer French Toast

Basic Recipes

Beef Stock
Chicken Stock
Lamb, Ham or Veal Stock

Basic Pastry
Basic Pastry Shell
Basic Pancakes

Soups

Broccoli Soup
Celeriac and Fennel Soup
Courgette Soup
'Creamed' Tomato Soup

'Cream' of Spinach Soup
Fresh Mushroom Soup
Leek and Cauliflower Soup
Tomato, Onion and Potato
  Soup
Vegetable Soup

Vegetables and Starters

Asparagus Quiche
Sweet-and-Sour Red
  Cabbage

Main Dishes

Beef and Vegetable Pie
Chicken-Mushroom
  Pancake Filling
Chicken in Wine
Chicken Peasant-Style
Chilli Veal Pie
Cod in Pepper Sauce
Cornish-Style Pasties
Egg, Onion and Fish Pie
Fish in Wine and Tomato
  Sauce
Fisherman's Pie
French Bread Four Ways
French Bread Pizza
Ham and Cabbage Pancake
  Filling
Homemade Beefburgers
Hot Chicken and Tomato
  Bisque
Lamb Curry
Lamb and Jam
Lambs' Kidneys in Mustard
  Sauce
Middle Eastern Lamb

Parsley Fish Cakes
Orange Lamb with
  Rosemary
Rose Chicken
Seafood Pancake Filling
Steak Braised in Beer
Sweet-and-Sour Meatballs
Tomato-Beef Stew
Turkey Pie
Tuna Mushroom Pie
Veal Escalopes with
  Cheese and Ham
Veal Balls with Fresh
  Tomato Sauce

Sauces and Dressings

Bechamel (White Sauce)
Fresh Tomato Sauce
Hot Tomato Sauce
Mushroom Sauce (1)
Mushroom Sauce (2)
Paprikash Sauce
Plum Sauce
Strawberry Sauce

Desserts and Snacks

'Apple Cake'
Apple Crumble
Apricot and Orange Frozen
  Dessert
Apricot and Pineapple
  Upside-Down Cake
Apricot Crunch
Apricot-Yogurt Sorbet
Coffee-Rum 'Ice Cream'
Ginger Biscuit Cones
Gooseberry Treat

Mango Sherbert   Rum-Raisin 'Ice Cream'
Peanut Butter Muffins   Sultana Biscuits
Plum Compote   Tropical Muffins
Rum and Orange Sorbet   Vanilla Fudge Swirl

Freezer French Toast

4 eggs, lightly beaten
½ oz (15 g) low-fat dry milk reconstituted with 2 tablespoons water
2 teaspoons vanilla flavouring
4 slices (4 oz/120 g) white bread
2 teaspoons vegetable oil or margarine

Combine eggs, milk and vanilla. Dip bread slices into egg
mixture, coating all sides; let bread soak in mixture until as
much liquid as possible has been absorbed. Heat oil or
margarine in large non-stick frying pan; add bread and pour an
equal amount of any remaining egg mixture over each slice.
Reduce heat and cook until bread is browned on underside;
turn slices and brown other side. Transfer toast to a baking
sheet; cool slightly, then freeze. Once frozen, wrap toast slices
individually or stack and wrap, using 2 sheets of wax paper
between each slice to separate. May be frozen for up to two
weeks. To serve, reheat in toaster or in an oven at 350°F,
180°C, Gas Mark 4.
Serving Suggestions: just before serving, top each heated slice
with 2 teaspoons low-calorie jam or pour 1 teaspoon golden
syrup over each heated slice.
Makes 4 servings.   *Per serving: 191 calories.*
                        Per serving: 209 calories with jam.
                Per serving: 211 calories with golden syrup.

Basic Pancakes

8 fl oz (240 ml) skim milk

3 oz (90 g) flour

2 large eggs

pinch salt

In blender or processor combine all ingredients and blend until smooth; let stand for 15 to 20 minutes. Heat a small non-stick frying pan (to test, sprinkle pan with drop of water; if water sizzles, pan is hot enough). Pour one eighth of batter into pan and quickly swirl batter so that it covers entire bottom of pan; cook over moderate heat until edges and underside are dry. Using palette knife, carefully turn pancake over; cook other side briefly just to dry, about 30 seconds. Slide pancake onto a plate and let cool. Repeat procedure 7 more times, using remaining batter and making 7 more pancakes. To freeze, stack cooled pancakes, using wax paper to separate; wrap stack in freezer wrap and label. Freeze for future use. Thaw at room temperature for 10 to 15 minutes before serving.

Makes 4 servings.   *Per serving: 140 calories.*

Chicken Stock

1 chicken carcass

1 small onion, chopped

1 sachet bouquet garni

1 stick celery, sliced

3-4 peppercorns

½ teaspoon salt

Place the chicken carcass in a large pan with the bouquet garni, vegetables and seasoning. Cover with 2 pints (1 litre 200 ml) water; bring to the boil and simmer, covered, for about 1½ hours, or cook for 30 minutes in a pressure cooker. Strain and discard solids. Refrigerate liquid until fat congeals on top. Remove and discard fat. Pour into freezer container, cover and freeze. Stock will also keep for 2 to 3 days in refrigerator. Use as required in recipes calling for stock.

Yields about 2 pints (1 litre 200 ml)

Basic Pastry

| 1 1/2 oz (45 g) flour |
| 2 tablespoons natural yogurt |

pinch salt

4 teaspoons margarine

2 tablespoons natural yogurt

Mix flour and salt in a mixing bowl. Rub in margarine until mixture resembles coarse breadcrumbs. Add yogurt and mix thoroughly. Form dough into 2 equal balls; cover each with plastic wrap and chill for 30 to 40 minutes (may be kept in refrigerator for up to 3 days), or wrap in plastic freezer wrap and freeze until ready to use. If dough has been frozen, thaw completely in refrigerator before using.

Note: For a shorter pastry use less yogurt. Pastry dough may be frozen in double quantities for larger quiches and flans, e.g. Yogurt-Caraway Quiche (page 145).

Per serving: 170 calories.

Variation: Cheese Pastry – Add 1 oz (30 g) grated Cheddar cheese to dry ingredients and proceed as directed.

Makes 2 servings. *Per serving: 230 calories.*

Basic Pastry Shell

4 oz (120 g) flour

1/2 teaspoon salt

8 teaspoons margarine

2 1/2 fl oz (75 ml) natural yogurt

Combine flour and salt; add margarine and rub in until mixture resembles coarse breadcrumbs. Add yogurt and mix thoroughly. Form dough into 2 equal balls; cover each with plastic wrap and chill for about 1 hour. Roll each ball between 2 sheets of wax paper, forming 2 circles, one about 1/8 inch (3 mm) thick, the other about 1/4 inch (5 mm) thick. Fit the 1/8-inch (3-mm) thick circle into an 8-inch (20-cm) quiche dish, the other into a 7-inch (17.5-cm) flameproof pie plate; flute edges if desired. Wrap in plastic freezer wrap, label and freeze for future use.*

*If shell is going to be used immediately, rather than frozen, prick bottom and sides in several places with the tines of a fork.

Makes 4 or 8 servings. *Per serving: 95 or 190 calories.*

Beef Stock

3 lb (1 kg 440 g) beef bones
4 oz (120 g) celery, chopped
1 medium carrot, sliced
1 medium onion, chopped
1 small turnip, chopped
1 clove garlic, crushed
6 pints (3 litres 500 ml) water
1 medium tomato, chopped
3-4 parsley sprigs
10 peppercorns, crushed
2 bay leaves
½ teaspoon thyme
2 cloves

Place bones on rack in roasting tin. Combine celery, carrots, onion, turnip and garlic in another roasting tin. Roast at 425°F, 210°C, Gas Mark 7, until bones and vegetables are brown. Combine bones, vegetables, water, tomatoes and seasonings in large saucepan. Bring to the boil; reduce heat and simmer, covered, for 3 hours. Strain and discard solids. Refrigerate liquid until fat congeals on top. Remove and discard fat. Pour into freezer container, cover and freeze. Stock will also keep for 2 to 3 days in refrigerator. Use as required in recipes calling for stock.

Yields about 6 pints (3 litres 500 ml)

Lamb, Ham or Veal Stock

1 lb 8 oz (720 g) lamb, ham or veal bones

3 pints (1 litre 750 ml) water

1 celery stick with leaves, sliced

1 medium carrot, sliced

1 medium onion, chopped

6 parsley sprigs

6 peppercorns

1 bay leaf

1 clove garlic, crushed

Place bones on rack in roasting tin. Roast at 425°F, 210°C, Gas Mark 7, until bones are browned. Combine bones with remaining ingredients in large saucepan. Bring to the boil; reduce heat and simmer, covered, for 1½ hours. Strain and discard solids. Refrigerate liquid until fat congeals on top. Remove and discard fat. Pour into freezer container, cover and freeze. Stock will also keep for 2 to 3 days in refrigerator. Use as required in recipes calling for stock.

Yields about 3 pints (1 litre 750 ml)

Broccoli Soup

1 lb 8 oz (720 g) broccoli, chopped

3 pints (1 litre 750 ml) chicken stock, prepared according to package directions

½ teaspoon salt

1 oz (30 g) low-fat dry milk, reconstituted with ¼ pint (150 ml) water

pinch nutmeg

pinch cayenne pepper

Combine broccoli, stock and salt in large saucepan; bring to the boil. Reduce heat and simmer for 15 minutes. Transfer half the mixture to blender, puree until smooth and pour into a bowl. Repeat with remaining mixture. Add remaining ingredients and return mixture to saucepan. Reheat, stirring often, until well heated through (do not boil). Cool, pour into freezer container, cover and freeze. To serve, thaw and reheat gently (do not boil). If preferred, freeze soup without milk and add milk when reheating.

Makes 6 servings.   *Per serving: 40 calories.*

Leek and Cauliflower Soup

12 oz (360 g) cauliflower florets

1 large leek, thinly sliced

4 tablespoons chopped parsley

2¼ pints (1 litre 250 ml) chicken stock, prepared according to package directions

1 tablespoon chopped onion

3 oz (90 g) low-fat dry milk, reconstituted with ¾ pint (450 ml) water

salt and pepper to taste

pinch nutmeg

parsley sprigs for garnish

Combine first 5 ingredients in large saucepan; bring to the boil. Reduce heat and simmer for about 10 minutes, or until vegetables are tender. Using a slotted spoon, transfer vegetables to blender; add 8 fl oz (240 ml) cooking liquid and puree until smooth. Return to saucepan containing remaining liquid; add milk and seasonings. Cool. Pour into freezer container, cover and freeze. To serve, thaw and reheat gently (do not boil). If preferred, freeze soup without milk and add milk when reheating. Garnish with parsley sprigs.

Makes 6 servings. *Per serving: 75 calories.*

Vegetable Soup

8 teaspoons margarine
6 oz (180 g) onions, chopped
9 oz (270 g) carrots, diced
6 oz (180 g) turnips, diced
2 pints (1 litre 200 ml) beef stock, prepared according to package directions
1 tablespoon chopped parsley
pinch thyme
pinch ground bay leaves
salt and pepper to taste
2 tablespoons cornflour

Heat margarine in a large non-stick saucepan, add onions and saute until lightly browned. Add carrots, turnips, stock, herbs and seasonings. Simmer for one hour. Transfer to blender and puree until smooth. Mix cornflour to a paste with a little cold water. Return soup to pan, reheat and thicken with cornflour paste. Cool. Divide between 4 small freezer containers, cover and freeze.

Makes 4 servings. *Per serving: 143 calories.*

'Cream' of Spinach Soup

16 fl oz (480 ml) chicken stock, prepared according to package directions

6 oz (180 g) cooked frozen chopped spinach

pinch nutmeg

salt and pepper to taste

1 oz (30 g) low-fat dry milk, reconstituted with ¼ pint (150 ml) water

1 tablespoon chopped chives

Combine stock and spinach in blender and puree until smooth. Pour into saucepan; season with nutmeg, salt and pepper. Bring to the boil; remove from heat. Slowly pour in milk. Cook for 2 minutes longer, stirring constantly. Cool. Pour into freezer container, cover and freeze. To serve, thaw and reheat gently (do not boil). If preferred, freeze soup without milk and add milk when reheating. Stir in chives.

Makes 4 servings.   *Per serving: 37 calories.*

'Creamed' Tomato Soup

4 teaspoons margarine

1 medium onion, finely chopped

2 x 15-oz (450-g) cans tomatoes, with juice

1¼ pints (750 ml) chicken stock, prepared according to package directions

1 tablespoon chopped parsley

2 teaspoons salt

¼ teaspoon pepper

2 oz (60 g) low-fat dry milk, reconstituted with ½ pint (300 ml) water

parsley sprigs for garnish

Heat margarine in large saucepan; add onions and saute until transparent. Puree tomatoes in blender, add to onions with stock, parsley, salt and pepper and bring to the boil. Reduce heat; simmer for 20 minutes, stirring frequently. Transfer ½ pint (300 ml) of the soup to a bowl. Gradually add milk, stirring constantly. Combine milk mixture with soup in saucepan, stirring constantly. Cool. Pour into freezer container, cover and freeze. To serve, thaw and reheat gently (do not boil). If preferred, freeze soup without milk and add milk when reheating. Garnish with parsley sprigs.

Makes 8 servings.   *Per serving: 65 calories.*

Celeriac and Fennel Soup

6 oz (180 g) celeriac
6 oz (180 g) celery
2 medium bulbs fennel
4 teaspoons margarine
1¾ pints (1 litre) chicken stock, prepared according to package directions
8 fl oz (240 ml) skim milk
salt and pepper to taste
pinch grated nutmeg
dill weed for garnish

Dice vegetables finely. Heat margarine in saucepan and saute vegetables for 8 to 10 minutes. Add stock, bring to the boil and simmer for 20 minutes. Puree in blender and return to saucepan. Add milk and season with salt, pepper and nutmeg. Cool, transfer to freezer container, cover and freeze. To serve, thaw, heat through gently and sprinkle with dill weed.

Makes 4 servings.   *Per serving: 74 calories.*

Courgette Soup

1 lb 4 oz (600 g) courgettes

1 pint 4 fl oz (720 ml) chicken stock (see page 144)

1 small onion, chopped

salt to taste

pinch nutmeg

1 oz (30 g) low-fat dry milk, reconstituted with ¼ pint (150 ml) water

freshly ground pepper to taste

Remove and finely chop the skin of 1 courgette. Reserve. Slice all courgettes. Combine sliced courgettes, stock, onion and salt in a saucepan. Bring to the boil; reduce heat, cover and simmer for 20 minutes or until vegetables are tender. Sprinkle with nutmeg, cool slightly. In 2 batches, puree mixture in blender and transfer to large bowl; stir in milk and chopped courgette skin. Cool. Pour into freezer container, cover and freeze. To serve, thaw and serve cold or reheat gently and serve hot. Sprinkle with freshly ground pepper.

Makes 4 servings.   *Per serving: 60 calories.*

Fresh Mushroom Soup

8 oz (240 g) mushrooms

8 teaspoons low-fat spread

2 tablespoons flour

¾ pint (450 ml) chicken stock, prepared according to package directions

½ pint (300 ml) skim milk

2 tablespoons finely chopped parsley

juice of ½ lemon

salt and pepper to taste

Chop mushrooms finely, then puree in blender or pass through the fine blade of vegetable mill. Melt low-fat spread in a saucepan, add flour and mix well. Cook gently, stirring, for 3 to 4 minutes. Gradually stir in stock and bring to the boil, stirring constantly. Add milk, mushrooms, parsley and lemon juice. Season to taste, cool and pour into freezer container. Cover and freeze. To serve, thaw and serve cold, or reheat gently and serve hot.

Makes 4 servings.   *Per serving: 98 calories.*

Tomato, Onion and Potato Soup

12 oz (360 g) potatoes
1 lb 8 oz (720 g) onions
1 pint (600 ml) water
2 lb (960 g) ripe tomatoes
4 tablespoons tomato puree
2 vegetable stock cubes
2 tablespoons hot water
salt and pepper to taste
¼ teaspoon basil
1 tablespoon chopped parsley

Peel potatoes and onions and slice thinly. Bring water to the boil in a saucepan, add sliced vegetables and simmer for 15 minutes. Skin and chop tomatoes and add to the pan. Mix in tomato puree. Crumble the stock cubes and blend with hot water. Add to the soup and mix well. Season to taste, stir in herbs and cool. Pour into freezer container, cover and freeze. To serve, thaw, reheat gently and divide between 4 warmed bowls.

Makes 4 servings.   *Per serving: 144 calories.*

Sweet-and-Sour Red Cabbage

1 lb (480 g) red cabbage, finely shredded

2 teaspoons salt

4 teaspoons margarine

4 oz (120 g) onion, chopped

4 medium cooking apples, peeled, cored and chopped

¼ pint (150 ml) boiling water

3 tablespoons vinegar

2 tablespoons sugar

Place shredded cabbage in a large bowl and cover with cold salted water. Leave to soak for 5 minutes. Melt the margarine in a large non-stick saucepan. Add the onion and saute gently for 4 to 5 minutes or until soft. Remove cabbage from salted water with a slotted spoon and add to saucepan, together with prepared apples, boiling water, vinegar and sugar. Simmer for 35-45 minutes, stirring occasionally. A further 1-2 fl oz (30-60 ml) of water may be added if needed but the mixture should not be too wet. Cool and divide into 4 equal portions. Freeze in freezer bags or boxes. To serve, thaw and reheat gently to just below boiling point, stirring occasionally.

Makes 4 servings.   *Per serving: 142 calories.*

Asparagus Quiche

double recipe Basic Pastry (see page 145), thawed

16 medium asparagus spears, cooked

3 oz (90 g) low-fat dry milk

½ pint (300 ml) water

4 eggs, beaten

1 teaspoon prepared mustard

1 teaspoon Worcestershire sauce

pinch nutmeg

salt and pepper to taste

Roll out pastry between 2 sheets of greaseproof paper and line a loose bottomed 9-inch (22.5-cm) flan tin. Cut 8 asparagus spears into ½-inch (1-cm) pieces. Mix dry milk with water. Combine asparagus, milk, eggs, mustard, Worcestershire sauce, nutmeg, salt and pepper. Prick pastry case with a fork; pour in asparagus and egg mixture and arrange remaining spears on top. Bake at 350°F, 180°C, Gas Mark 4 for 40 minutes, or until knife inserted in centre comes out clean. Allow to cool completely before removing from tin.

Makes 4 servings.   *Per serving: 260 calories.*

Turkey Pie

2 teaspoons flour

6 fl oz (180 ml) chicken stock, prepared according to package directions

3 oz (90 g) carrot, thinly sliced

1 tablespoon chopped onion

8 oz (240 g) skinned and boned cooked turkey, diced

3 oz (90 g) frozen peas

¼ teaspoon poultry seasoning

pinch pepper

1 recipe Basic Pastry (see page 145)

Blend flour and stock in large saucepan; bring to the boil. Add carrot and onion. Reduce heat to low, cover and cook until carrot slices are tender, about 10 minutes. Add all remaining ingredients except pastry dough. Cook uncovered, stirring occasionally, for 5 minutes. Divide mixture evenly into two individual casseroles. Roll 1 ball of dough between 2 sheets of wax paper, forming a circle slightly larger than top of casserole. Lift dough onto 1 filled dish. Using a fork, press edges of dough to rim of dish; gently pierce top of dough to allow steam to escape. Repeat procedure. Pies may now be wrapped and frozen for future use. To cook, preheat oven to 375°F, 190°C, Gas Mark 5. Bake on baking sheet until crust is lightly browned for 45 to 50 minutes. If pies have not been frozen, bake for 30 to 35 minutes.

Makes 2 servings.   *Per serving: 378 calories.*

Chicken-Mushroom Pancake Filling

4 teaspoons margarine

3 oz (90 g) chopped onion

3 oz (90 g) sliced mushrooms

3 tablespoons flour

12 fl oz (360 ml) chicken stock, prepared according to package directions

12 oz (360 g) skinned and boned cooked chicken, cut into ½-inch (1-cm) cubes

½ teaspoon each salt and thyme

¼ teaspoon white pepper

6 oz (180 g) frozen petit pois

Heat margarine in large saucepan until bubbly and hot; add onions and saute until softened, 1 to 2 minutes. Add mushrooms and saute for 3 minutes; add flour and cook, stirring constantly, for 3 minutes longer. Remove pan from heat and gradually stir in stock; return to heat and bring to the boil. Reduce heat and simmer for 5 minutes. Add chicken and seasonings and simmer 3 minutes longer; stir in peas and cook until tender, about 3 more minutes. Let cool, then divide evenly into plastic freezer bags, label, and freeze for future use. Thaw overnight in refrigerator before using.
Makes 4 servings.   *Per serving: 236 calories.*

Ham and Cabbage Pancake Filling

4 teaspoons margarine

6 oz (180 g) chopped onions

1 garlic clove, crushed

4 oz (120 g) carrot, cut in matchstick pieces

12 oz (360 g) finely shredded green cabbage

10 oz (300 g) boiled ham, cut in matchstick pieces

¼ teaspoon pepper

8 fl oz (240 ml) water

Heat margarine in large frying pan until bubbly and hot; add onions and garlic and saute until onions are transparent, 2 to 3 minutes. Add carrots and saute for 3 minutes; add cabbage, ham and pepper and saute until cabbage is wilted, about 5 minutes. Stir in water and bring to the boil. Reduce heat and let simmer, stirring occasionally, until almost all liquid has evaporated, 5 to 10 minutes. Let cool, then divide evenly into plastic freezer bags, label and freeze for future use. Thaw overnight in refrigerator before using.

Makes 4 servings.   *Per serving: 190 calories.*

Chilli Veal Pie

1 teaspoon vegetable oil

3 oz (90 g) each chopped onion and chopped green pepper

2 garlic cloves, crushed

10 oz (300 g) veal

1½ teaspoons chilli powder

½ teaspoon each oregano and ground cumin

pinch salt

dash hot pepper sauce

3 oz (90 g) drained canned haricot beans

4 oz (120 g) canned tomatoes, crushed

4 teaspoons tomato puree

1 recipe Basic Pastry (see page 145)

Heat oil in non-stick frying pan over moderate heat; add onion, green pepper and garlic and saute until onion is transparent, about 5 minutes. Add veal and seasonings to vegetables and cook, stirring constantly, until meat loses its pink colour, about 3 minutes. Add beans, tomatoes and tomato puree and cook, stirring occasionally, for 5 to 8 minutes longer. Divide mixture evenly into two individual casseroles. Cover with pastry and freeze (see Turkey Pie page 155). Cook as for Turkey Pie.

Makes 2 servings.   *Per serving: 420 calories.*

Seafood Pancake Filling

4 teaspoons margarine

1 tablespoon minced celery

2 tablespoons chopped shallots or onion

6 oz (180 g) mushrooms, sliced

2 tablespoons lemon juice

4 teaspoons dry sherry

6 oz (180 g) each drained canned crab meat and prawns, chopped

½ teaspoon salt

pinch white pepper

Heat margarine over a moderate heat until bubbly and hot; add celery and shallots or onion and saute until vegetables are soft, about 3 minutes. Add mushrooms, lemon juice and sherry and cook, stirring occasionally, until most of the liquid has evaporated, about 5 minutes. Stir in seafood and seasonings and cook until heated. Let cool, then divide evenly into plastic freezer bags, label and freeze for future use. Thaw overnight in refrigerator before using.

Makes 4 servings.   *Per serving: 131 calories.*

Lambs' Kidneys in Mustard Sauce

2 tablespoons low-fat spread

2 tablespoons finely chopped shallots

4 fl oz (120 ml) chicken stock, prepared according to package directions

1 teaspoon French mustard

1 lb (480 g) lambs' kidneys, cored and sliced

Melt low-fat spread in a non-stick frying pan; add shallots and cook until tender. Add stock, mustard and kidneys and cook, stirring frequently, for about 10 minutes or until kidneys are tender. Cool and pack into a large foil freezer container, cover and freeze.

Makes 4 servings.   *Per serving: 132 calories.*

Beef and Vegetable Pie

1 teaspoon vegetable oil

3 oz (90 g) chopped onion

1 garlic clove, crushed

6 oz (180 g) grilled stewing steak, cut in ½-inch (1-cm) cubes

6 fl oz (180 ml) water

3 oz (90 g) each chopped carrot and celery

2 oz (60 g) mushrooms, chopped

1 teaspoon tomato puree

½ chicken stock cube, crumbled

1 small bay leaf

1 clove

pinch thyme

pinch pepper

2 teaspoons flour

chilled Cheese Pastry (see page 145)

Heat oil in large saucepan over moderate heat; add onion and garlic and saute until onion is transparent, about 5 minutes. Add all remaining ingredients except flour and pastry dough. Cover pan, reduce heat to low, and cook until meat is fork-tender, about 45 minutes. Sprinkle flour over beef mixture and mix well. Cook uncovered, stirring occasionally, until thickened. Remove and discard bay leaf and clove. Divide mixture into two individual casseroles. Cover with pastry dough and freeze (see Turkey Pie, page 155). Cook as for Turkey Pie.

Makes 2 servings.   *Per serving: 437 calories.*

Cornish-Style Pasties
double recipe Basic Pastry (page 145)
Filling

10 oz (300 g) lean minced beef
6 oz (180 g) cooked potato, mashed
1 medium onion, cooked and chopped
salt and pepper to taste

Form minced beef into small patties and grill on a rack, turning once until juices stop running, approximately 3 minutes each side. Cool and mash with a fork. Mix beef, potato and onion and season with salt and pepper. Divide pastry into 4 equal-sized pieces. Roll each out into 6-7-inch (15-18-cm) rounds, moisten edges with water, put equal amounts of filling on each, fold rounds in half over filling, press edges well together to seal. Crimp edges with fork; place pasties on flat dish and open-freeze until firm. Transfer to a large freezer container, cover and replace in freezer. To serve, thaw and bake at 375°F, 190°C, Gas Mark 5 for 45 to 50 minutes or until golden brown.

Makes 4 servings.   *Per serving: 255 calories.*

Veal Escalopes with Cheese and Ham

4 x 3-oz (90-g) veal escalopes
4 slices (1 oz/30 g each) lean ham
4 slices (1 oz/30 g each) Emmental cheese
4 tablespoons flour
1 egg, beaten
2 slices (2 oz/60 g) bread, made into crumbs, mixed with pinch each sage, garlic salt and pepper
4 teaspoons vegetable oil

Beat escalopes between 2 sheets cling film until thin. Place a slice each of ham and cheese on each escalope. Fold in half so that cheese is now in the centre of the escalope. Dip each escalope into flour, then into egg and finally into breadcrumb mixture, coating each evenly. Open-freeze on a tray. When

Monte
Cristo
Sandwiches

Orange
'Cream'
Pancakes

Blackberry
Cheesecake

Carrot Cake

Corned Beef Cottage Pie

Quick Liver, Tomato and Onion Saute

Rose
Chicken

Asparagus
Quiche

frozen, wrap escalopes individually in cling film and pack in freezer bag or covered container. To serve, thaw escalopes and gently saute each individually in 1 teaspoon vegetable oil in a non-stick pan for 3 to 4 minutes on each side until veal is cooked through and golden.

Makes 4 servings.   *Per serving: 394 calories.*

Veal Balls with Fresh Tomato Sauce

1 lb 4 oz (600 g) lean veal, finely minced
1 tablespoon finely chopped onion
1 slice (1 oz/30 g) bread, made into crumbs
1 egg, beaten
2 teaspoons olive oil
2 fl oz (60 ml) chicken stock, prepared according to package directions
1 tablespoon finely chopped parsley
1 teaspoon oregano
½ teaspoon nutmeg
pinch each ground bay leaf, salt and black pepper
1 clove garlic, crushed
¾ oz (20 g) flour
2 tablespoons vegetable oil

Mix veal with onion, breadcrumbs, egg, olive oil, stock, herbs, spices and crushed garlic. Shape mixture into small balls and coat evenly with flour. Heat oil in non-stick pan and saute balls gently over low heat until golden brown. Cool. Open-freeze on trays and pack into bags. To serve, thaw veal balls and reheat thoroughly in 1 pint (600 ml) Fresh Tomato Sauce, thawed (see page 177).

Makes 4 servings.   *Per serving: 297 calories.*

Homemade Beefburgers

1 lb 4 oz (600 g) lean minced beef

1 egg, beaten

1 medium onion, finely chopped

2 slices (2 oz/60 g) bread, made into crumbs

2 teaspoons beef extract

½ teaspoon mixed herbs

dash Worcestershire sauce

dash soy sauce

½ teaspoon garlic salt

pinch black pepper

Mix all ingredients well together. Shape into 8 round flat cakes. Open-freeze on a tray. When frozen, pack in a bag, separating beefburgers with circles of cling film or greaseproof paper. Return to freezer. To serve, thaw and grill under moderate heat for 3 to 4 minutes each side.

Makes 4 servings.   *Per serving: 306 calories.*

Tomato-Beef Stew

1 lb 4 oz (600 g) lean stewing steak

2 tablespoons flour seasoned with salt and pepper

2 tablespoons vegetable oil

6 oz (180 g) onion, chopped

6 oz (180 g) carrots, sliced

4 oz (120 g) swede, diced

16 fl oz (480 ml) tomato juice

½ pint (300 ml) beef stock, prepared according to package directions

1 teaspoon basil

salt and pepper to taste

Trim all fat from steak, place on rack under grill and cook, turning once, until juices stop running, approximately 3 minutes each side. Cut into 1-inch (2.5-cm) cubes and toss in seasoned flour. Heat oil in large non-stick saucepan and cook meat cubes briskly until browned on all sides; lift meat from pan and add onion, carrot and swede. Saute, stirring frequently, for 3 to 4 minutes. Return beef to pan, add tomato juice, stock and basil. Add salt and pepper to taste. Bring to the boil, lower heat, cover pan and simmer until meat is tender, approximately 1 to 1¼ hours. Cool. Transfer to large freezer container, cover and freeze.

Makes 4 servings.   *Per serving: 395 calories.*

Sweet-and-Sour Meatballs

Meatballs

1 lb 2 oz (540 g) minced veal

1 tablespoon dried onion flakes, reconstituted in 1 tablespoon hot water

2 teaspoons chopped parsley

¼ teaspoon cinnamon

¼ teaspoon salt

pepper to taste

Sweet-and-Sour Sauce

6 oz (180 g) canned tomatoes with juice, pureed in blender

2 tablespoons steak sauce

2 tablespoons red wine

2 teaspoons brown sugar

3 cloves

½ bay leaf

To Prepare Meatballs: Combine first 6 ingredients and mix well. Divide evenly into 24 balls. Brown meatballs on all sides in preheated non-stick frying pan, cook 5 to 7 minutes or until done.

To Prepare Sauce: Combine remaining ingredients in medium saucepan. Simmer 10 minutes. Remove cloves and bay leaf. To freeze, put meatballs in large foil container and top with sauce. Cover and freeze.

Makes 6 servings.   *Per serving: 113 calories.*

Egg, Onion and Fish Pie

1 medium onion chopped

4 teaspoons margarine

4 teaspoons flour

½ pint (300 ml) skim milk

2 tablespoons parsley

salt and pepper to taste

4 oz (120 g) canned salmon, flaked

4 hard-boiled eggs, chopped

2 oz (60 g) Cheddar cheese, grated

2 medium tomatoes, skinned and sliced

Cook onion in a little salted water until just tender; drain and set aside. Melt margarine in a small non-stick saucepan and stir in flour slowly; add milk and stir until well mixed. Add parsley and salt and pepper to taste. Bring to the boil and cook, stirring, for 2 to 3 minutes. Remove pan from heat and add onion. Arrange salmon and chopped egg in a large foil dish and pour the sauce over. Arrange tomato slices on fish mixture and sprinkle with grated cheese. Freeze.

Makes 4 servings.   *Per serving: 292 calories.*

Parsley Fish Cakes

14 oz (420 g) cooked white fish

12 oz (360 g) cooked mashed potatoes

1 tablespoon chopped parsley

1 tablespoon margarine, melted

salt and pepper to taste

2 eggs

6 tablespoons seasoned breadcrumbs

1 tablespoon vegetable oil (to serve)

Flake cooked fish and mix with mashed potato, parsley, melted margarine and seasoning. Bind mixture with 1 beaten egg. Divide mixture into 12 equal portions and shape into flat round cakes. Beat the second egg and dip each cake into the egg and then into the breadcrumbs. Place on a sheet of foil on baking tray and open-freeze. Transfer carefully to freezer container, storing fish cakes flat in one layer or separating them with foil. To serve, cook fish cakes when just thawed. Heat oil in a non-stick frying pan and cook fish cakes over medium heat, turning once, until golden.

Makes 4 servings, 3 fish cakes each.   *Per serving: 295 calories.*

Fisherman's Pie

| 1 lb 2 oz (540 g) white fish |
| 1 pint (600 ml) tomato juice |
| 2 tablespoons lemon juice |
| salt and pepper |
| 4 teaspoons cornflour |
| 2 tablespoons low-fat dry milk |
| 12 oz (360 g) mashed cooked potato |
| 4 tablespoons grated Parmesan cheese |
| 1 teaspoon curry powder |

Poach fish in tomato and lemon juices seasoned with salt and pepper until it flakes easily with a fork. Lift out fish and flake into a large foil freezer dish. Mix cornflour to a paste with a little water and stir into cooking liquid with dry milk. Bring to the boil and, stirring constantly, cook until thickened, 2 to 3 minutes. Cool. Mix mashed potato with grated cheese and curry powder. Pour cooled sauce over fish and spread potato evenly over mixture. Cover and freeze.

Makes 4 servings.   *Per serving: 287 calories.*

Orange Lamb with Rosemary

10 oz (300 g) lamb, cubed

2 teaspoons vegetable oil

3 oz (90 g) spring onions, chopped

¾ pint (450 ml) chicken stock, prepared according to package directions

4 oz (120 g) cooked pearl barley

2 medium oranges, unpeeled, thinly sliced

2 tablespoons lemon juice

1 teaspoon rosemary

pinch each salt and pepper

On a rack in a baking tin, bake lamb at 350°F, 180°C, Gas Mark 4, until rare; reduce oven temperature to 300°F, 150°C, Gas Mark 2. While lamb is baking, heat oil in a flameproof casserole; saute spring onions until lightly browned. Add lamb and all remaining ingredients; stir to combine. Cover and bake for about 1 hour or until lamb is just tender. Cool, transfer to freezer container, cover and freeze.

Makes 2 servings.   *Per serving: 396 calories.*

Middle Eastern Lamb

2 tablespoons diced onion

2 cloves garlic, crushed

2 medium tomatoes, chopped

8 oz (240 g) cooked lamb, cut into small cubes

¼ teaspoon each ground allspice, mace, coriander, cinnamon, ginger, salt and pepper

8 fl oz (240 ml) chicken stock, prepared according to package directions

1 medium eating apple, cored and chopped

½ teaspoon powdered turmeric, or to taste

Place the onion in a non-stick pan with the garlic, tomatoes and lamb. Mix the spices and stir into the lamb mixture. Add the chicken stock, heat gently and simmer for 5 minutes. Add the apple and cook for 5 to 6 minutes. Cool, pack in foil container, cover and freeze.

Makes 2 servings. *Per serving: 260 calories.*

Lamb and Jam

1 lb (480 g) lamb, cut in 1-inch (2.5-cm) cubes
12 oz (360 g) button mushrooms
4 tablespoons low-calorie raspberry jam
2 tablespoons Worcestershire sauce
2 tablespoons lemon juice
1 teaspoon ground nutmeg
salt and pepper to taste
2 tablespoons margarine
2 tablespoons flour
½ pint (300 ml) beef stock, prepared according to package directions

Place lamb on rack and grill under high heat until well browned. Transfer to casserole with the mushrooms. Place jam, Worcestershire sauce, lemon juice and nutmeg in a saucepan and stir over low heat until jam is melted. Season to taste. Melt margarine in separate saucepan, stir in flour, mix well and cook, stirring, for 1 minute. Blend in stock and jam mixture. Bring to the boil and simmer for 2 minutes. Adjust seasoning and pour over lamb. Cover and cook in the oven at 300°F, 150°C, Gas Mark 2 for 1 hour. Cool, transfer to freezer container, cover and freeze. To serve, thaw, reheat gently and simmer for 7 to 10 minutes.

Makes 4 servings. *Per serving: 305 calories.*

Lamb Curry

10 oz (300 g) lamb, cubed

2 teaspoons olive oil

2 oz (60 g) onion, chopped

¾ pint (450 ml) chicken stock, prepared according to package directions

1 medium apple, cored and chopped

1 teaspoon curry powder

1 teaspoon sugar

½ teaspoon each salt and ground ginger

pinch pepper

1 oz (30 g) raisins

Place lamb cubes on rack in grill pan and grill until rare. Heat oil in non-stick frying pan; add lamb and all remaining ingredients except raisins. Cover and simmer for about 1 hour or until lamb is tender. Add raisins and cook for 15 minutes more or until raisins are plumped and soft. Cool, transfer to freezer container, cover and freeze.

Makes 2 servings. *Per serving: 358 calories.*

Steak Braised in Beer

1 lb 8 oz (720 g) lean braising steak

4 teaspoons vegetable oil

6 oz (180 g) onions, sliced

8 teaspoons flour

½ pint (300 ml) beer

¾ pint (450 ml) beef stock, prepared according to package directions

2 teaspoons brown sugar

pinch basil

salt and pepper to taste

Preheat oven to 350°F, 180°C, Gas Mark 4. Cut steak into 4 equal slices and grill on a rack until juices stop running, approximately 3 minutes each side. Heat oil in a non-stick frying pan and saute onions until lightly browned. Drain onions and transfer to a large casserole; lay steak slices over onions. Add flour to juice in frying pan and cook for 1 minute. Gradually add beer to pan and stir until sauce thickens. Add stock, sugar, basil and seasoning to taste. Bring to the boil and pour over steak and onions in the casserole. Cover and cook in oven for 1½ hours. Cool. Transfer to freezer container, cover and freeze.

Makes 4 servings. *Per serving: 423 calories.*

Tuna Mushroom Pie

1 teaspoon margarine

3 oz (90 g) chopped spring onions or onion

1 tablespoon chopped pimentos

3 oz (90 g) sliced mushrooms

2 teaspoons flour

4 fl oz (120 ml) chicken stock, prepared according to package directions

2 fl oz (60 ml) dry sherry

½ oz (15 g) low-fat dry milk, reconstituted with 2 fl oz (60 ml) water

1 oz (30 g) Cheddar cheese, grated

2 tablespoons chopped parsley

6 oz (180 g) drained canned tuna, flaked

1 recipe Basic Pastry (see page 145)

Heat margarine in frying pan over moderate heat until bubbly and hot; add onions and pimentos and saute briefly, about 3 minutes. Add mushrooms and cook, stirring constantly, until most of the liquid has evaporated. Sprinkle flour over vegetables and stir to combine; gradually stir in stock and sherry and cook, stirring constantly, until thickened. Stir in milk, cheese and parsley and bring to a simmer (do not boil); add tuna and stir until thoroughly combined. Divide evenly into two individual casseroles. Cover with pastry dough and freeze. Cook as for Turkey Pie (see page 155).

Makes 2 servings. *Per serving: 498 calories.*

Chicken in Wine

8 oz (240 g) lean back bacon

8 x 8-oz (240-g) chicken portions, skinned

16 small onions or shallots, peeled

8 teaspoons margarine

8 teaspoons vegetable oil

salt and pepper to taste

1 tablespoon tomato puree

16 fl oz (480 ml) red wine

4 fl oz (120 ml) chicken stock, prepared according to package directions

1 tablespoon chopped parsley

pinch rosemary

pinch ground bay leaves

pinch ground mace

8 oz (240 g) mushrooms, sliced

1 garlic clove, crushed

1 tablespoon cornflour

Grill bacon on a rack until crisp. Allow to cool and chop finely; set aside. Heat 5 teaspoons margarine with the oil in a large non-stick pan and saute onions until lightly brown. Remove from pan and saute chicken portions for 10 minutes. Return onions to pan, cover and cook over low heat for a further 10 minutes. Season with salt and pepper. Add chopped bacon, tomato puree, wine, stock, herbs, mace and crushed garlic. Cover and simmer over moderate heat for 1 to 1¼ hours. Meanwhile saute mushrooms in remaining margarine until cooked; remove chicken pieces from pan and place in freezer container with mushrooms. Mix cornflour to a paste with a little water and add to cooking liquid, bring to the boil and cook until thickened, approximately 3 minutes; pour over chicken and mushrooms. Cool. Transfer to freezer container, cover and freeze.

Makes 8 servings.   *Per serving: 412 calories.*

Rose Chicken

2 teaspoons flour

½ teaspoon salt

pinch pepper

1 lb (480 g) chicken portions, skinned

4 teaspoons vegetable oil

2 tablespoons finely chopped onion

1 garlic clove, crushed

1 medium green pepper, seeded and cut into 1-inch (2.5-cm) squares

4 oz (120 g) mushrooms, quartered

6 oz (180 g) canned tomatoes, crushed

4 fl oz (120 ml) rose wine

½ teaspoon chopped parsley

Combine flour, ¼ teaspoon salt and the pepper on a sheet of greaseproof paper. Dredge chicken portions in flour mixture, turning to coat all sides. Heat oil in large non-stick frying pan; add chicken portions and brown on all sides. Transfer to large casserole. Saute onion, garlic, peppers and mushrooms in the same pan for 2 minutes; add tomatoes, wine, thyme and parsley and bring to the boil. Simmer 2 minutes and pour over chicken portions. Cover casserole and bake in moderate oven, 350°F, 180°C, Gas Mark 4, for 1¼ hours or until chicken is tender. Cool. Transfer chicken and sauce to large foil freezer container, cover and freeze.

Makes 2 servings.   *Per serving: 456 calories.*

Chicken Peasant-Style

4 x 6-oz (180-g) chicken portions, skinned

salt, pepper, garlic powder and paprika to taste

12 oz (360 g) mushrooms, quartered

6 oz (180 g) carrots, thinly sliced

4 oz (120 g) onion, chopped

4 fl oz (120 ml) tomato juice

2 tablespoons tomato puree

2 chicken stock cubes, crumbled

2 large garlic cloves, finely chopped

1 teaspoon gravy browning

1 bay leaf

¼ teaspoon thyme

freshly ground pepper to taste

16 fl oz (480 ml) water

2 tablespoons red wine vinegar

2 teaspoons cornflour, mixed with 2 tablespoons water

3 oz (90 g) pickled silver-skin onions

Season chicken with salt, pepper, garlic powder and paprika. Grill, turning once, for 10 minutes on each side or until browned. In a large saucepan combine next 11 ingredients and cook for 10 minutes. Add water and vinegar and bring to the boil. Reduce heat and simmer for 5 minutes. Stir in cornflour and simmer for 2 to 3 minutes longer or until sauce thickens. Remove chicken from bones and put in casserole. Add sauce and top with onions. Cover and cook at 350°F, 180°C, Gas Mark 4 for 30 to 35 minutes or until chicken is tender. Cool. Pour into freezer container, cover and freeze.

Makes 4 servings.   *Per serving: 192 calories.*

Hot Chicken and Tomato Bisque

2 teaspoons vegetable oil

4 oz (120 g) celery, chopped

5 oz (150 g) carrots, chopped

3 oz (90 g) onion, chopped

2 teaspoons chicken stock powder

1 lb (480 g) canned tomatoes, chopped

12 fl oz (360 ml) water

2 tablespoons dry white wine

1 teaspoon chopped parsley

4 cloves

1 small bay leaf

pinch thyme

salt and pepper to taste

1 oz (30 g) low-fat dry milk, reconstituted with ¼ pint (150 ml) water

Heat oil in a saucepan and saute celery, carrots and onion for 5 minutes, stirring frequently. Mix in stock powder. Add tomatoes, water, wine, parsley, cloves, bay leaf, thyme, salt and pepper and bring to the boil. Reduce heat; cover and simmer 40 minutes. Remove and discard cloves and bay leaf. In batches, puree mixture in blender. Return to saucepan; cook 3 minutes. Add milk. Cool. Pour into freezer container, cover and freeze. To serve, thaw and reheat gently. Do not boil. If preferred, freeze soup without milk and add milk when reheating.

Makes 4 servings.   *Per serving: 84 calories.*

French Bread Pizza

4 x 3-oz (90-g) portions French bread
8 teaspoons margarine
15 oz (450 g) canned tomatoes with juice
1 tablespoon oregano
1 clove garlic, crushed
2 tablespoons brown sugar
½ teaspoon Worcestershire sauce
salt and pepper to taste
12 oz (360 g) Cheddar cheese, thinly sliced

Slice each portion of bread in half lengthwise and spread each cut side with 1 teaspoon margarine. Put canned tomatoes with juice in a blender and puree until smooth. Put pureed tomatoes, oregano, garlic, brown sugar and Worcestershire sauce in a non-stick saucepan, bring to the boil and simmer for 15 to 20 minutes until sauce thickens. Season to taste. Cool. Spread cut sides of each piece of bread with an eighth of the sauce. Top each portion with 1½ oz (45 g) cheese. Wrap in foil and seal. Freeze. To serve, unwrap bread and thaw at room temperature for 1 hour. Bake at 375°F, 190°C, Gas Mark 5 for 25 minutes.

Makes 4 servings. 2 pieces each.   *Per serving: 663 calories.*

If liked, the following toppings may be added to each portion before baking:

1 tablespoon chopped onions with 1 tablespoon chopped green peppers.
Per serving: 667 calories.

1 oz mushrooms, thinly sliced.
Per serving: 665 calories.

2 anchovy fillets with 2 green olives.
Per serving: 683 calories.

French Bread Four Ways

Each spread is enough for 1 x 8-oz (240-g) French loaf.

Onion Spread

3 oz (90 g) chopped onion

8 teaspoons margarine, softened

Per serving: 108 calories.

Garlic-Herb 'Butter'

8 teaspoons margarine, softened

¼ teaspoon each oregano and basil

pinch each garlic powder and onion powder

pinch each salt and cayenne pepper

Per serving: 106 calories.

Cheese Spread

2 tablespoons grated Parmesan cheese

8 teaspoons margarine, softened

pinch paprika

prepared mustard to taste

Per serving: 121 calories.

Anchovy 'Butter'

8 teaspoons margarine, softened

4 anchovy fillets, mashed

1 teaspoon lemon juice

Per serving: 111 calories.

Combine ingredients for chosen spread, stirring until smooth. Cut loaf in half lengthwise and spread mixture evenly over surface of one cut side. Place bread halves together and wrap entire loaf in heavy-duty foil; freeze. When ready to use, preheat oven to 350°F, 180°C, Gas Mark 4; bake wrapped frozen loaf until bread is hot and spread is melted, 20 to 30 minutes. Slice into 8 equal portions.
Makes 8 servings.

Fish in Wine and Tomato Sauce

4 x 6-oz (180-g) haddock fillets, skinned

salt and pepper to taste

2 tablespoons vegetable oil

1 small onion, chopped

pinch garlic powder

15 oz (450 g) canned tomatoes, with juice

1 teaspoon chervil or dill

3 tablespoons white wine

Cut each fish fillet in half and season with salt and pepper. Heat oil over moderate heat, add fish and cook briskly until fish is brown on both sides or flakes easily with a fork. Transfer fish to a plate and set aside. Add onion and garlic powder to the pan and saute until lightly browned. Add rest of ingredients and cook, stirring occasionally, for 10 minutes. Arrange fish in a large foil freezer container and cover with sauce. Cool, cover and freeze.

Makes 4 servings.   *Per serving: 221 calories.*

Cod in Pepper Sauce

1½ lb (720 g) cod fillets, skinned

4 tablespoons lemon juice

Sauce

1 green pepper

1 red pepper

3 oz (90 g) button mushrooms

½ pint (300 ml) tomato juice

¼ pint (150 ml) chicken stock, prepared according to package directions

¼ teaspoon salt

¼ teaspoon pepper

1 teaspoon oregano

Sprinkle cod fillets with lemon juice and grill on both sides until cooked through. Set aside to cool. To make the sauce, wash peppers and remove stalks and seeds. Slice peppers into thin strips. Wash and slice mushrooms. Combine remaining ingredients in a saucepan. Bring to the boil and add peppers and mushrooms. Simmer until tender. Cool sauce. Put cod fillets into large foil freezer container, add sauce, cover and freeze.

Makes 4 servings.   *Per serving: 155 calories.*

Fresh Tomato Sauce

There is nothing like the flavour of homemade tomato sauce. This sauce may be frozen for up to 3 months or refrigerated for up to 2 weeks.

2½ lb (1 kg 200 g) very ripe tomatoes, cut into halves
4 tablespoons chopped basil
3 garlic cloves, halved
1 teaspoon salt
pinch freshly ground pepper

Combine all ingredients in a large saucepan; cover and bring to the boil. Reduce heat and let simmer for 15 to 20 minutes. Remove sauce from heat and let cool. Remove skin and other solids by pressing mixture through a food mill or coarse sieve into a large bowl. Divide into 2-fl oz (60-ml), 4-fl oz (120-ml) and 8-fl oz (240-ml) freezer containers, label, and freeze. When ready to use, thaw only the amount needed.

2 fl oz, 18 calories.
4 fl oz, 36 calories.
8 fl oz, 72 calories.

Hot Tomato Sauce

4 oz (120 g) canned tomatoes, with juice, pureed in blender

4 tablespoons tomato ketchup

2 tablespoons cider vinegar

1 tablespoon Worcestershire sauce

dash hot pepper sauce

Combine all ingredients in small saucepan; cover and simmer for 10 minutes. Cool. Pour into freezer container, cover and freeze. To serve, thaw and serve at room temperature with Chinese-style dishes.

Makes 4 servings.   *Per serving: 19 calories.*

Bechamel (White Sauce)

2 tablespoons margarine

3 tablespoons flour

16 fl oz (480 ml) skim milk, heated

pinch each salt and white pepper

pinch ground nutmeg (optional)

Heat margarine in a fairly large saucepan until bubbly and hot; add flour and cook over low heat, stirring constantly, for 3 minutes. Remove pan from heat. Gradually stir in milk and continue stirring until mixture is smooth. Add remaining ingredients and cook over moderate heat, stirring constantly, until sauce is thickened. Reduce heat to low and cook for 10 minutes longer, stirring occasionally. Let cool, then divide evenly into freezer containers, label and freeze for future use. Transfer to refrigerator to thaw for about 8 hours before using.

Makes 4 servings.   *Per serving: 130 calories.*

Mushroom Sauce (1)

2 tablespoons low-fat spread

8 oz (240 g) mushrooms, sliced

2 tablespoons flour

¼ teaspoon dill weed

8 fl oz (240 ml) skim milk

salt and pepper to taste

Melt low-fat spread in saucepan, add mushrooms and cook over low heat, stirring occasionally, until mushrooms are tender. Stir in flour and dill weed and mix well. Gradually add milk, stirring constantly. Bring to the boil, lower heat and simmer, still stirring, until sauce thickens. Season to taste. Cool, pour into freezer container, cover and freeze.

Makes 6 servings. *Per serving: 50 calories.*

Mushroom Sauce (2)

8 oz (240 g) mushrooms, sliced

12 fl oz (360 ml) beef stock, prepared according to package directions

4 teaspoons cornflour mixed with 2 tablespoons water

salt and pepper to taste

Combine mushrooms and 2 tablespoons stock in saucepan. Cover and cook for 3 to 5 minutes or until mushrooms are tender. Add remaining stock and stir in cornflour. Continue to stir and cook until thickened. Season with salt and pepper. Cool. Pour into freezer container, cover and freeze.

Makes 8 servings. *Per serving: 12 calories.*

Plum Sauce

4 canned plums with 2 tablespoons juice

1 medium pear, peeled, cored and chopped

2 tablespoons red wine vinegar

2 teaspoons sugar

1 slice fresh ginger root, chopped

1 garlic clove, crushed

½ teaspoon soy sauce

¼ teaspoon lemon juice

2 teaspoons cornflour mixed with 2 tablespoons water

Remove and discard plum stones. In blender combine plums with all remaining ingredients except cornflour; blend until smooth. Pour mixture into small saucepan. Bring to the boil; reduce heat. Stir in cornflour. Simmer for 10 minutes or until mixture thickens, stirring constantly. Cool, pour into freezer container, cover and freeze. To serve, thaw and serve at room temperature with Chinese-style dishes.

Makes 4 servings.   *Per serving: 47 calories.*

Paprikash Sauce

1 medium onion, finely chopped

1 medium carrot, finely chopped

3 sticks celery, finely chopped

2 teaspoons paprika

2 teaspoons sugar (optional)

1 bay leaf

½ teaspoon each garlic powder, thyme, salt and Worcestershire sauce

¼ teaspoon freshly ground pepper

1½ pints (900 ml) chicken stock, prepared according to package directions

15 oz (450 g) canned tomatoes with juice, pureed in blender

Combine all ingredients except water and tomatoes in a saucepan. Cook for 3 to 5 minutes, stirring occasionally. Add water and tomato puree. Bring to the boil; reduce heat and simmer for 25 minutes or until vegetables are tender. Remove from heat and remove bay leaf. Cool. Pour into freezer container, cover and freeze. To serve, reheat gently. Serve with roast meats.

Makes 8 servings. *Per serving: 22 calories.*

Strawberry Sauce

1 lb 14 oz (900 g) ripe strawberries

6 teaspoons sugar

2-3 teaspoons lemon juice (optional)

Hull strawberries and puree in blender with the sugar (blend in batches). Add lemon juice to taste and divide between 6 small freezer containers. Cover and freeze. Thaw before serving with sorbets, ice cream etc.

Makes 12 servings. *Per serving: 26 calories.*

'Apple Cake'

1 lb (480 g) cooking apples, peeled, cored and chopped

4 tablespoons water

3 tablespoons brown sugar

pinch ground cloves

2 tablespoons margarine

3 slices (3 oz/90 g) wholemeal bread, made into crumbs

Cook apples in the water with 1 tablespoon sugar and the ground cloves until they are soft. Cool. Heat margarine in a non-stick frying pan and saute breadcrumbs gently until golden brown. Mix the breadcrumbs with the remainder of the sugar. In a foil freezer container, beginning and ending with a layer of crumbs, arrange alternate layers of crumbs and apples. Press down firmly. Cool. Cover and freeze. To serve, remove lid and thaw at room temperature for 1 hour. Alternatively, heat, without lid, in a moderately hot oven, 375°F, 190°C, Gas Mark 5, for 25 minutes.

Makes 4 servings. *Per serving: 193 calories.*

Apricot and Pineapple Upside-Down Cake

8 teaspoons margarine
2 tablespoons brown sugar
6 canned pineapple slices, drained
4 oz (120 g) canned apricot halves, drained
6 oz (180 g) flour
1 tablespoon baking powder
¼ teaspoon salt
2 tablespoons caster sugar
3 small eggs
4 fl oz (120 ml) skim milk
1 teaspoon vanilla flavouring

Preheat oven to 350°F, 180°C, Gas Mark 4. Combine 4 teaspoons margarine with the brown sugar and dot bottom of 8 x 8 x 2-inch (20 x 20 x 5-cm) non-stick baking tin with mixture. Using paper towels, pat pineapple slices and apricots dry and arrange fruit in bottom of the tin; set aside. Sift together flour, baking powder and salt; set aside. Cream remaining 4 teaspoons margarine with caster sugar; add eggs and, using electric mixer, beat until thoroughly combined. Add milk, then beat in sifted flour, one third at a time and continue beating until thoroughly combined; beat in vanilla. Pour batter over fruit in baking tin; bake for 35 to 40 minutes (until top is lightly browned and a skewer inserted in centre comes out clean). Transfer tin to wire rack and let cake cool in tin; invert cake on to serving dish. Serve immediately or freeze for future use. To freeze, cut cake in half, then cut each half into thirds and wrap each piece in plastic freezer wrap. Freeze. To serve, thaw at room temperature. Serve each portion with 2 oz (60 g) vanilla ice cream (optional).

Makes 6 servings. *Per serving: 263 calories.*
Per serving: 360 calories with ice cream.

Apricot and Orange Frozen Dessert

4 medium oranges
4 oz (120 g) dried apricots
1 tablespoon caster sugar
1 egg white

Wash and dry oranges, cut off tops and reserve. Scoop out the contents with a small spoon, discard membranes and place pulp in saucepan with dried apricots and sugar. Simmer gently until the apricots are cooked. Place fruit mixture in blender and puree until smooth. Cool. Beat egg white until stiff peaks form. Fold egg white into fruit puree. Fill orange cases with the mixture, top with lids. Open-freeze on a tray until firm. Wrap in foil and place in bags. Return to freezer. To serve, thaw at room temperature for 2 to 3 hours.

Makes 4 servings. *Per serving: 106 calories.*

Plum Compote

8 canned plums with 4 fl oz (120 ml) juice
2 tablespoons water
2 teaspoons sugar
1 cinnamon stick
2 cloves
pinch nutmeg
2 teaspoons cornflour mixed with 2 tablespoons water
½ teaspoon vanilla flavouring

Combine plum juice, water, sugar, cinnamon, cloves and nutmeg in a small saucepan. Bring to the boil. Reduce heat; simmer 10 minutes. Remove and discard cinnamon and cloves. Add cornflour and cook, stirring constantly, until mixture thickens. Stir in vanilla. Place 2 plums in each of 4 small freezer containers. Pour an equal amount of syrup over each portion of plums, cover and freeze. To serve, thaw and serve at room temperature.

Makes 4 servings. *Per serving: 57 calories.*

Apricot Crunch

8 oz (240 g) canned apricots

1½ oz (45 g) plain flour

⅓ teaspoon baking powder

1½ oz (45 g) rolled oats

5 teaspoons brown sugar

2 tablespoons margarine

Place apricots in a foil container. Mix together flour, baking powder, oats and sugar; rub in margarine. Sprinkle mixture over apricots. Cover with lid and freeze. To serve, remove lid and bake at 400°F, 200°C, Gas Mark 6 for 45 minutes.
Makes 2 servings. *Per serving: 382 calories.*

Gooseberry Treat

1 lb 4 oz (600 g) ripe gooseberries

4 tablespoons water

3 tablespoons soft brown sugar

4 tablespoons margarine

6 slices (6 oz/180 g) bread, made into crumbs

Cook gooseberries in water with 1 tablespoon sugar until soft. Cool. Gently melt margarine and 1 tablespoon of sugar in a non-stick frying pan. Add the breadcrumbs and saute until crisp and golden. Cool. Stir in the remaining sugar. Arrange layers of crumbs and gooseberries in a foil freezer dish, beginning and ending with crumbs. Cover and freeze. To serve, thaw at room temperature for 3 hours.
Makes 4 servings. *Per serving: 288 calories.*

Apple Crumble

8 medium apples, peeled, cored and sliced

2 tablespoons lemon juice

2 teaspoons cinnamon

pinch ground cloves

pinch ground ginger

8 slices (8 oz/240 g) currant bread, toasted and made into crumbs

3 tablespoons low-fat spread

Arrange apple slices in bottom of large, shallow baking tin.
Sprinkle with lemon juice, then ½ teaspoon cinnamon and the
cloves and ginger. Mix remaining 1½ teaspoons cinnamon
with remaining ingredients. Mixture should be crumbly.
Sprinkle crumb mixture over apples. Bake at 375°F, 190°C,
Gas Mark 5 for 35 minutes or until apples are tender when
tested with a skewer. Cool, cover and freeze. When required,
thaw and serve cold or reheat in moderate oven.
Makes 8 servings.   *Per serving: 136 calories.*

Mango Sherbert

2 very ripe small mangoes, peeled, stoned and cut into small
pieces

1 oz (30 g) low-fat dry milk, reconstituted with ¼ pint (150 ml)
water

4 teaspoons granulated sugar

2 teaspoons lemon juice

¼ teaspoon vanilla flavouring

In a blender or processor combine all ingredients and process
until smooth. Divide mixture into 4 freezer-proof dessert
dishes (or into 2 freezer trays); cover with plastic wrap and
freeze until firm. Allow to soften slightly before serving. If
trays are used, divide into dessert dishes just before serving.
Makes 4 servings.   *Per serving: 95 calories.*

Ginger Biscuit Cones

2 tablespoons brown sugar
2 tablespoons margarine, melted
1 tablespoon golden syrup
½ teaspoon lemon juice
½ teaspoon ground ginger
1½ oz (45 g) flour

Preheat oven to 350°F, 180°C, Gas Mark 4. Combine sugar, margarine and syrup, stirring until smooth. Add lemon juice, ginger and flour; mix to a smooth batter. Using 1½ tablespoons of batter, drop batter onto a 14 x 17-inch (35 x 42-cm) non-stick baking sheet, forming 3 equal biscuits and leaving a space of about 6 inches (15 cm) between each. Using your fingertips, carefully flatten each biscuit into a ¼-inch (5-mm) thick circle. Bake until golden brown, 5 to 6 minutes, (batter will spread to form lacy biscuit, each about 5 inches (12.5 cm) in diameter). Remove baking sheet from oven and let biscuits cool until slightly firm, 1 to 2 minutes. Using a palette knife, carefully remove biscuits from sheet; shape each into a cone by wrapping it round the handle of a wooden spoon (if biscuit becomes too firm to shape, reheat in oven for 15 to 20 seconds). Transfer cones to wire rack, seamside down; let cool. Use remaining batter to make 3 more cones. Transfer cooled cones to a freezer container until ready to use, or store in an airtight container in the refrigerator. Just before serving, fill each cone with 2 oz (60 g) softened vanilla ice cream or lay each cone in a dessert dish and fill with 2½ oz (75 g) strawberries and top with 1 tablespoon whipped dessert topping.

Makes 6 servings.   *Per serving: 90 calories.*
Per serving: 185 calories with ice cream.
Per serving: 140 calories with strawberries etc.

Apricot-Yogurt Sorbet

12 oz (360 g) canned apricot halves with 12 fl oz (360 ml) juice
1 tablespoon unflavoured gelatine
8 fl oz (240 ml) natural yogurt
4 teaspoons sugar
dash almond flavouring or to taste

Pour juice from apricots into saucepan. Sprinkle gelatine over juice and allow to soften. Heat, stirring constantly, until gelatine is dissolved. In blender or food processor combine apricots, yogurt, sugar, almond flavouring and gelatine mixture; blend until smooth. Pour mixture into bowl and place in freezer; freeze until almost solid. Remove from freezer and beat. Repeat freezing and beating procedure twice more. Sorbet may be softened in refrigerator for 1 hour before serving. Divide evenly into 12 sundae dishes. Serve with Strawberry Sauce (page 181).

Makes 12 servings.   *Per serving: 43 calories.*

Vanilla Fudge Swirl

8 oz (240 g) vanilla ice cream
8 teaspoons chocolate sauce
4 teaspoons toasted desiccated coconut

Using an electric mixer at low speed, soften the vanilla ice cream in a large mixing bowl. Add the chocolate sauce and stir it lightly through the dessert to create a swirl effect. Do not mix. Divide mixture into 4 freezer-proof sundae dishes and cover with plastic wrap. Freeze until hard. If you prefer, freeze in larger container and scoop into dishes just before serving. Top each serving with 1 teaspoon toasted coconut.

Makes 4 servings.   *Per serving: 150 calories.*

Rum-Raisin 'Ice Cream'

2 oz (60 g) seedless raisins
8 oz (240 g) vanilla ice cream
½ teaspoon rum flavouring
4 tablespoons whipped dessert topping

Soak raisins in warm water to cover until plumped.
Meanwhile, soften the ice cream in another bowl. Drain raisins
and add to the ice cream with the rum flavouring. Stir well
together. Divide the mixture between 2 freezer-proof ice
cream or dessert dishes and cover with plastic wrap. Freeze
until hard. If you prefer, freeze in larger container and scoop
into dishes just before serving. To serve, top each portion with
1 tablespoon whipped dessert topping.
Makes 4 servings.   *Per serving: 155 calories.*

Coffee-Rum 'Ice Cream'

2 oz (60 g) low-fat dry milk
¼ pint (150 ml) cold water
1 teaspoon instant coffee powder
2 teaspoons hot water
½ teaspoon vanilla flavouring
½ teaspoon rum flavouring
2 tablespoons sugar
1 teaspoon unflavoured gelatine
1 tablespoon hot water

Mix low-fat dry milk with cold water. Mix coffee powder with
hot water and the vanilla and rum flavourings. Mix with milk
and add sugar. Dissolve gelatine in hot water, mix well. Add to
the flavoured milk and stir well. Pour into freezer container
and freeze for 20 to 30 minutes. Remove from freezer and
transfer to large mixing bowl. Whip with electric mixer until
mixture has trebled in volume. Pour into freezer container,
cover and freeze.
Makes 5 servings.   *Per serving: 63 calories.*

Rum and Orange Sorbet

4 oz (120 g) low-fat dry milk, reconstituted with 1 pint (600 ml) water

3 tablespoons sugar

2 fl oz (60 ml) frozen orange juice concentrate, thawed

1 tablespoon lemon juice

½ teaspoon vanilla flavouring

½ teaspoon rum flavouring

Mix all ingredients in a bowl. Freeze, stirring often, until ice crystals form throughout and mixture is firm. Transfer to refrigerator for about 30 minutes to soften slightly before serving.

Makes 6 servings.   *Per serving: 103 calories.*

Tropical Muffins

9 oz (270 g) flour

2 tablespoons sugar

1 tablespoon baking powder

6 tablespoons margarine

6 oz (180 g) canned crushed pineapple

1 teaspoon vanilla flavouring

½ teaspoon coconut flavouring

Preheat oven to 375°F, 190°C, Gas Mark 5. Mix flour, sugar and baking powder. Rub in margarine until mixture resembles coarse breadcrumbs. Add remaining ingredients and stir until mixture just forms a sticky dough and leaves sides of bowl (do not over-mix). Divide pineapple mixture evenly between 12 deep non-stick bun tins. Bake until muffins are golden brown, 30 to 35 minutes. Remove muffins to a wire rack and let cool. Serve immediately or wrap individually and freeze until ready to use. To thaw or reheat, see Peanut Butter Muffins (page 191).

Makes 12 servings.   *Per serving: 141 calories.*

Sultana Biscuits

1½ oz (45 g) bran-flakes-with-sultana cereal
1½ oz (45 g) self-raising flour
1 oz (30 g) sultanas
1 tablespoon brown sugar
2 fl oz (60 ml) skim milk
1 tablespoon margarine, melted

Preheat oven to 400°F, 200°C, Gas Mark 6. Combine cereal, flour, sultanas and brown sugar, stirring with a fork until well mixed; add milk and margarine and stir until thoroughly combined. Drop batter by heaping tablespoonfuls onto non-stick baking sheet, making 4 equal biscuits and leaving a space of about 2 inches (5 cm) between each. Bake until golden brown, 10 to 12 minutes. Remove biscuits to a wire rack and let cool. Serve immediately or wrap individually and freeze until ready to use; thaw or reheat as directed in Peanut Butter Muffins (page 191). Just before serving, dust each biscuit with ¼ teaspoon icing sugar (an easy method for doing this is to press sugar through a mesh tea strainer).

Makes 4 servings.   *Per serving: 149 calories.*

Peanut Butter Muffins

4½ oz (135 g) self-raising flour
4 tablespoons caster sugar
8 fl oz (240 ml) skim milk
4 eggs, lightly beaten
12 tablespoons crunchy peanut butter
4 teaspoons margarine, melted

Preheat oven to 400°F, 200°C, Gas Mark 6. Sift together flour and sugar; add remaining ingredients and stir until combined (batter will be lumpy). Do not beat or over-mix. Fill 12 deep non-stick bun tins with equal amounts of the batter (each tin will be about two-thirds full). Bake until muffins are golden brown, about 20 minutes. Remove muffins to wire rack and let cool. Serve cooled muffins or wrap individually and freeze until ready to use. Just before serving, spread each muffin with 1 teaspoon low-calorie jam. Frozen muffins may be thawed at room temperature or reheated in oven at 300°F, 150°C, Gas Mark 2 for about 10 minutes. Good for breakfast as well as a dessert or snack.

Makes 12 servings.   *Per serving: 198 calories.*

GUESTS ARE COMING

Isn't it strange that some hostesses are always cool and collected when entertaining, while others invariably seem to panic? Planning and simplicity are the keynotes to success with dinner parties and formal entertaining. Do as much as you can before your guests arrive, even down to little things like checking the salt and pepper and chopping the parsley. Polish the wine glasses, put the flowers on the table and have a gorgeous bowl of fruit in case your guests don't eat desserts.

Simplicity is essential when you are a single-handed cook and hostess combined. Don't forget that your friends are coming to see *you* and enjoy a meal in your company. They won't enjoy it if you are disappearing into the kitchen all the time! Try to arrange your menu so that only one dish requires last minute attention. If you are serving a hot main dish, have a tempting cold starter and a cold dessert all ready in the fridge.

Entertaining, though, doesn't always mean a pre-planned three course meal. If you have some good soups in the freezer and cheeses and salads in the fridge, you can rustle up a relaxed and happy meal at any time. Friends love being made to feel welcome when they drop in and most of us can remember an impromptu meal which turned into a lovely occasion, simply because no one had to work too hard!

Soups and Starters

Avocado Salad
Avocado and Cheese Creams
Avocado and Pink Grapefruit Starter with Creamy Cheese Sauce
Cheese, Prawn and Pear Cocktail
Crab Mousse
Cream of Pea and Asparagus Soup
Salmon Mousse
Savoury Prawn Starter
Smoked Cod's Roe Pate
Stuffed Pasta Shell Starter
Tuna and Parsley Pate
Warming Winter Soup

Salads and Side Dishes

Apple and Sweet Potato
Asparagus with Sesame 'Butter'
Aubergine Provencale
Cauliflower Provencale
Italian Salad
Marinated Roasted Peppers
Spinach-Stuffed Mushrooms
Tangy Broccoli Salad

Main Dishes

Chicken-Mushroom Pancakes
Chicken Veronique
Chicken with Ham and Cheese
Chinese-Style Pork
Crispy Cinnamon-Chicken Bake
Curried Chicken with Melon
Fiesta Chicken
Fish Salad with Chilli Mayonnaise
'Frying Pan' Broccoli Souffle
Haddock Provencale
Ham and Cabbage Pancakes
Ham, Rice and Orange Salad
Lamb Korma
Leek and Cheese Crumble
Meat-Loaf Wellington

Nutty Stuffed Chicken Breasts
Orange-Ginger-Glazed Pork Chops
Oriental Chicken Livers en Brochette
Oriental Marinated Cod
Oven-Fried Chicken with Orange-Teriyaki Sauce
Prawn Fandango
Prawns and Noodles with Tangy Tomato Sauce
Rabbit Stew in White Wine Sauce
Rolled, Stuffed Plaice Fillets
Salmon Kedgeree
Sauteed Chilli Prawns
Seafood Pancakes
Tuna Crunch
Tuna and Tomato Quiche
Veal Patties in Parsley Sauce
Yogurt-Caraway Quiche

Desserts and Snacks

Apricot-Raisin Crescents
Carrot Cake
Chocolate and Banana Crunch Pie
Fabulous Fruit Cup
Festive Melon Baskets
Fruit Flapjacks
Ginger Kisses
Glazed Apricot Dessert
Mandarin Cheesecake
Mince Pies
Orange 'Cream' Pancakes
Orange Loaf

Pineapple Cheesecake
Pineapple Fizz
Spiced Scones
Strawberry Cheesecake
Strawberry Chiffon
Sweet Jam Biscuits
Swiss Pudding
Wine-Poached Pears

Apple-Ale Punch
Banana Flip
Cheddar-Beer Crackers
Cheese Straws
Cocktail Toasties
Golden 'Eggnog'
Ham and Cheese Buffet
  Whirls
'Martini'
Mimosa
'Orange-Cream' Stuffed
  Prunes
Orange Tonic
Tropical Wine Punch

Drinks and Cocktail Snacks

Avocado Cocktail Canapes

Avocado Salad

1 medium avocado pear
2 medium tomatoes, peeled and chopped
¼ medium cucumber, peeled and chopped
2 tablespoons olive oil
2 tablespoons wine vinegar
2 teaspoons mild French mustard
freshly ground black pepper to taste
finely shredded iceberg lettuce
16 black olives, stoned and sliced, for garnish

Halve and stone avocado. Peel thinly and chop. Mix with tomato and cucumber. Combine oil, vinegar, mustard and black pepper in a small screwtop jar and shake vigorously; pour over salad ingredients. Arrange a layer of shredded lettuce on each of four small plates and spoon a quarter of the avocado mixture into the centre of the lettuce. Garnish with black olive slices. Chill before serving.

Makes 4 servings.   *Per serving: 230 calories.*

Avocado and Pink Grapefruit Starter with Creamy Cheese Sauce

1 medium, ripe avocado pear
2 medium pink grapefruit (ordinary grapefruit may be used as an alternative)
5 oz (150 g) low-fat soft cheese
2 tablespoons tomato ketchup
1 teaspoon Worcestershire sauce

Halve avocado pear and remove stone; peel thinly and cut each half into 8 thin slices. Remove peel from grapefruit with a sharp knife, making sure to remove all the white pith. Carefully slide each segment of fruit from the membrane with a small knife. Beat cheese with ketchup and Worcestershire sauce. On 4 small plates, arrange alternating pieces of avocado and grapefruit in a circle. Spoon an equal quantity of cheese mixture in the middle of each plate. Chill before serving.
Makes 4 servings.   *Per serving: 213 calories.*

Warming Winter Soup

15 oz (450 g) canned tomatoes
6 oz (180 g) carrots, grated
2 oz (60 g) leeks, finely chopped
½ pint (300 ml) chicken stock, prepared according to package directions
pinch mixed herbs
1 teaspoon brown sugar
salt and pepper to taste

Place canned tomatoes in blender and puree until smooth. Transfer to a saucepan with all remaining ingredients, bring to the boil and simmer for 30 minutes.
Makes 4 servings.   *Per serving: 33 calories.*

Avocado and Cheese Creams

10 oz (300 g) avocado flesh (approximately 2 medium sized)

15 oz (450 g) low-fat soft cheese

juice of 1 lemon

2 teaspoons finely chopped onion

1 teaspoon salt

dash Worcestershire sauce

¼ teaspoon green food colouring

3 tablespoons single cream

Place all ingredients in blender and puree until smooth. Serve in individual ramekins.
Makes 6 servings.   *Per serving: 222 calories.*

Cheese, Prawn and Pear Cocktail

4 medium, ripe pears

1 tablespoon lemon juice

5 oz (150 g) low-fat soft cheese

4 fl oz (120 ml) natural yogurt

grated rind of 1 lemon

1 teaspoon dill weed

shredded iceberg lettuce

4 oz (120 g) peeled prawns

Halve pears and remove core; brush cut halves with lemon juice. Beat together low-fat soft cheese, lemon rind, yogurt and dill. Put cheese mixture into a piping bag and, using a serrated nozzle, pipe mixture into the centre of each pear half. Arrange pears on a bed of shredded lettuce; cut prawns into halves and use to garnish pears.
Makes 4 servings (2 halves each).   *Per serving: 148 calories.*

Stuffed Pasta Shell Starter

6 oz (180 g) large pasta shells
4 teaspoons vegetable oil
4 cloves garlic, finely chopped
4 tablespoons finely chopped onion
1 lb (480 g) cooked turkey, finely minced
½ pint (300 ml) apple juice
1 chicken stock cube, crumbled
4 teaspoons tomato puree
1 teaspoon mixed herbs
4 tablespoons grated Parmesan cheese
shredded lettuce
2 medium tomatoes, sliced
2 lemons, cut in wedges

Cook pasta in boiling salted water for 8 to 10 minutes, drain and keep hot. Heat oil in large non-stick frying pan. Add garlic and onion and saute for 2 to 3 minutes or until transparent. Add turkey, apple juice and stock cube and cook, stirring, for 4 to 5 minutes. Add tomato puree and mixed herbs and continue cooking for a further 5 minutes. Fill pasta shells with turkey mixture and arrange in a shallow flameproof casserole. Sprinkle with grated cheese and brown quickly under a hot grill. Serve each portion garnished with shredded lettuce, tomato slices and lemon wedges.

Makes 8 servings.   *Per serving: 233 calories.*

Savoury Prawn Starter

| 5 fl oz (150 ml) natural yogurt |
| 1 small clove garlic, finely chopped |
| 2 teaspoons lemon juice |
| 2 tablespoons tomato ketchup |
| 2 teaspoons tomato puree |
| 2 tablespoons finely chopped celery |
| 2 tablespoons finely chopped cucumber |
| 4 oz (120 g) peeled prawns |
| salt and pepper to taste |
| 8 tablespoons finely chopped lettuce |
| 4 black olives for garnish |

Mix yogurt with garlic, lemon juice, tomato ketchup and puree and beat until well combined. Add celery, cucumber, prawns and salt and pepper to taste. Mix well. Put 2 tablespoons finely chopped lettuce in each of 4 long-stemmed glasses; divide prawn mixture evenly between the glasses. Garnish with olives. Chill before serving.

Makes 4 servings. *Per serving: 69 calories.*

Smoked Cod's Roe Pate

| 12 oz (360 g) smoked cod's roe |
| pinch garlic powder |
| 2 oz (60 g) fresh white breadcrumbs |
| 1 fl oz (30 ml) water |
| 6 tablespoons olive oil |
| 2 tablespoons lemon juice |
| black pepper to taste |
| 1 teaspoon finely chopped parsley |
| 6 slices (6 oz/180 g) wholemeal bread, toasted and cut in fingers |

Remove cod's roe from the skin with a teaspoon and place in basin. Beat with garlic powder until smooth. Soak breadcrumbs in the water for 2 minutes. Squeeze out excess moisture and add breadcrumbs to the cod's roe. Stir to combine. Transfer mixture to blender and puree, alternately adding oil and the lemon juice, a tablespoon at a time. Transfer mixture to bowl and season with black pepper. Beat in chopped parsley. Serve with fingers of toast.

Makes 6 servings.   *Per serving: 283 calories.*

Salmon Mousse

6 oz (180 g) drained, canned salmon
6 tablespoons low-calorie mayonnaise
5 fl oz (150 ml) natural yogurt
1 teaspoon dill weed
1 teaspoon lemon juice
1 small onion, grated
1 medium pickled cucumber, chopped
salt and pepper
3 tablespoons hot water
1 tablespoon unflavoured gelatine
chunk of cucumber, sliced thinly for garnish
watercress for garnish

Discard skin from the salmon. Mash salmon and stir in the mayonnaise, yogurt, dill weed, lemon juice, onion and pickled cucumber. Season to taste. Pour hot water into a cup and sprinkle the gelatine over; stir to dissolve. Stir into the salmon mixture. Turn into a 1-pint (600-ml) mould or deep dish. Chill until set. Turn out and garnish with cucumber and watercress.

Makes 6 servings.   *Per serving: 114 calories.*

Crab Mousse

4 teaspoons unflavoured gelatine

3 fl oz (90 ml) hot water

5 oz (150 g) low-fat soft cheese

2 eggs, separated

6 tablespoons white wine

salt and pepper to taste

6 oz (180 g) crab meat

8 strips lemon peel

Dissolve gelatine in hot water, set aside to cool. Beat cheese until soft and smooth, add egg yolks and beat well. Add wine, salt and pepper and dissolved gelatine; beat until smooth. Leave until just on the point of setting, then fold in crab meat and stiffly beaten whites of eggs. Divide evenly between 8 stemmed glasses and garnish with strips of lemon.
Makes 8 servings.   *Per serving: 90 calories.*

Tuna and Parsley Pate

6 oz (180 g) drained canned tuna

4 teaspoons mayonnaise

1 tablespoon tomato ketchup

1 tablespoon lemon juice

2-3 drops hot pepper sauce

1 teaspoon Worcestershire sauce

2 tablespoons chopped parsley

12 water biscuits

3 medium tomatoes, quartered, and 12 lettuce leaves for garnish

Flake tuna with a fork, add next 6 ingredients and mix well. Spoon mixture into a dish and chill. To serve, divide pate into 6 equal portions. Serve each portion with 2 water biscuits and garnish with 2 tomato quarters and 2 lettuce leaves.
Makes 6 servings.   *Per serving: 151 calories.*

Cream of Pea and Asparagus Soup

16 oz (480 g) canned asparagus spears

8 oz (240 g) canned peas

1½ pints (900 ml) chicken stock, prepared according to package directions

salt and pepper to taste

6 tablespoons single cream

2 tablespoons dry sherry

Reserve tips of asparagus spears for garnish. Put remainder in blender with peas and can liquid and puree until smooth. Pour into a large saucepan, add stock and salt and pepper; bring to the boil and simmer for 2 to 3 minutes. Remove from the heat and stir in cream, sherry and reserved asparagus tips. Reheat but do not boil. Serve at once.

Makes 4 servings.   *Per serving: 115 calories.*

Asparagus with Sesame 'Butter'

24 asparagus spears, woody ends removed

1 teaspoon salt

4 teaspoons each margarine and lemon juice

2 teaspoons sesame seeds

parsley sprigs and lemon slices for garnish

Arrange asparagus spears in saucepan large enough to hold them in 1 layer; sprinkle with salt, add water to cover, and bring to the boil. Reduce heat and let simmer until cut ends of spears are tender, 5 to 8 minutes; drain. Transfer asparagus to a warm dish; set aside and keep warm. In a saucepan combine margarine, lemon juice and sesame seeds; cook over low heat, stirring occasionally, until margarine is melted and seeds are golden. Spoon mixture evenly over asparagus spears. Garnish with parsley sprigs and lemon slices.

Makes 4 servings.   *Per serving: 57 calories.*

Cauliflower Provencale

1 lb 4 oz (600 g) cauliflower florets

1 tablespoon olive oil

1 garlic clove, finely chopped

2 tablespoons finely chopped onion

6 oz (180 g) canned tomatoes, crushed

8 stoned black olives, sliced

¼ teaspoon basil

dash Worcestershire sauce

pinch pepper

1 tablespoon chopped parsley for garnish

Cook florets in boiling salted water for 4 to 5 minutes; drain. Heat oil in large non-stick frying pan with lid; add garlic and onion and saute for 2 minutes. Do not brown. Add tomatoes, olives, basil, Worcestershire sauce and pepper to taste. Cook, stirring, for 2 to 3 minutes; add cauliflower, cover and simmer for 10 minutes or until florets are tender. Serve sprinkled with parsley.

Makes 2 servings. *Per serving: 138 calories.*

Apple and Sweet Potato

1 tablespoon margarine

2 medium eating apples, cored, peeled and cut into cubes

2 tablespoons finely chopped onion

2 teaspoons brown sugar

1 teaspoon lemon juice

¼ teaspoon salt

pinch ground cinnamon

pinch ground nutmeg (optional)

6 oz (180 g) peeled cooked sweet potatoes, chilled and cut into 1-inch (2.5-cm) cubes

Heat margarine in frying pan until bubbly and hot; add apples and onion and saute, stirring occasionally, until apples are

soft, 4 to 5 minutes. Sprinkle evenly with sugar, lemon juice and seasonings and cook, stirring constantly, until sugar is melted; add sweet potato cubes and cook, stirring occasionally, until sweet potatoes are well heated through.
Makes 2 servings.   *Per serving: 201 calories.*

Aubergine Provencale

2 teaspoons olive oil
1 teaspoon margarine
1 tablespoon chopped onion
1 garlic clove, crushed
¼ teaspoon salt
6 oz (180 g) peeled and cubed aubergine (1-inch/2.5-cm) cubes
1 medium tomato, blanched, peeled and chopped
1 tablespoon chopped fresh basil or ½ teaspoon dried
pinch pepper

Combine oil and margarine in non-stick frying pan and heat until bubbly and hot; add onion and garlic and saute until onion is transparent. Add aubergine and cook, stirring occasionally, until lightly browned; stir in tomato and basil. Reduce heat to low, cover pan and let simmer until aubergine is soft and mixture thickens slightly, 15 to 20 minutes.
Makes 2 servings.   *Per serving: 84 calories.*

Tangy Broccoli Salad

1 tablespoon each wine vinegar and sesame oil
1 teaspoon each soy sauce and prepared mustard
10 oz (300 g) frozen broccoli spears, steamed until tender-crisp and drained*

Combine vinegar, oil, soy sauce and mustard in salad bowl; add broccoli and toss to coat. Serve chilled as a starter or hot as a vegetable.
*6 oz (180 g) fresh broccoli florets may be substituted for the broccoli spears.
Makes 2 servings.   *Per serving: 106 calories.*

Italian Salad

1½ oz (45 g) tiny pasta shapes, cooked according to package directions

6 small tomatoes, cut into quarters

1 small green pepper, seeded and cut into thin strips

2 sticks celery, sliced diagonally

4 stoned black olives, sliced

1 tablespoon each olive oil, wine vinegar and lemon juice

2 teaspoons grated Parmesan cheese

½ teaspoon each garlic powder and basil

¼ teaspoon salt

pinch pepper

Combine all ingredients in a salad bowl and toss well. Cover and chill lightly. Toss again just before serving.
Makes 2 servings. *Per serving: 215 calories.*

Spinach-Stuffed Mushrooms

8 large mushrooms (each about 2 inches (5 cm) in diameter)

1 tablespoon margarine

2 tablespoons finely chopped shallots or onion

8 oz (240 g) well-drained cooked chopped spinach (fresh or frozen)

4 oz (120 g) cooked long-grain rice

2 oz (60 g) Mozzarella cheese, grated

pinch each salt and freshly ground pepper

2 fl oz (60 ml) chicken stock, prepared according to package directions

Rinse mushrooms and, using paper towels, gently dry. Remove and chop stems, reserving caps. Heat margarine in non-stick frying pan until bubbly and hot; add chopped mushroom stems and shallots or onion, and saute until all liquid has evaporated. Add spinach, rice, cheese, salt and pepper and stir to combine. Preheat oven to 400°F, 200°C, Gas Mark 6. Fill each reserved mushroom cap with an equal amount of spinach mixture; transfer stuffed mushrooms to an

8 x 8 x 2-inch (20 x 20 x 5-cm) baking pan. Add stock to pan and bake until mushrooms are tender when pierced with a fork, 20 to 25 minutes. Serve hot.

Makes 2 servings.   *Per serving: 257 calories.*

Rabbit Stew in White Wine Sauce

4 teaspoons vegetable oil

1 lb 8 oz (720 g) rabbit, cut into pieces

3 oz (90 g) onion, chopped

1 garlic clove, crushed

1 medium green pepper, seeded and cut into 1-inch (2.5-cm) squares

3 oz (90 g) mushrooms, sliced

2 teaspoons flour

3 medium tomatoes, blanched, peeled, seeded and chopped

4 fl oz (120 ml) white wine

2 fl oz (60 ml) chicken stock, prepared according to package directions

¼ teaspoon each thyme, salt and pepper

2 teaspoons chopped parsley

Heat 3 teaspoons oil in large pressure cooker; add rabbit a few pieces at a time, and cook until evenly browned on all sides. Set rabbit pieces aside. Add remaining teaspoon of oil to cooker and heat; add onion and garlic and saute until onion is soft. Add green pepper and mushrooms and continue sauteing until pepper is tender-crisp; sprinkle vegetable mixture with flour and cook, stirring constantly, for 2 minutes longer. Stir in tomatoes and wine and bring to the boil; add stock, thyme, salt, pepper and browned rabbit and stir to combine. Close cover securely, bring to pressure and cook for 15 minutes. Hold cooker under running cold water to reduce pressure. Transfer rabbit to serving dish and cook sauce over high heat until slightly thickened, about 2 minutes. Pour over rabbit and sprinkle with parsley.

Makes 4 servings.   *Per serving: 223 calories.*

Marinated Roasted Peppers

2 medium red peppers

2 medium green peppers

1 tablespoon freshly squeezed lemon juice

2 anchovy fillets, mashed

pinch pepper

Preheat grill. On baking sheet grill red and green peppers 3 inches (7.5 cm) from heat source, turning frequently until charred on all sides; remove peppers and let stand until cool enough to handle. Place strainer over large bowl and peel peppers into it; remove and discard stem ends and seeds, allowing juice from peppers to drip into bowl. Cut each pepper into strips and add to bowl; add remaining ingredients and stir to combine. Cover and let marinade for at least 30 minutes.
Makes 2 servings.   *Per serving: 46 calories.*

Ham and Cabbage Pancakes

4 servings frozen Bechamel (see page 178), thawed

8 teaspoons dry sherry

pinch each salt and ground nutmeg

4 servings frozen Ham and Cabbage Pancake Filling (see page 156), thawed

8 frozen pancakes (see Basic Pancakes page 144), thawed

ground nutmeg for garnish

Preheat oven to 400°F, 200°C, Gas Mark 6. Combine thawed Bechamel, sherry, salt and nutmeg in a saucepan and heat (do not boil). In bowl combine thawed filling with one third of the Bechamel mixture. Spoon an equal amount of filling mixture onto centre of each pancake and fold sides of pancake over filling to enclose. Place 2 pancakes, seam-side down, in each of 4 small shallow non-stick baking tins. Spoon an equal amount of remaining Bechamel mixture over each portion of pancakes and bake until well heated through, about 10 minutes. Serve sprinkled with nutmeg.
Makes 4 servings.   *Per serving: 114 calories excluding filling.*

Ham, Rice and Orange Salad

6 oz (180 g) long-grain rice

8 oz (240 g) drained canned mandarin orange segments

1 lb (480 g) lean ham, diced

2 medium tomatoes, skinned and chopped

1 bunch watercress, washed and chopped

4 tablespoons mayonnaise

black pepper

Cook rice until tender, following package directions, and leave until cool. Mix rice with orange segments, ham, tomatoes and chopped watercress. Add black pepper to mayonnaise and fold into rice mixture. Chill lightly before serving.

Makes 4 servings. *Per serving: 430 calories.*

Chicken with Ham and Cheese

2 tablespoons vegetable oil

4 x 3-oz (90-g) skinned and boned chicken breasts

salt and pepper to taste

1 tablespoon cornflour

6 tablespoons white wine

½ pint (300 ml) chicken stock, prepared according to package directions

4 slices (1 oz/30 g each) ham

2 oz (60 g) Cheddar cheese, grated

Heat oil in a non-stick frying pan. Gently saute chicken breasts for 4 to 5 minutes each side until tender. Season to taste and leave in pan. Mix cornflour with wine. Pour stock and cornflour mixture into pan and cook, stirring constantly, until sauce thickens and bubbles. Lay 1 slice ham over each chicken breast. Sprinkle ½ oz (15 g) grated cheese on each ham slice. Cover the pan and simmer gently until ham is hot and cheese melted, approximately 2 minutes.

Makes 4 servings. *Per serving: 288 calories.*

Meat-Loaf Wellington

5 oz (150 g) minced beef

2½ oz (75 g) low-fat soft cheese

1 egg

3 tablespoons plain dried breadcrumbs

2 tablespoons each chopped celery and parsley

1 tablespoon water

2 teaspoons chopped shallot or onion

1 teaspoon Worcestershire sauce

¼ teaspoon salt

pinch pepper

3 oz (90 g) cooked potato

2 tablespoons skim milk

2 teaspoons each margarine and grated Parmesan cheese

Combine first 10 ingredients; shape into a loaf. Transfer to rack in roasting pan and bake at 425°F, 220°C, Gas Mark 7, for 25 to 30 minutes. Combine potato, milk, margarine and grated cheese and, using electric mixer, whip until smooth. Transfer meat loaf to an 8 x 8-inch (20 x 20-cm) ovenproof serving dish; spread with potato mixture, coating entire loaf. Using a fork, make ridges in coating to form a design. Bake at 425°F, 220°C, Gas Mark 7 until lightly browned, about 15 minutes.

Makes 2 servings.   *Per serving: 401 calories.*

Leek and Cheese Crumble

1 lb (480 g) leeks, trimmed

2 tablespoons flour

2 tablespoons white wine

4 tablespoons low-fat dry milk

8 oz (240 g) Cheddar cheese, grated

2 tablespoons margarine

3 oz (90 g) flour

pinch cayenne pepper

2 teaspoons paprika

1 teaspoon dry mustard

Cut leeks into 1-inch (2.5-cm) lengths and cook in boiling lightly salted water for 6 to 8 minutes, or until tender but still firm. Drain, reserving liquid, and arrange in an ovenproof dish. Make cooking liquid up to 1 pint (500 ml) with water, mix flour to a thin paste with wine and add to cooking liquid with dry milk. Bring slowly to the boil, stirring, and cook for about 2 minutes or until thickened. Add half the cheese, stir until melted and pour over leeks. Rub margarine into flour until mixture resembles coarse breadcrumbs. Add cayenne, paprika, dry mustard and remaining cheese; mix well and sprinkle over leek mixture. Bake at 400°F, 200°C, Gas Mark 6 for 15 to 20 minutes or until the top is bubbling and golden brown.

Makes 4 servings.   *Per serving: 467 calories.*

Oriental Chicken Livers en Brochette

2 tablespoons each wine vinegar and soy sauce

1½ teaspoons brown sugar

1 teaspoon each finely chopped and peeled ginger root and crushed garlic

10 oz (300 g) chicken livers

1 medium green pepper, seeded and cut into 1-inch (2.5-cm) squares

2 tomatoes, cut in halves

8 medium mushroom caps (about 1½ inches (3.5 cm) in diameter)

Combine vinegar, soy sauce, sugar, ginger and garlic; add livers and toss to coat. Cover and refrigerate for at least 4 hours, tossing once. (If preferred, livers may be marinated overnight). Preheat grill. Onto each of 4, 12-inch (30-cm) skewers, thread an equal amount of livers, a quarter of the pepper squares, 2 tomato halves and 2 mushroom caps, alternating ingredients; reserve marinade. Place skewers on rack in grill pan and grill, turning once and brushing frequently with reserved marinade, until livers are browned and firm, 4 to 5 minutes on each side. Arrange skewers on serving dish.

Makes 2 servings.   *Per serving: 236 calories.*

Chicken Veronique

1 lb 4 oz (600 g) skinned and boned chicken breasts

4 teaspoons vegetable oil

8 oz (240 g) mushrooms, sliced

4 oz (120 g) onion, sliced

8 fl oz (240 ml) chicken stock, prepared according to package directions

4 teaspoons cornflour

6 oz (180 g) seedless green grapes, halved

4 tablespoons white wine

8 oz (240 g) hot cooked rice

Cut chicken breasts into ½-inch (1-cm) slivers. Heat oil in a

large non-stick frying pan. Add mushrooms and onions and
saute until onions are transparent. Add chicken and cook,
turning frequently, for approximately 10 minutes. Mix
cornflour with stock, add to the pan and bring to the boil. Add
grapes and wine and cook for 1 minute. Serve with hot cooked
rice.
Makes 4 servings. *Per serving: 345 calories.*

Yogurt-Caraway Quiche
Crust

double recipe Basic Pastry (page 145), thawed

Filling

2 teaspoons margarine

4 oz (120 g) chopped onions

1 oz (30 g) cooked ham, chopped

4 eggs, beaten

2 fl oz (60 ml) natural yogurt

3 oz (90 g) Emmental cheese, grated

½ teaspoon caraway seeds

pinch pepper

pinch salt (optional)

To Prepare Crust: Preheat oven to 400°F, 200°C, Gas Mark 6.
Roll out pastry and line an 8-inch (20-cm) quiche or flan tin.
Prick pastry shell in several places with a fork; line shell with
foil and bake for 5 minutes. Remove foil and bake until golden
brown, 5 to 8 minutes longer. Remove crust from oven and
reduce oven temperature to 350°F, 180°C, Gas Mark 4.
To Prepare Quiche: Heat margarine in small non-stick pan
until bubbly and hot; add onions and ham and saute until
onions are transparent. Beat eggs lightly with yogurt to
combine; stir in onion mixture and remaining ingredients for
filling. Pour into baked crust; bake until set, about 20 minutes.
Serve warm.
Makes 4 servings. *Per serving: 305 calories.*

Haddock Provencale

1 lb 4 oz (600 g) filleted haddock, cut into 1-inch (2.5-cm) pieces

3 tablespoons flour

¼ teaspoon each salt and pepper

4 teaspoons vegetable oil

2 teaspoons olive oil

1 garlic clove, crushed

2 medium tomatoes, cut into wedges

4 teaspoons dry sherry

2 teaspoons chopped fresh basil or ½ teaspoon dried

Rinse fish in cold water; pat dry with paper towels. Mix flour, salt and pepper; dredge fish in flour mixture, coating all sides and using up all the mixture. Pour oils into a large non-stick frying pan and heat over moderate heat; add fish and garlic and saute until lightly browned. Reduce heat, add remaining ingredients and cook until hot.
Makes 4 servings.   *Per serving: 220 calories.*

Prawn Fandango

1 tablespoon vegetable oil

1 tablespoon each chopped yellow and red peppers

1 garlic clove, crushed

10 oz (300 g) peeled prawns

2 fl oz (60 ml) dry sherry

2 oz (60 g) mange-tout peas (stem ends and strings removed), steamed until tender-crisp

2 oz (60 g) carrots, cut in matchstick pieces, steamed until tender-crisp

1½ oz (45 g) spring onions, sliced

pinch salt

dash hot pepper sauce

4 oz (120 g) cooked long-grain rice, hot (optional)

Heat oil in frying pan until bubbly and hot; add peppers and garlic and saute until peppers are tender, about 2 minutes. Increase heat to high; add prawns and cook, stirring constantly, for about 2 minutes. Add sherry; continue to stir and cook until liquid is reduced, about 2 minutes. Add all remaining ingredients except rice; cook, stirring constantly, until heated through. If liked, serve over hot rice.

Makes 2 servings.   *Per serving: 346 calories.*

Fiesta Chicken

4 teaspoons margarine
5 oz (150 g) each onions and green peppers, chopped
1 lb 4 oz (600 g) skinned and boned chicken breasts, cut into cubes
16 oz (480 g) canned tomatoes, crushed
3 oz (90 g) uncooked long-grain rice
8 large pimento-stuffed green olives, thinly sliced
1 teaspoon salt
¼ teaspoon garlic powder
¼ teaspoon saffron or turmeric
pinch pepper

Preheat oven to 400°F, 200°C, Gas Mark 6. Heat margarine in a large flameproof casserole over moderate heat until bubbly and hot; add onions and green peppers and saute until vegetables are tender, 2 to 3 minutes. Remove casserole from heat and add remaining ingredients; stir until thoroughly combined. Cover casserole and bake until rice has absorbed liquid, 30 to 35 minutes.

Makes 4 servings.   *Per serving: 317 calories.*

Crispy Cinnamon-Chicken Bake

1½ oz (45 g) cornflakes, crushed

4 teaspoons brown sugar

2 teaspoons each ground cinnamon and grated orange peel

½ teaspoon salt

5 fl oz (150 ml) natural yogurt

3 lb (1 kg 440 g) chicken portions, skinned

4 teaspoons vegetable oil

Preheat oven to 400°F, 200°C, Gas Mark 6. In blender or processor combine crushed cornflakes, sugar, cinnamon, orange peel and salt and blend well. Pour mixture onto a plate or sheet of greaseproof paper. Dip chicken portions into yogurt, then coat with crumb mixture, pressing crumbs into chicken and being sure to use all the yogurt and crumb mixture. Using oil, grease a non-stick baking pan large enough to hold chicken in 1 layer; add coated chicken portions and bake until tender, about 30 minutes.

Makes 4 servings. *Per serving: 410 calories.*

Oven-Fried Chicken with Orange-Teriyaki Sauce

10 oz (300 g) skinned and boned chicken breasts, cut into 4 pieces

1½ oz (45 g) cornflakes, crushed

2 tablespoons grated orange peel

2 tablespoons thawed frozen concentrated orange juice

2 teaspoons margarine

2 tablespoons thinly sliced spring onion

½ garlic clove, crushed

2 tablespoons soy sauce

4 teaspoons orange marmalade

1 tablespoon water

To Prepare Chicken: Preheat oven to 350°F, 180°C, Gas Mark 4. Mix cornflake crumbs and orange peel. Pour juice into small bowl. Dip chicken pieces into juice, then into crumb mixture, coating thoroughly and pressing any remaining crumbs firmly

onto chicken. Arrange coated chicken on baking sheet and bake for 10 to 15 minutes; turn pieces over and bake until chicken is tender and coating is crisp, about 5 minutes longer.
To Prepare Sauce: While chicken is baking, heat margarine in small saucepan until bubbly and hot; add spring onion and garlic and saute until onion slices are soft. Reduce heat to low, add remaining ingredients and cook until sauce is hot and slightly thickened. Serve with chicken.
Makes 2 servings. *Per serving: 345 calories.*

Curried Chicken with Melon

1 lb (480 g) chicken portions, skinned

2 teaspoons flour

½ teaspoon curry powder

¼ teaspoon salt

pinch pepper

2 teaspoons margarine

1 tablespoon chopped onion

6 fl oz (180 ml) chicken stock, prepared according to package directions

2 tablespoons natural yogurt

10 oz (300 g) cubed melon

Pat chicken dry. Mix together 1 teaspoon flour, ½ teaspoon curry powder and salt and pepper; dredge chicken in mixture. Heat half the margarine in frying pan until bubbly and hot; add chicken and brown on all sides. Remove from pan. In same pan heat remaining margarine; add onion and saute until softened, 1 to 2 minutes. Return chicken to pan; add stock and bring to the boil. Reduce heat, cover and let simmer until chicken is tender, about 40 minutes. Remove chicken to serving dish; reserve pan juices. Combine yogurt and remaining flour and curry powder, mixing well; add to pan juices along with melon cubes. Cook, stirring gently, until melon is heated through and sauce is thickened; serve over chicken.
Makes 2 servings. *Per serving: 382 calories.*

Nutty Stuffed Chicken Breasts

4 x 3-oz (90-g) boned chicken breasts

6 tablespoons crunchy peanut butter

8 oz (240 g) onion, finely chopped and blanched

2 cloves garlic, finely chopped

4 teaspoons paprika

salt and pepper to taste

4 tablespoons margarine

2 teaspoons cornflour

Using a meat mallet or rolling pin, beat chicken breasts until ¼ inch (5 mm) thick. Mix peanut butter, chopped onion, garlic, paprika, salt and pepper. Divide mixture evenly and spread over chicken breasts. Roll up chicken breasts, folding in the ends, and secure with wooden cocktail sticks. Place seam-side down in a small baking tin. Dot rolls with margarine, add a little water to the baking tin, cover tin with foil and bake in a moderately hot oven, 375°F, 190°C, Gas Mark 5 for 35 to 40 minutes, occasionally removing foil and basting chicken rolls. When cooked, remove rolls to a serving dish and keep hot. Mix cornflour to a paste with a little water, add to juices in the pan and cook, stirring, until thickened. Spoon over chicken rolls and serve at once.

Makes 4 servings. *Per serving: 384 calories.*

Orange-Ginger-Glazed Pork Chops

2 x 6-oz (180-g) pork loin chops

2 teaspoons vegetable oil

1 tablespoon finely chopped shallots or onion

4 fl oz (120 ml) orange juice

4 teaspoons undiluted low-calorie orange drink

1 teaspoon each brown sugar, prepared mustard and soy sauce

¼ teaspoon ground ginger

1 medium orange, sliced

Grill chops on a rack for about 3 minutes on each side. While chops are grilling, heat oil in small non-stick saucepan; add shallots or onion and saute briefly, being careful not to burn. Add all remaining ingredients, except chops, and bring to the boil. Cook over high heat, stirring constantly, until mixture is reduced and thickened, about 5 minutes. Arrange chops in shallow flameproof casserole, large enough to hold them in 1 layer. Using some of the glaze, spread both sides of each chop evenly and grill, turning once, until glaze is browned, about 3 minutes on each side. Serve with orange slices and remaining glaze.

Makes 2 servings.   *Per serving: 325 calories.*

Chinese-Style Pork

1 lb (480 g) fillet of pork

Marinade

¾ teaspoon five spice powder

3 tablespoons soy sauce

3 tablespoons hot water

1 tablespoon honey

pinch black pepper

4 cloves garlic, finely crushed

salt to taste

8 oz (240 g) hot cooked rice

12 oz (360 g) cooked mange-tout peas

Using a sharp knife, make deep cuts in the meat at ½-inch (1-cm) intervals. Mix marinade ingredients. Pour marinade over meat in a shallow dish and leave for 6 hours, turning from time to time. Remove meat from marinade, place under medium grill and cook, turning frequently, until cooked through. Heat marinade and serve over pork. Serve each portion of pork with 2 oz (60 g) hot cooked rice and 3 oz (90 g) cooked mange-tout peas.

Makes 4 servings.   *Per serving: 303 calories.*

Chicken-Mushroom Pancakes

4 servings frozen Chicken-Mushroom Pancake Filling (see page 156), thawed

8 frozen pancakes (see Basic Pancakes page 144), thawed

2 tablespoons chopped parsley

Preheat oven to 400°F, 200°C, Gas Mark 6. Spoon half serving of thawed filling on to centre of each pancake and fold sides of pancake over to enclose filling. Arrange pancakes, seam-side down, in a shallow non-stick baking dish or casserole large enough to take them in one layer. Bake until heated through and lightly browned, 15 to 20 minutes. Serve sprinkled with parsley.

Makes 4 servings.

For 6 or 8 servings, use 6 or 8 servings of filling and 12 or 16 pancakes.

Seafood Pancakes

4 servings frozen Seafood Pancake Filling (see page 158), thawed

4 servings frozen Bechamel (see page 178), thawed

8 frozen pancakes (see Basic Pancakes page 144), thawed

ground nutmeg for garnish

Preheat oven to 400°F, 200°C, Gas Mark 6. Mix thawed filling with quarter of thawed Bechamel, stirring well. Spoon an equal amount of filling mixture onto centre of each pancake and fold sides of pancake over filling to enclose. Place 2 pancakes, seam-side down in each of 4 small shallow non-stick baking tins. Spoon an equal amount of remaining Bechamel over each portion of pancakes and bake until well heated through, about 10 minutes. Serve sprinkled with nutmeg.

Makes 4 servings.   *Per serving: 103 calories excluding filling.*

For 6 or 8 servings, use 6 or 8 servings each of the filling and the Bechamel and 12 or 16 pancakes.

Oriental Marinated Cod

4 tablespoons each soy sauce and water

8 teaspoons dry sherry

2 cloves garlic, chopped

½ teaspoon ground ginger

1 lb 4 oz (600 g) cod fillets, skinned

Mix soy sauce, water, sherry, garlic and ginger. Arrange fillets in baking dish and pour soy mixture over fillets; turn fish over to coat other side. Cover dish and leave to marinate for 1 hour. Bake in hot oven, 425°F, 220°C, Gas Mark 7, for 15 to 20 minutes or until fish flakes easily with a fork.

Makes 4 servings.   *Per serving: 120 calories.*

Salmon Kedgeree

4 hard-boiled eggs

4 teaspoons margarine

4 oz (120 g) drained canned salmon, skinned and flaked

pinch each salt and freshly ground black pepper

8 oz (240 g) long-grain rice, cooked

2 teaspoons curry powder

5 fl oz (150 ml) natural yogurt

paprika for garnish

Chop one whole egg and whites of other 3, reserving yolks. Mix eggs with salmon and season with salt and pepper. Melt margarine in a small saucepan; add egg and salmon mixture and heat thoroughly, shaking from time to time to prevent sticking. Add rice and stir in curry powder and yogurt; heat through but do not boil. Sieve reserved egg yolks. Transfer rice mixture to a hot serving dish and garnish with sieved egg yolks and paprika.

Makes 4 servings.   *Per serving: 402 calories.*

Lamb Korma

12 oz (360 g) lamb
4 cloves garlic, peeled
1-inch (2.5-cm) piece fresh ginger, peeled and chopped
7 fl oz (210 ml) water
1 tablespoon vegetable oil
10 whole cardamom pods
6 cloves
1-inch (2.5-cm) piece cinnamon stick
6 oz (180 g) onions, chopped
1 teaspoon ground coriander
2 teaspoons ground cumin
½ teaspoon cayenne pepper
1 teaspoon salt or to taste
10 fl oz (300 ml) natural yogurt
4 oz (120 g) hot cooked long-grain rice

Grill lamb on a rack under moderate heat for 10 minutes and reserve. Place garlic and ginger in blender with 3 fl oz (90 ml) water and puree to make a paste. Heat oil in a flameproof casserole and add the cardamom, cloves, cinnamon and chopped onions. Saute, stirring well, until the onions begin to brown. Add garlic paste from the blender, the coriander, cumin and cayenne. Cook together, stirring, for 4 minutes. Add lamb, salt, yogurt and remaining 4 fl oz (120 ml) water. Bring to the boil, cover and transfer to the oven. Cook for 1 hour at 350°F, 180°C, Gas Mark 4. Remove whole spices before serving with hot rice.

Makes 2 servings.   *Per serving: 511 calories.*

Tuna and Tomato Quiche

Pastry*

4 tablespoons margarine
6 oz (180 g) plain flour
cold water

Filling

4 oz (120 g) onion, finely chopped
12 oz (360 g) drained canned tuna
6 oz (180 g) canned tomatoes
1 teaspoon oregano
2 eggs
½ pint (300 ml) skim milk
2 oz (60 g) Cheddar cheese, grated

Preheat oven to 400°F, 200°C, Gas Mark 6.

Pastry: Rub margarine into flour until mixture resembles coarse breadcrumbs; add enough cold water to make a firm dough. Roll out between 2 sheets of greaseproof paper and line a 7-8-inch (17.5-20-cm) loose-bottomed flan tin.

Filling: Mix onion, tuna, tomatoes and oregano and put into the pastry case. Whisk eggs with the milk and pour over tuna mixture. Sprinkle grated cheese on top. Bake for 15 minutes, then reduce heat to 350°F, 180°C, Gas Mark 4, for a further 20 minutes.

*Or use a double recipe Basic Pastry (page 145).

Makes 4 servings.   *Per serving: 579 calories.*

Sauteed Chilli Prawns

2 tablespoons olive oil
12 oz (360 g) broccoli florets
5 oz (150 g) each onions and red or green peppers, chopped
1 lb 4 oz (600 g) shelled prawns
1 garlic clove, crushed, or pinch garlic powder
2 fl oz (60 ml) chilli sauce
1/4 teaspoon each salt and thyme
lemon wedges for garnish

Heat oil until bubbly and hot in wok or large frying pan; add broccoli florets and saute until tender-crisp, about 3 minutes. Add onions and peppers to broccoli and saute until onions are transparent, about 2 minutes. Push vegetables to side of pan and add prawns and garlic; saute, stirring constantly, for 2 to 3 minutes. Add all remaining ingredients except garnish and stir all ingredients in pan together to combine; cook for 3 to 4 minutes or until mixture is piping hot. Serve garnished with lemon wedges.

Makes 4 servings. *Per serving: 257 calories.*

'Frying Pan' Broccoli Souffle

1 teaspoon olive or vegetable oil
2 garlic cloves, crushed
5 oz (150 g) well-drained cooked chopped broccoli (reserve 2 cooked florets for garnish)
1/4 teaspoon salt
5 oz (150 g) low-fat soft cheese
2 eggs, separated (at room temperature)
1 tablespoon chopped parsley
2 teaspoons grated Parmesan cheese
pinch freshly ground pepper
1 teaspoon margarine

In small frying pan with an ovenproof or removable handle, heat oil over moderate heat; add garlic and saute briefly, about

30 seconds (do not brown). Add broccoli and salt and cook, stirring occasionally, for about 3 minutes to blend flavours. Remove broccoli to a plate and wipe pan clean; set aside. Preheat oven to 400°F, 200°C, Gas Mark 6. In large mixing bowl combine soft cheese, egg yolks, parsley, Parmesan cheese and pepper; beat until smooth. In separate bowl, using clean beaters, beat egg whites until stiff peaks form; fold egg whites alternately with broccoli into cheese mixture. Heat margarine in the frying pan until bubbly and hot; pour in broccoli mixture and, using spatula, gently smooth top. Remove pan to oven and bake for 15 to 20 minutes (until puffed and lightly browned); serve immediately, garnished with reserved broccoli florets.

Makes 2 servings.   *Per serving: 267 calories.*

Tuna Crunch

2 teaspoons vegetable oil
4 oz (120 g) onions, sliced
12 oz (360 g) canned baked beans
4 oz (120 g) drained canned tuna
pinch each mixed herbs, salt and pepper
dash anchovy essence (optional)
2 slices (2 oz/60 g) brown bread, made into crumbs
2 oz (60 g) Cheddar cheese, grated

Heat oil in a non-stick frying pan and saute onions until lightly brown. Add baked beans, tuna, herbs, salt, pepper and anchovy essence and cook until heated through, 3 to 5 minutes. Transfer mixture to an ovenproof dish. Mix breadcrumbs and cheese and scatter over the fish mixture. Place under a hot grill until golden brown.

Makes 4 servings.   *Per serving: 230 calories.*

Prawns and Noodles with Tangy Tomato Sauce

2 tablespoons olive oil

3 oz (90 g) onion, chopped

4 garlic cloves, crushed

2 anchovy fillets, mashed

1 lb 4 oz (600 g) peeled prawns

1 lb 12 oz (840 g) canned tomatoes, chopped

5 oz (150 g) mushrooms, thinly sliced

1 tablespoon drained capers, rinsed

2 tablespoons chopped fresh basil or 2 teaspoons dried

½ teaspoon cayenne pepper

8 oz (240 g) cooked noodles, hot

fresh basil or mint leaves for garnish

Heat half the oil in a large non-stick frying pan; add half each of the onion and garlic and saute briefly, about 2 minutes. Add anchovies and stir to combine; add prawns and cook over high heat, stirring constantly, for 2 to 3 minutes. Immediately transfer mixture to bowl; set aside. In same pan heat remaining oil; add remaining onion and garlic and saute briefly, about 2 minutes. Add tomatoes and bring to the boil; add mushrooms, capers, basil and pepper and cook over moderate heat, stirring occasionally, for 15 to 20 minutes. Add prawn mixture and cook until heated through; serve over hot noodles and garnish with basil or mint leaves.

Makes 4 servings. *Per serving: 325 calories.*

Veal Patties in Parsley Sauce

1 oz (30 g) low-fat dry milk, reconstituted with ¼ pint (150 ml) water

1 slice (1 oz/30 g) white bread, torn into pieces

1 tablespoon margarine

1 tablespoon chopped onion

8 oz (240 g) minced veal

1 egg

¼ teaspoon salt

pinch pepper

pinch each ground nutmeg and ground allspice

1 tablespoon chopped parsley

6 fl oz (180 ml) water

2 chicken stock cubes

1 teaspoon flour

Place half the milk and bread in blender or food processor and blend for about 30 seconds; let stand for 5 minutes. Heat one third of the margarine in a small frying pan until bubbly and hot; add onion and saute until softened. Add onion, veal, egg, salt and spices to blender or processor and puree until smooth; add one third of the parsley and blend again. Refrigerate, covered, for 15 minutes. Using moist hands, shape veal mixture into 4 patties. Heat remaining margarine in a medium frying pan; add patties and cook, turning once, until evenly browned. Add water and crumbled stock cubes, cover and let simmer for 15 minutes, turning patties once. Remove patties from pan and keep hot; reserve pan juices. Combine flour with remaining milk, stirring to dissolve. Stir into pan juices; stirring constantly, bring to the boil, lower heat and simmer until thickened. Stir in remaining parsley; serve over patties.
Makes 2 servings.   *Per serving: 334 calories.*

Fish Salad with Chilli Mayonnaise

5 oz (150 g) each onion, celery and carrot, chopped

4 lemon slices

pinch each salt and pepper

8 fl oz (240 ml) water

10 oz (300 g) fish fillets (any firm white fish)

2 tablespoons chopped spring onions

4 teaspoons chilli sauce

1 tablespoon each mayonnaise, natural yogurt and lemon juice

8 lettuce leaves

Combine onion, celery, carrot, lemon slices, salt and pepper in non-stick frying pan; add water and bring to the boil. Add fish and spoon some vegetables over fillets; return liquid to the boil. Reduce heat, cover and let simmer until fish flakes easily when tested with a fork but is still firm, about 5 minutes. Remove fish to a plate, discarding liquid and vegetables. Let fish cool slightly, then cover and refrigerate until lightly chilled. Combine all remaining ingredients except lettuce; mix well. Cover and chill lightly. Cut fish into bite-size pieces and serve on lettuce leaves. Spoon sauce over fish.

Makes 2 servings.   *Per serving: 221 calories.*

Rolled, Stuffed Plaice Fillets

2 teaspoons margarine

3 oz (90 g) onion, finely chopped

1 garlic clove, crushed

1 tablespoon each finely chopped celery and carrot

1 tablespoon finely chopped red pepper

6 oz (180 g) mushrooms, thinly sliced

pinch each salt, white pepper and thyme

2 tablespoons chopped parsley

4 x 5-oz (150-g) plaice fillets

4 teaspoons each grated Parmesan cheese and mayonnaise

½ teaspoon French mustard

1 tablespoon lemon juice

lemon slices and parsley for garnish

Heat margarine in small non-stick frying pan until bubbly and hot; add onion and garlic and saute briefly. Add celery, carrot and red pepper; cover and cook over moderately low heat, stirring occasionally, until vegetables are tender, about 5 minutes. Add mushrooms and seasonings, stirring to combine. Increase heat to moderately high and cook, uncovered, until all moisture has evaporated; stir in half the parsley. Spoon an equal amount of mixture onto centre of each fillet and roll fish to enclose. Place stuffed fish rolls in a layer, seam-side down, in shallow casserole. Preheat oven to 400°F, 200°C, Gas Mark 6. Combine cheese, mayonnaise and mustard; spread mixture evenly over fillets and sprinkle with lemon juice. Bake until fish is lightly browned and flakes easily when tested with a fork, about 20 minutes; sprinkle with remaining parsley. Serve garnished with lemon slices and parsley sprigs.

Makes 4 servings. *Per serving: 218 calories.*

Carrot Cake

2 lb (960 g) carrots, grated

1 pint (600 ml) skim milk

8 oz (240 g) raisins

3 oz (90 g) fine oatmeal

3 oz (90 g) porridge oats

2 teaspoons ground ginger

2 teaspoons mixed spice

4 eggs

4 tablespoons caster sugar

Put grated carrots and milk in a saucepan and bring to the boil. Lower heat and simmer until carrots are cooked and milk is absorbed. Add raisins, oatmeal, porridge oats, ground ginger and mixed spice and leave to cool. Beat eggs with sugar and beat into cooked mixture. Pour into a large loose-bottomed cake tin and bake in a moderate oven, 350°F, 180°C, Gas Mark 4, for approximately 45 to 50 minutes. Leave cake in the tin until quite cold before removing.

Makes 16 servings.   *Per serving: 140 calories.*

Pineapple Cheesecake

1 teaspoon vegetable oil

3 digestive biscuits made into crumbs

2½ oz (75 g) low-fat soft cheese

1 large egg

8 teaspoons low-fat dry milk

4 teaspoons flour

2 teaspoons margarine

1 teaspoon caster sugar

½ teaspoon vanilla flavouring

¼ teaspoon grated lemon peel

4 oz (120 g) canned crushed pineapple

Preheat oven to 350°F, 180°C, Gas Mark 4. Rub inside of

individual non-stick baking tins with vegetable oil and sprinkle tins with an equal amount of crumbs, covering bottom and sides, and set aside. In blender or processor, combine all remaining ingredients except pineapple and blend until smooth, scraping down sides of container as necessary. Stir pineapple into cheese mixture (do not blend). Divide pineapple mixture into tins and transfer tins to 8 x 8 x 2-inch (20 x 20 x 5-cm) baking tin; pour hot water into tin to a depth of about 1 inch (2.5 cm). Bake until cheesecakes are set and lightly browned on top, 15 to 20 minutes. Remove tins to wire rack and let cool; cover each with plastic wrap and refrigerate until chilled, at least 1 hour. Serving suggestion: Top each portion with 1 tablespoon whipped dessert topping.

Makes 2 servings.   *Per serving: 372 calories.*

Mandarin Cheesecake

8 digestive biscuits
8 teaspoons margarine, melted
10 oz (300 g) low-fat soft cheese
8 oz (240 g) mandarin orange segments, with 8 tablespoons juice
½ teaspoon orange flower water (optional)
2 tablespoons caster sugar
4 teaspoons unflavoured gelatine
4 fl oz (120 ml) hot water
1 teaspoon grated orange peel

Crumble biscuits and add to melted margarine; mix until all margarine has been absorbed into biscuit crumbs. Spread mixture over base of 6-7-inch (15-17.5-cm) loose-bottomed cake tin. Chill in refrigerator. Combine cheese, mandarin segments, juice, orange flower water and sugar in blender; puree until smooth. Sprinkle gelatine over hot water and stir until dissolved. Add to contents of blender and process for a few seconds. Pour over chilled biscuit base. Put in refrigerator until firm. Sprinkle with grated orange peel to serve.

Makes 8 servings.   *Per serving: 196 calories.*

Festive Melon Baskets

2 medium-sized honeydew or Ogen melons

10 oz (300 g) strawberries, hulled

2 medium peaches, stoned and sliced

2 tablespoons clear honey with 1 tablespoon lemon juice

4 sprigs mint for garnish

Cut the melons in halves, serrating the edges with a small pointed knife, if liked. Scoop out melon flesh with a melon baller or teaspoon; put in a large bowl. Reserve 12 strawberries, slice the rest and add to the melon with the peach slices. Pour honey and lemon mixture over the fruit and toss well; leave to marinate. When ready to serve, spoon equal amounts of fruit into each melon shell. Top with the reserved strawberries and garnish with mint. Serve at once.

Makes 4 servings.   *Per serving: 104 calories.*

Mince Pies

Pastry

6 oz (180 g) plain flour

4 tablespoons margarine

2½ fl oz (75 ml) natural yogurt

Mincemeat

1 oz (30 g) sultanas

1 oz (30 g) currants

1 oz (30 g) raisins

1 medium apple, peeled and grated

1 teaspoon lemon juice

pinch ground allspice

¼ teaspoon almond flavouring

¼ teaspoon rum flavouring

2 tablespoons demerara sugar

Sieve flour into basin, rub in fat until mixture resembles fine breadcrumbs; add yogurt to make a firm dough. Roll out, cut into 8 rounds and fit into bun tins. Mix all mincemeat ingredients together and divide evenly between pastry cases. Roll out remaining pastry, divide evenly and cut into small rounds or crescents to decorate pies. Bake in a moderate oven, 350°F, 180°C, Gas Mark 4 for about 20 minutes or until pastry is golden.

Makes 8 servings.   *Per serving: 187 calories.*

Chocolate and Banana Crunch Pie

Base

8 digestive biscuits
4 tablespoons margarine, melted

Filling

12 fl oz (360 ml) skim milk
4 teaspoons cornflour
2 tablespoons cocoa
2 tablespoons caster sugar
2 tablespoons margarine
1 tablespoon unflavoured gelatine
3 medium bananas (2 mashed and 1 sliced)
9 tablespoons single cream

Crush biscuits and stir into melted margarine. Line flan dish with mixture, pressing down with a wooden spoon. Whisk milk, cornflour, cocoa, sugar and margarine together in a saucepan; bring to the boil and cook for 1 minute. Dissolve gelatine in a little hot water and stir into milk mixture. Leave to cool, then stir in 2 mashed bananas and the cream. Pour onto biscuit base and chill until set. To serve, decorate with remaining sliced banana.

Makes 6 servings.   *Per serving: 323 calories.*

Wine-Poached Pears

14 fl oz (420 ml) dry red wine

2 teaspoons sugar

2-inch (5-cm) cinnamon stick

4 firm but ripe medium pears, peeled (stems left on)

Combine wine, sugar and cinnamon stick in saucepan large enough to hold pears in 1 layer, bring to the boil. Add pears, cover pan and cook over moderate heat for 5 to 8 minutes, until pears are tender, turning pears once during cooking. Using a slotted spoon, transfer each pear to an individual dish; cook wine mixture, uncovered, until liquid is reduced by half. Remove and discard cinnamon stick and pour an equal amount of remaining liquid over each pear. Serve at room temperature.

Makes 4 servings. *Per serving: 128 calories.*

Glazed Apricot Dessert

4 teaspoons low-fat spread

2 digestive biscuits, crushed

12 canned apricot halves

1 teaspoon arrowroot

4 tablespoons canned juice

1 tablespoon water

To make base, melt low-fat spread in a basin over a pan of hot water; add crushed biscuits and stir until all melted spread is absorbed. Divide mixture evenly between 2 small dessert dishes or ramekin dishes. Arrange apricot halves on top of the biscuit crumbs in overlapping circles. Chill in refrigerator. Meanwhile, make the glaze. Mix arrowroot to a paste with the water, put juice in a non-stick pan and add arrowroot. Bring to the boil and cook, stirring, for 1 minute or until mixture becomes transparent. Pour mixture over apricots, dividing evenly.

Makes 2 servings. *Per serving: 167 calories.*

Orange 'Cream' Pancakes

Filling

5 oz (150 g) low-fat soft cheese

2 teaspoons sugar

1 teaspoon grated orange peel

¼ teaspoon ground cinnamon

Pancakes

4 frozen pancakes (see Basic Pancakes, page 144), thawed for about 15 minutes)

Sauce

1 medium orange

4 fl oz (120 ml) orange juice

4 teaspoons low-calorie orange marmalade

1 teaspoon grated orange peel

To Prepare Filling: Combine cheese, sugar, orange peel and cinnamon, mixing well; set aside.

To Prepare Sauce: Peel and divide orange into segments over small saucepan to catch juice, adding segments to pan; add orange juice, marmalade and orange peel and bring to the boil. Reduce heat and let simmer, stirring occasionally, until sauce is syrupy and reduced to about 4 fl oz (120 ml); let cool.

To Serve: Spoon an equal amount of filling onto centre of each pancake and fold sides over filling to enclose; arrange pancakes, seam-side down, on serving dish and top with sauce.

Makes 2 servings. *Per serving: 246 calories.*

Pineapple Fizz

2 tablespoons thawed frozen concentrated orange juice

4 teaspoons thawed frozen concentrated pineapple juice

2 teaspoons freshly squeezed lemon juice

½ teaspoon sugar

dash rum flavouring

4 fl oz (120 ml) soda water

2 lemon slices for garnish

Chill two small tumblers. In blender or processor combine all ingredients except soda water and garnish; blend until frothy. Turn off motor and add soda water; blend until just combined. Divide mixture into chilled glasses and garnish each portion with a lemon slice; serve immediately.

Makes 2 servings.   *Per serving: 44 calories.*

Ginger Kisses

8 teaspoons margarine

2 tablespoons golden syrup

3 oz (90 g) self-raising flour

1½ teaspoons ground ginger

¼ teaspoon mixed spice

pinch salt

1 tablespoon icing sugar, sieved

Preheat oven to 350°F, 180°C, Gas Mark 4. Place margarine and syrup in a basin over hot water and stir occasionally until margarine has melted. Sift together flour, ginger, mixed spice and salt. Add flour mixture to basin and mix to a firm dough. If necessary, add a few drops of water to bind. On greaseproof paper, roll out dough to approximately ⅛-inch (3-mm) thickness. Using tiny biscuit cutters, cut out approximately 3 dozen biscuits. Place on foil or greaseproof paper on baking tray and bake 6 to 8 minutes or until golden. Allow to cool on tray. Dust evenly with sieved icing sugar. Store in airtight container.

Makes 4 servings.   *Per serving: 199 calories.*

Strawberry Chiffon

1 strawberry jelly

¾ pint (450 ml) boiling water

1 lb 4 oz (600 g) strawberries

8 oz (240 g) vanilla ice cream, softened slightly

1 egg white

Combine jelly and water in a 1½-pint (900-ml) bowl, stirring until jelly is completely dissolved; cover and refrigerate until syrupy, 15 to 20 minutes. Set aside 8 strawberries for garnish; puree remaining strawberries in blender. Stir pureed strawberries and ice cream into jelly. Using an electric mixer, beat egg white until stiff peaks form. Fold into strawberry mixture. Divide chiffon into 8 dessert bowls; cover lightly and refrigerate until set, about 4 hours. To serve, garnish with reserved strawberries.

Makes 8 servings.   *Per serving: 103 calories.*

Fruit Flapjacks

3 tablespoons margarine

2 tablespoons golden syrup

4½ oz (135 g) porridge oats

6 oz (180 g) sultanas

3 eggs, lightly beaten

2 tablespoons brown sugar

Plump sultanas in boiling water for 3 to 4 minutes, drain and pat dry with paper towel. Melt margarine and syrup over gentle heat. Remove from heat and add porridge oats, sultanas, eggs and sugar. Mix well. Spoon into a shallow 8 x 10-inch (20 x 25-cm) baking tin and smooth with a knife. Bake at 375°F, 190°C, Gas Mark 5, for 20 to 25 minutes or until golden brown. When cold, cut into 12 portions.

Makes 6 servings (2 pieces each).   *Per serving: 301 calories.*

Swiss Pudding

3 oz (90 g) pudding rice, washed and drained

1½ pints (900 ml) skim milk

2 oz (60 g) sultanas

3 tablespoons caster sugar

2 medium cooking apples, peeled, cored and chopped

4 teaspoons low-fat spread

½ teaspoon ground cinnamon

Put rice, milk, sultanas and half the sugar in a saucepan. Bring to the boil, stir and cover. Simmer for 30 to 40 minutes or until rice is tender and most of the liquid absorbed. Cool. Meanwhile, rinse prepared apples and put in a saucepan with low-fat spread, cinnamon and remainder of sugar; cover and cook very gently over low heat until the apples are fluffy. Remove from heat and beat to a puree. Cool. Layer the rice and apples in a large glass serving dish beginning and ending with a layer of rice. Chill well before serving.
Makes 4 servings. *Per serving: 272 calories.*

Spiced Scones

4 tablespoons margarine

3 oz (90 g) self-raising flour

4 tablespoons natural bran

1 oz (30 g) currants

1 oz (30 g) sultanas

4 teaspoons caster sugar

2 teaspoons baking powder

2 teaspoons mixed spice

pinch salt

3-4 drops vanilla flavouring

2 fl oz (60 ml) skim milk

Rub fat into flour until mixture resembles fine breadcrumbs. Add next 7 ingredients and mix well. Add vanilla flavouring to milk, reserving 2 teaspoons milk; add the rest to the dry mixture and stir to a soft dough. Divide into 4 or 8 equal bun shapes. Prick with a fork, brush with reserved milk and bake in a moderate oven, 350°F, 180°C, Gas Mark 4, for 25 to 30 minutes or until well risen and golden.

Makes 4 servings.   *Per serving: 265 calories.*

Strawberry Cheesecake

8 teaspoons margarine
8 digestive biscuits, crumbled
2 tablespoons natural bran
4 eggs
3 tablespoons caster sugar
10 oz (300 g) low-fat soft cheese
3 oz (90 g) self-raising flour
½ teaspoon vanilla flavouring
1 teaspoon grated lemon rind
10 oz (300 g) strawberries, hulled
4 tablespoons reduced-sugar strawberry jam

Melt 7 teaspoons margarine in a saucepan. Add crumbled biscuits and bran and form into a ball. Grease the sides of a 9-in (22.5-cm) cake tin with remaining margarine. Place mixture on base of tin and press out until base is covered. Put eggs and sugar in blender, or beat with a whisk, until mixture is frothy. Add cheese and puree until smooth. Pour into large basin, fold in flour, vanilla flavouring and lemon rind. Pour over crumb base and bake on centre shelf of oven, 325°F, 160°C, Gas Mark 3, for 1 hour. Do not open oven door during baking. With heat turned off, leave to cool for a further hour, so that the cake holds together. Loosen edge of cake from tin with a knife and turn out carefully, keeping biscuit crumb base on bottom. Slice strawberries and arrange over top of cake. Warm jam and spoon over strawberries. Chill thoroughly before serving.

Makes 8 servings.   *Per serving: 200 calories.*

Apricot-Raisin Crescents

Basic Pastry (page 145), thawed

2 oz (60 g) dried apricot halves, chopped

2 oz (60 g) seedless raisins, chopped

2 teaspoons each granulated sugar and apricot jam

1 teaspoon sifted icing sugar

Preheat oven to 400°F, 200°C, Gas Mark 6. Roll dough between 2 sheets of wax paper, forming a circle about ⅛ inch (3 mm) thick; cut into 12 equal wedges. Combine all remaining ingredients except icing sugar. Spoon an equal amount of mixture on to each wedge near curved end; roll each curved end towards point. Stand each roll on its edge and bend into a crescent shape. Place crescents on non-stick baking tin and bake until golden brown; about 20 minutes. Transfer crescents to wire rack to cool. Just before serving, sprinkle each with an equal amount of icing sugar.
Makes 2 servings.   *Per serving: 259 calories.*

Fabulous Fruit Cup

½ small pineapple

3 medium kumquats

4 medium golden plums

10 oz (300 g) strawberries; reserve 1 strawberry for garnish

2 medium kiwi fruits

6 oz (180 g) black grapes

3 oz (90 g) green grapes

12 tablespoons whipped dessert topping

Slice pineapple and cut into segments. Slice kumquats and plums. Select a few best of the other fruits, slice strawberries and kiwi fruits; halve grapes; reserve these for lining the bowl. Chop remaining fruit ready for putting in centre of the bowl. Arrange all the kumquat slices in the bottom of the bowl. Stand half the sliced strawberries on top of kumquats round edge of bowl and hold in position with half the chopped strawberries. Do the same with the kiwi fruits. Put in a layer of sliced plums. Stand halved black grapes round edge of bowl and support with remainder of black grapes. Do the same with the rest of the strawberries, then add a layer of pineapple segments. Finish with a ring of halved green grapes. Top with whipped topping and garnish with reserved strawberry.

Makes 4 servings.   *Per serving: 215 calories.*

Sweet Jam Biscuits

1½ oz (45 g) flour
¼ teaspoon baking powder
pinch salt
4 teaspoons margarine
2 teaspoons sugar
½ teaspoon vanilla flavouring
1 tablespoon ice water
2 teaspoons apricot or raspberry jam
1 teaspoon icing sugar

Sift together flour, baking powder and salt; set aside. Cream margarine with sugar; add vanilla and stir to combine. Mix in sifted dry ingredients; add water and mix to form dough (if mixture is dry and crumbly, add up to an additional teaspoon ice water to adjust consistency). Preheat oven to 375°F, 190°C, Gas Mark 5. Between 2 sheets of wax paper roll dough to about ¼-inch (5-mm) thickness; remove paper and, using 2-inch (5-cm) round biscuit cutter, cut out biscuits. Roll scraps of dough and continue cutting until all dough has been used (should yield 12 biscuits). Transfer biscuits to non-stick baking sheet and bake for 10 minutes; remove biscuits to wire rack and let cool. Top centre of each biscuit with an equal amount of jam and sprinkle each with an equal amount of icing sugar.

Makes 2 servings.   *Per serving: 207 calories.*

Orange Loaf

3 oz (90 g) flour

1 egg

2 tablespoons thawed frozen concentrated orange juice

4 teaspoons orange marmalade

2 teaspoons each sugar and margarine

½ teaspoon vanilla flavouring

Preheat oven to 350°F, 180°C, Gas Mark 4. Combine all ingredients in a small mixing bowl and, using an electric mixer on low speed, beat for 30 seconds or until just combined. Pour into 1-lb (480-g) non-stick loaf tin and bake for about 25 minutes (until knife inserted in centre comes out clean). Remove loaf from pan and cool on wire rack. Slice into 4. 2 slices per serving.

Makes 2 servings. *Per serving: 315 calories.*

Cheddar-Beer Crackers

1½ oz (45 g) flour

¼ teaspoon baking powder

pinch salt

2 teaspoons margarine

2 fl oz (60 ml) beer

1 oz (30 g) strong Cheddar cheese, grated

½ teaspoon poppy seeds

Preheat oven to 450°F, 230°C, Gas Mark 8. Combine first 3 ingredients, then rub in margarine until mixture resembles coarse breadcrumbs. Add beer and cheese and stir to combine. Drop batter onto non-stick baking sheet by heaping teaspoonsful, forming 16 mounds and leaving a space of about 1 inch (2.5 cm) between each. Sprinkle each mound with an equal amount of poppy seeds and bake until lightly browned, 8 to 10 minutes. Remove crackers to wire rack to cool.

Makes 2 servings. *Per serving: 182 calories.*

Apple-Ale Punch

1 pint (600 ml) low-calorie ginger ale
½ pint (300 ml) chilled apple juice
3 tablespoons freshly squeezed lemon juice
2 teaspoons clear honey
2 lemons, thinly sliced

Combine all ingredients, except lemon slices, in punch or serving bowl and stir to mix; float lemon slices in punch and serve chilled. Place punch or serving bowl in a larger bowl lined with ice (punch will be chilled but not diluted).
Makes 4 servings.   *Per serving: 31 calories.*

Orange Tonic

6 fl oz (180 ml) low-calorie tonic water
2 tablespoons thawed frozen concentrated orange juice
ice cubes (optional)

Chill a large tumbler. Combine tonic water and concentrated orange juice in blender or processor and blend until frothy. Pour into chilled glass and add ice cubes, if liked. Serve immediately.
Makes 1 serving.   *Per serving: 40 calories.*

Banana Flip

2 medium bananas
1 pint (600 ml) skim milk
12 tablespoons single cream
1 tablespoon lemon juice
2 tablespoons caster sugar

Mash bananas and place in blender with milk, cream, lemon juice and sugar. Puree until smooth. Chill well and divide between 4 long-stemmed wine glasses.
Makes 4 servings.   *Per serving: 210 calories.*

Golden 'Eggnog'

4 fl oz (120 ml) skim milk
2 oz (60 g) vanilla ice cream
1 tablespoon whipped dessert topping
½ teaspoon sugar
dash each rum and brandy flavourings
pinch ground nutmeg

In blender or processor combine all ingredients except nutmeg and blend until smooth; pour into champagne glass and sprinkle with nutmeg.
Makes 1 serving.   *Per serving: 171 calories.*

Ham and Cheese Buffet Whirls

4 oz (120 g) cooked lean ham, thinly sliced
1-2 teaspoons English mustard
5 oz (150 g) low-fat soft cheese
1 tablespoon chopped chives

Spread ham slices evenly with mustard. Mix soft cheese with the chives and spread evenly over ham. Roll each slice up like a Swiss roll. Chill in refrigerator until cheese is firm. To serve, slice each roll into 4 rings.
Makes 12 servings.   *Per serving: 29 calories.*

'Orange-Cream' Stuffed Prunes

6 large stoned prunes
8 fl oz (240 ml) hot water
1 oz (30 g) low-fat soft cheese
½ teaspoon sugar
¼ teaspoon grated orange peel
ground cinnamon

Put prunes into hot water; let stand until prunes are softened, about 10 minutes. Combine cheese, sugar and orange peel, mixing well. Drain prunes, discarding liquid. Stuff each prune

with an equal amount of cheese mixture and sprinkle each with
pinch of cinnamon.
Makes 2 servings.   *Per serving: 37 calories.*

Tropical Wine Punch

14 fl oz (420 ml) chilled low-calorie ginger ale

½ pint (300 ml) chilled pineapple juice

8 fl oz (240 ml) chilled dry white wine

1 lemon, thinly sliced

1 lime, thinly sliced

Combine first 3 ingredients in punch or serving bowl, stirring
to mix; float lemon and lime slices in punch and place bowl in
larger bowl lined with ice. Serve chilled.
Makes 4 servings.   *Per serving: 58 calories.*

Avocado Cocktail Canapes

1 ripe medium avocado pear

2 tablespoons lemon juice

1 small green pepper, seeded and finely chopped

1 small onion, finely chopped

1 small clove garlic, finely chopped

freshly ground black pepper

8 cream crackers

watercress sprigs for garnish

Halve and stone avocado. Scoop out flesh and mash with
lemon juice. Add green pepper, onion and ground black
pepper and mix well. Cut each cream cracker into 4 and spread
with avocado mixture. Arrange on a serving dish and garnish
with watercress sprigs.
Makes 8 servings.   *Per serving: 116 calories.*

Cocktail Toasties

1 teaspoon olive oil

1 tablespoon finely chopped onion

½ garlic clove

1 tablespoon blanched, peeled, seeded and chopped tomato

2 anchovy fillets, mashed

pinch each oregano and freshly ground pepper

2 slices French bread (2 oz/60 g each), toasted

1 teaspoon grated Parmesan cheese

Preheat oven to 400°F, 200°C, Gas Mark 6. Heat oil in non-stick frying pan; add onion and garlic and saute over moderate heat until onion is transparent. Remove and discard garlic. Add tomatoes, anchovies, oregano and pepper to onion and cook, stirring occasionally, for about 3 minutes. Place bread slices on sheet of foil and place on baking sheet; spread an equal amount of anchovy mixture over each slice. Sprinkle each with ½ teaspoon cheese and bake until top is browned, 10 to 15 minutes. Serve hot.
Makes 2 servings.   *Per serving: 177 calories.*

Cheese Straws

1½ oz (45 g) flour

pinch each oregano, garlic powder, cayenne pepper and salt

4 tablespoons margarine

2 tablespoons natural yogurt

4 teaspoons grated Parmesan cheese

Combine flour and seasonings and rub in margarine until mixture resembles coarse breadcrumbs. Add yogurt and mix thoroughly to form dough. Form dough into a ball, wrap in plastic wrap and refrigerate until chilled, about 1 hour. Preheat oven to 400°F, 200°C, Gas Mark 6. Between 2 sheets of wax paper roll dough to about ⅛-inch (3-mm) thickness; remove paper and cut dough into strips, each about 4 inches (10 cm) long and ½ inch (1 cm) wide. Fold each strip in half, forming 2-inch (5-cm) long strips, and twist each slightly.

Place strips on non-stick baking sheet and sprinkle each with an equal amount of cheese; bake until golden brown, about 15 minutes. Serve warm.

Makes 4 servings.　　　　　　　　　　　　*Per serving: 180 calories.*

'Martini'

3 fl oz (90 ml) each dry sherry and dry vermouth

½ teaspoon freshly squeezed lemon juice

4 ice cubes

2 green olives

Chill two stemmed cocktail glasses and a cocktail shaker; shake sherry, vermouth and lemon juice to combine. Add ice cubes and shake until mixture is thoroughly chilled. Strain 'martini' mixture into chilled glasses, add 1 olive to each, and serve immediately.

Makes 2 servings.　　　　　　　　　　　　*Per serving: 103 calories.*

Mimosa

4 fl oz (120 ml) each chilled dry champagne and soda water

1 tablespoon thawed frozen concentrated orange juice

2 mint sprigs for garnish

Chill 2 tulip champagne glasses. In blender or processor combine all ingredients except garnish and blend until smooth and frothy, about 30 seconds. Divide mixture into chilled glasses and garnish each with a mint sprig; serve immediately.

Makes 2 servings.　　　　　　　　　　　　*Per serving: 43 calories.*

If you need to lose weight and want to maintain that weight loss, Weight Watchers is for you!

Weight Watchers uses the most famous and effective programme in the world, and probably has a class near you.

For information about that class, look at the Yellow Pages under 'Health Clubs'.

WEIGHT WATCHERS MAGAZINE, published bi-monthly, gives a wealth of information and tips on losing weight as well as recipes, regular features and fashion. Get your copy from your local newsagent now.

If you would like to know more about the Weight Watchers organisation, phone Windsor 856751 or write to:

Weight Watchers (UK) Ltd
11 Fairacres
Dedworth Road
Windsor
Berkshire
SL4 4UY

Please Note: FOOD EXCHANGES ARE GIVEN BY THE RECIPE TITLE, ABBREVIATED AS FOLLOWS:
Pro. Ex (Protein Exchange), Brd. Ex (Bread Exchange), Veg. Ex (Vegetable Exchange), Fruit Ex, Milk Ex, Cal. Opt. Ex (Calories Optional Exchange).

FAST AND FUN

Bacon-Corn Fritters
Each serving provides: 1 Pro. Ex, 1 Brd. Ex, 2 Fat Ex, 120 Cal. Opt. Ex.

Cheese and Tomato Toast
Each serving provides: 1 Pro. Ex, 1 Brd. Ex, 1 Veg. Ex.

French Toast with Mushrooms
Each serving provides: 1 Pro. Ex, 1 Brd. Ex, 1 Veg. Ex, 1 Fat Ex.

Cream of Asparagus Soup
Each serving provides: 2 Veg. Ex, 1 Fat Ex, 1 Milk Ex, 20 Cal. Opt. Ex.

Sauteed Tomatoes
Each serving provides: 1½ Veg. Ex, 1½ Fat Ex, 15 Cal. Opt. Ex.

Mushroom Saute
Each serving provides: 2 Veg. Ex, 1½ Fat Ex, 10 Cal. Opt. Ex.

Orange Rice
Each serving provides: 1 Brd. Ex, ½ Veg. Ex, 1½ Fat Ex, 1 Fruit Ex, 15 Cal. Opt. Ex.

Cream Tomato Vegetable Soup
Each serving provides: ½ Veg. Ex, 1 Fat Ex, ½ Fruit Ex, ½ Milk Ex, 20 Cal. Opt. Ex.

Shrimp and Pasta Soup
Each serving provides: 1 Pro. Ex, ¼ Brd. Ex, 1 Veg. Ex, 5 Cal. Opt. Ex.

Vegetable Risotto
Each serving provides: 1 Brd. Ex, 2 Veg. Ex, 1 Fat Ex.

Cream of Artichoke Soup
Each serving provides: 1½ Veg. Ex, 1 Fat Ex, ¼ Milk Ex, 20 Cal. Opt. Ex.

Chicken with Hot Peanut Sauce
Each serving provides: 3½ Pro. Ex, 1 Brd. Ex, ½ Veg. Ex, 3 Fat Ex, 30 Cal. Opt. Ex.

Lemon Butter Baked Sole
Each serving provides: 3 Pro. Ex, 1½ Fat Ex, 40 Cal. Opt. Ex.

Curried Livers in Wine Sauce
Each serving provides: 4 Pro. Ex, 1 Veg. Ex, 1 Fat Ex, 35 Cal. Opt. Ex.

Parmesan Chicken
Each serving provides: 3½ Pro. Ex, 1 Brd. Ex, 2 Fat Ex, 30 Cal. Opt. Ex.

'Waldorf' Chicken Salad
Each serving provides: 4 Pro. Ex, ½ Veg. Ex, 1½ Fat Ex, 1 Fruit Ex, 40 Cal. Opt. Ex.

Curried Aubergine and Lamb Stew
Each serving provides: 4 Pro. Ex, 2 Veg. Ex, ½ Fat Ex.

Chicken and Chick Peas
Each serving provides: 3½ Pro. Ex, 2 Veg. Ex, 1 Fat Ex, 10 Cal. Opt. Ex.

Chicken Cordon Bleu
Each serving provides: 4 Pro. Ex, 1 Fat Ex, 20 Cal. Opt. Ex.

Hot Open Roast Beef Sandwich
Each serving provides: 4 Pro. Ex, 1 Brd. Ex, 1 Veg. Ex, 1 Fat Ex, 20 Cal. Opt. Ex.

Spiced Vegetable-Egg Bake
Each serving provides: 2 Pro. Ex, 1 Veg. Ex, 50 Cal. Opt. Ex.

Oriental Beef and Vegetable Stir-Fry
Each serving provides: 4 Pro. Ex, 1 Brd. Ex, 1 Veg. Ex, 40 Cal. Opt. Ex.

Grilled Ham and Cheese with Mustard Dressing
Each serving provides: 3 Pro. Ex, 1 Brd. Ex, ½ Veg. Ex, 25 Cal. Opt. Ex.

Potato-Carrot Fritters
Each serving provides: 1 Pro. Ex,

1 ½ Brd. Ex, 1 Veg. Ex, 2 Fat Ex, 80 Cal. Opt. Ex.

Prawn Supreme
Each serving provides: 5 Pro. Ex, 1 ½ Fat Ex.

Hot Open Turkey Sandwich
Each serving provides: 4 Pro. Ex, 1 Brd. Ex, 1 Veg. Ex, 1 Fat Ex, 10 Cal. Opt. Ex.

Cheesy Vegetable Pasta
Each serving provides: 1 Pro. Ex, 1 Brd. Ex, 1 ½ Veg. Ex.

Grilled Fish with Wine Sauce
Each serving provides: 4 Pro. Ex, 2 Fat Ex, 30 Cal. Opt. Ex.

Monte Cristo Sandwich
Each serving provides: 3 Pro. Ex, 2 Brd. Ex, 1 Fat Ex, 30 Cal. Opt. Ex.

Courgette and Corn Saute
Each serving provides: 1 Brd. Ex, 3 ½ Veg. Ex, 2 Fat Ex.

Cauliflower Polonaise
Each serving provides: ½ Pro. Ex, ½ Brd. Ex, 2 Veg. Ex, 1 ½ Fat Ex.

Sweet and Sour Spinach-Mushroom Salad
Each serving provides: 1 Veg. Ex, ½ Fat Ex, 10 Cal. Opt. Ex.

Pan-Fried Marrow
Each serving provides: 3 ½ Veg. Ex, 1 ½ Fat Ex.

Bacon-Flavoured Corn Chowder
Each serving provides: ½ Brd. Ex, 1 Veg. Ex, 1 Fat Ex, 65 Cal. Opt. Ex.

Cauliflower and Carrot Stir-Fry
Each serving provides: 1 ½ Veg. Ex, 1 Fat Ex.

Braised Sweet and Sour Red Cabbage
Each serving provides: 1 Veg. Ex, 1 Fat Ex, 1 Fruit Ex, 40 Cal. Opt. Ex.

Oriental Vegetable Stir-Fry
Each serving provides: 1 ½ Veg. Ex, ¾ Fat Ex, 5 Cal. Opt. Ex.

Courgette and Apple Saute
Each serving provides: 2 ½ Veg. Ex, 2 Fat Ex, 1 Fruit Ex.

Hot Fruit Compote with Coconut Topping
Each serving provides: 1 Fat Ex, 2 Brd. Ex, 1 ¼ Fruit Ex, 15 Cal. Opt. Ex.

Crunchy Pineapple Dessert
Each serving provides: 1 Fruit Ex, 50 Cal. Opt. Ex.

Marmalade-Glazed Fruit Kebabs
Each serving provides: 1 ½ Fruit Ex, 20 Cal. Opt. Ex.

Bilberry Topping
Each serving provides: 1 Fruit Ex, 25 Cal. Opt. Ex.

Chocolate Topping
Each serving provides: ½ Milk Ex, 35 Cal. Opt. Ex.

Pineapple Topping
Each serving provides: ½ Fruit Ex, 15 Cal. Opt. Ex.

Mixed Fruit Chutney
Each serving provides: ½ Veg. Ex, 1 Fruit Ex, 15 Cal. Opt. Ex.

Pepper Relish
Each serving provides: ½ Veg. Ex, 5 Cal. Opt. Ex.

Spicy Tomato Sauce
Each serving provides: 4 Veg. Ex, 1 Fat Ex.

Sweet and Sour Barbecue Sauce
Each serving provides: ½ Fruit Ex, 25 Cal. Opt. Ex.

COOKING ON A SHOESTRING

Banana-Honey Breakfast Drink
Each serving provides: 1 Pro. Ex, ½ Milk Ex, 1 Fruit Ex, 60 Cal. Opt. Ex.

Savoury Grill
Each serving provides: 1 Pro. Ex, 1 Brd. Ex, 1 Veg. Ex, 15 Cal. Opt. Ex.

Hot Cereal
Each serving provides: 1 Brd. Ex, 1 Fruit Ex, ½ Milk Ex, 50 Cal. Opt. Ex.

Cauliflower and Tomato Soup
Each serving provides: 2 Veg. Ex,
10 Cal. Opt. Ex.

Tomato, Cauliflower and Tarragon Soup
Each serving provides: 3 Veg. Ex,
50 Cal. Opt. Ex.

Smoky Mac Pate
Each serving provides: 1½ Pro.
Ex, 1 Brd. Ex, ½ Veg. Ex.

Carrots au Gratin
Each serving provides: ½ Pro. Ex,
1 Veg. Ex, 1 Fat Ex, 40 Cal. Opt. Ex.

Cream of Celery Soup
Each serving provides: 2 Veg. Ex,
1 Fat Ex, 60 Cal. Opt. Ex.

Soft Cream Cheese with Herbs and Garlic
Each serving provides: 1 Pro. Ex,
25 Cal. Opt. Ex.

Beetroot and Orange Soup
Each serving provides: 1½ Veg.
Ex, 35 Cal. Opt. Ex.

Easy Vegetable-Barley Soup
Each serving provides: 1 Brd. Ex, 2
Veg. Ex, 1 Fat Ex.

Onion Popovers
Each serving provides: ½ Pro. Ex,
1 Brd. Ex, ½ Fat Ex, 30 Cal. Opt.
Ex.

Variation: Cheese Popovers Add 5
Cal. Opt. Ex.

Creamy Cauliflower Soup
Each serving provides: 1½ Veg.
Ex, 1 Fat Ex, 10 Cal. Opt. Ex.

Potato Soup
Each serving provides: 1 Brd. Ex, 1
Veg. Ex, ¾ Fat Ex, ¼ Milk Ex.

Norfolk Cheese Dumplings in Tomato Soup
Each serving provides: 1 Pro. Ex,
1½ Veg. Ex, ½ Brd. Ex, 25 Cal.
Opt. Ex.

Bacon-Liver Burgers
Each serving provides: 4 Pro. Ex, 1
Veg. Ex, 1 Fat Ex, 1 Brd. Ex, 45 Cal.
Opt. Ex.

Fruity Lamb Pilaf
Each serving provides: 4 Pro. Ex, 1
Veg. Ex, 2 Fat Ex, ¼ Milk Ex, 2 Brd.
Ex, ½ Fruit Ex.

Curried Cheese Crunch
Each serving provides: 2 Pro. Ex, 2
Veg. Ex, 2 Fat Ex, 1 Fruit Ex, 20 Cal.
Opt. Ex.

Mexican Liver
Each serving provides: 4 Pro. Ex, 1
Veg. Ex, 1 Fat Ex, ½ Brd. Ex, 20
Cal. Opt. Ex.

Shoulder of Lamb with Savoury Apricot Bake
Each serving provides: 1 Veg. Ex,
1 Brd. Ex, 1 Fruit Ex.

Grilled White Fish with Tomato and Mushroom Sauce
Each serving provides: 4 Pro. Ex, 2
Veg. Ex, 1 Fat Ex.

Cheese, Onion and Potato Layer
Each serving provides: 2 Pro. Ex,
1½ Veg. Ex, 1 Fat Ex, ¼ Milk Ex, 2
Brd. Ex, 20 Cal. Opt. Ex.

Spring Hot Pot
Each serving provides: 4 Pro. Ex,
1½ Veg. Ex, 20 Cal. Opt. Ex.

All-in-One Fish Dish
Each serving provides: 4 Pro. Ex, 3
Veg. Ex, 1 Fat Ex, 1 Brd. Ex, 15 Cal.
Opt. Ex.

Carrot Pudding
Each serving provides: 2 Pro. Ex,
1½ Veg. Ex, 1 Fat Ex, 1 Brd. Ex, 15
Cal. Opt. Ex.

West Indian Lamb
Each serving provides: 3 Pro. Ex,
½ Veg. Ex, ½ Fruit Ex, 35 Cal. Opt.
Ex.

Rich Cheese Sauce and Spaghetti
Each serving provides: ½ Pro. Ex,
1½ Fat Ex, 1½ Brd. Ex, 10 Cal.
Opt. Ex.

Lentil Curry
Each serving provides: 2 Pro. Ex, 2
Veg. Ex, 1 Fat Ex, 1 Brd. Ex, 10 Cal.
Opt. Ex.

Quick Liver, Tomato and Onion Sauté
Each serving provides: 3 Pro. Ex, 2 Veg. Ex, 2 Fat Ex, 40 Cal. Opt. Ex.

Chilli Con Carne
Each serving provides: 3 Pro. Ex, 2½ Veg. Ex, 10 Cal. Opt. Ex.

Orange Chicken with Rosemary
Each serving provides: 4 Pro. Ex, ½ Veg. Ex, 1 Fat Ex, 1 Fruit Ex.

Beef Sausage Rissoles
Each serving provides: 4 Pro. Ex, ½ Veg. Ex, ½ Brd. Ex, 15 Cal. Opt. Ex.

Shoulder of Lamb with Redcurrant Sauce
Each serving provides: 4 Pro. Ex, 50 Cal. Opt. Ex.

Potato Cheese Pie
Each serving provides: 2 Pro. Ex, ½ Veg. Ex, 1 Brd. Ex.

Greek-Style Lamb
Each serving provides: 4 Pro. Ex, 2½ Veg. Ex, 2 Fat Ex, ¼ Milk Ex, 1 Brd. Ex, 35 Cal. Opt. Ex.

Khitchari (Bean Kedgeree)
Each serving provides: 2 Pro. Ex, 1 Veg. Ex, 1 Brd. Ex.

Potato Souffle
Each serving provides: 1 Pro. Ex, 1 Veg. Ex, 2 Fat Ex, 1 Milk Ex, ½ Brd. Ex, 45 Cal. Opt. Ex.

Whitebait Minceur
Each serving provides: 4 Pro. Ex, 3 Fat Ex, 40 Cal. Opt. Ex.

Sausages with Barbecued Beans
Each serving provides: 3 Pro. Ex, ½ Veg. Ex, 1 Fat Ex, 1 Fruit Ex, 25 Cal. Opt. Ex.

Crispy Cauliflower
Each serving provides: 2 Pro. Ex, 2 Veg. Ex, 1 Fat Ex, ½ Brd. Ex, 115 Cal. Opt. Ex.

Pan-Fried Liver with Vegetables
Each serving provides: 4 Pro. Ex, 2 Veg. Ex, 2½ Fat Ex, 1 Brd. Ex, 40 Cal. Opt. Ex.

Calico Beans
Each serving provides: 2 Pro. Ex, ½ Veg. Ex, 45 Cal. Opt. Ex.

Cheesy Pasta
Each serving provides: 2 Pro. Ex, 2 Fat Ex, ¼ Milk Ex, 2 Brd. Ex, 135 Cal. Opt. Ex.

Main Meal Minestrone
Each serving provides: 3 Pro. Ex, 2 Veg. Ex, 1 Fat Ex, 1 Brd. Ex, ½ Fruit Ex.

Creamy Pasta with Broccoli
Each serving provides: 1 Pro. Ex, 1 Veg. Ex, 1 Fat Ex, 1½ Brd. Ex, 10 Cal. Opt. Ex.

Liver Baked in Foil
Each serving provides: 4 Pro. Ex, 2 Veg. Ex, 1 Fat Ex, 1 Brd. Ex.

Peppered Chicken
Each serving provides: 5 Pro. Ex, 2 Veg. Ex. ¼ Milk Ex, 1 Brd. Ex.

Hawaiian Liver
Each serving provides: 5 Pro. Ex, ½ Veg. Ex, 1 Fat Ex, 2 Brd. Ex, 1 Fruit Ex, 40 Cal. Opt. Ex.

Savoury Stuffed Heart
Each serving provides: 4 Pro. Ex, ½ Veg. Ex, 1 Brd. Ex, 20 Cal. Opt. Ex.

Yogurt Topped Beef Pie
Each serving provides: 4½ Pro. Ex, 2 Veg. Ex, 2 Fat Ex, ½ Milk Ex, 1½ Brd. Ex, 10 Cal. Opt. Ex.

Spanish Style Tripe
Each serving provides: 4 Pro. Ex, 1½ Veg. Ex, 1½ Fat Ex.

Mustard Cod
Each serving provides: 4 Pro. Ex, 1 Fat Ex, ½ Milk Ex.

Curried Chicken
Each serving provides: 4 Pro. Ex, 1 Veg. Ex, 1 Fat Ex, 1 Brd. Ex, ½ Fruit Ex, 20 Cal. Opt. Ex.

Bacon-Stuffed Hearts
Each serving provides: 4 Pro. Ex, 1 Brd. Ex, 105 Cal. Opt. Ex.

Beef Risotto
Each serving provides: 3 Pro. Ex, 1 Veg. Ex, 1 Fat Ex, 1 Brd. Ex.

Toad in the Hole
Each serving provides: 4 Pro. Ex, 1½ Fat Ex, ¼ Milk Ex, 1½ Brd. Ex.

Cheesy Fish Pie
Each serving provides: 4 Pro. Ex, ½ Veg. Ex, ¾ Fat Ex, 1¼ Brd. Ex, 65 Cal. Opt. Ex.

Chilli-Cheese Corn Fritters
Each serving provides: 2 Pro. Ex, 1½ Fat Ex, 1 Brd. Ex.

Main Meal Lamb and Split Pea Soup
Each serving provides: 4 Pro. Ex, 1 Veg. Ex, 1½ Fat Ex, 1 Brd. Ex.

Barbecued Butter Beans
Each serving provides: 2 Pro. Ex, 1 Veg. Ex, 50 Cal. Opt. Ex.

Liver-Stuffed Marrow
Each serving provides: 4 Pro. Ex, 4 Veg. Ex, 1 Fat Ex, 1 Brd. Ex, 20 Cal. Opt. Ex.

Onion and Cheese Scramble
Each serving provides: 2 Pro. Ex, ½ Veg. Ex, 1 Fat Ex, 1 Brd. Ex, 10 Cal. Opt. Ex.

Fruity Lamb Curry
Each serving provides: 4 Pro. Ex, 2½ Veg. Ex, 1 Brd. Ex, 2 Fruit Ex, 20 Cal. Opt. Ex.

Baked Kipper Loaf
Each serving provides: 3 Pro. Ex, ½ Fat Ex, ½ Brd. Ex, 15 Cal. Opt. Ex.

Cheese and Vegetable Pudding
Each serving provides: 2 Pro. Ex, 3 Veg. Ex, ½ Milk Ex, 1 Brd. Ex.

Chicken Liver Croustades with Caper Sauce
Each serving provides: 4 Pro. Ex, ½ Veg. Ex, 1 Fat Ex, 1 Brd. Ex, 60 Cal. Opt. Ex.

Mild Curried Chicken with Banana Rice
Each serving provides: 4 Pro. Ex, 1 Veg. Ex, 1 Fat Ex, 1 Brd. Ex, 1 Fruit Ex, 50 Cal. Opt. Ex.

Marrow Hot Pot
Each serving provides: 2 Pro. Ex, 2 Veg. Ex, 1 Brd. Ex.

Vegetable-Pasta Medley in Onion-Cheddar Sauce
Each serving provides: 1 Pro. Ex, 1½ Veg. Ex, 1 Fat Ex, ¼ Milk Ex, 1 Brd. Ex, 35 Cal. Opt. Ex.

Main Meal Kidney Bean and Ham Soup
Each serving provides: 3 Pro. Ex, 2 Veg. Ex, 1 Fat Ex.

Spiced Meat Balls
Each serving provides: 4 Pro. Ex, 2 Veg. Ex, 2 Brd. Ex, 10 Cal. Opt. Ex.

Traditional Tripe and Onions with Mashed Potato
Each serving provides: 4 Pro. Ex, 1½ Veg. Ex, 3 Fat Ex, ½ Milk Ex, 2 Brd. Ex, 5 Cal. Opt. Ex.

Chicken with Buckwheat
Each serving provides: 3½ Pro. Ex, 1 Veg. Ex, ½ Fat Ex, 1 Brd. Ex, 30 Cal. Opt. Ex.

Danish Haddock
Each serving provides: 4 Pro. Ex, 2 Veg. Ex, ½ Fat Ex, 100 Cal. Opt. Ex.

Italian-Style Scalloped Potatoes
Each serving provides: ½ Pro. Ex, 2 Veg. Ex. 1½ Fat Ex, 1 Brd. Ex, 5 Cal. Opt. Ex.

Parmesan-Topped Stuffed Potato
Each serving provides: 1 Veg. Ex, 1 Fat Ex, 1½ Brd. Ex, 30 Cal. Opt. Ex.

Hot Potato Salad
Each serving provides: 1 Veg. Ex, 1 Fat Ex, 1½ Brd. Ex, 10 Cal. Opt. Ex.

Broccoli-Stuffed Potato
Each serving provides: 1 Pro. Ex, 1 Veg. Ex, 1 Fat Ex, 1½ Brd. Ex.

Brown Sugar Custard
Each serving provides: ½ Pro. Ex, ¼ Milk Ex, 45 Cal. Opt. Ex.

Yogurt 'Cream' Ice with Orange
Each serving provides: 1 Milk Ex, 1 Fruit Ex, 50 Cal. Opt. Ex.

Bread Pudding
For 4 servings – Each serving provides: 1½ Fat Ex, 2 Brd. Ex, 66 Cal. Opt. Ex.
For 8 servings – Each serving provides: ¾ Fat Ex, 1 Brd. Ex, 33 Cal. Opt. Ex.

Raisin-Bread Pudding
Each serving provides: ½ Pro. Ex, 2 Fat Ex, 50 Cal. Opt. Ex.

Orange Spanish 'Cream'
Each serving provides: ¼ Pro. Ex, ½ Fruit Ex, ¼ Milk Ex, 30 Cal. Opt. Ex.

Apricot Surprise
Each serving provides: ½ Pro. Ex, ½ Fat Ex, ½ Milk Ex, 1 Brd. Ex, 1 Fruit Ex, 25 Cal. Opt. Ex.

Blackberry Cheesecake
Each serving provides: ½ Pro. Ex, ¾ Fat Ex, 1 Brd. Ex, ½ Fruit Ex, 55 Cal. Opt. Ex.

Spicy Apple Crumble
Each serving provides: ¾ Fat Ex, 2 Brd. Ex, 1 Fruit Ex, 40 Cal. Opt. Ex.

NON-COOK CREATIONS

Coconut-Bilberry Parfait
Each serving provides: ½ Milk Ex, 1 Brd. Ex, ½ Fruit Ex, 20 Cal. Opt. Ex.

Banana Split Breakfast
Each serving provides: 1 Pro. Ex, 1 Fruit Ex, 30 Cal. Opt. Ex.

Apricot Muesli
Each serving provides: 1 Milk Ex, 2 Brd. Ex, 1 Fruit Ex.

Banana and Peanut Breakfast
Each serving provides: 1 Pro. Ex, 1 Fat Ex, 1 Brd. Ex, 1 Fruit Ex.

Smoked Salmon and Horseradish Relish Appetiser
Each serving provides: 1 Pro. Ex, ½ Veg. Ex, 30 Cal. Opt. Ex.

'Creamy' Cucumber and Lime Starter
Each serving provides: ½ Pro. Ex, ½ Veg. Ex, 1½ Fat Ex, 50 Cal. Opt. Ex.

Tangy Cheese Dip
Each serving provides: ½ Pro. Ex, ½ Veg. Ex, ½ Brd. Ex, 15 Cal. Opt. Ex.

Cucumber-Yogurt Dip
Each serving provides: 2 Veg. Ex, 25 Cal. Opt. Ex.

Honeydew Refresher
Each serving provides: 1 Fruit Ex.

Melon Melange
Each serving provides: 1½ Fruit Ex, 45 Cal. Opt. Ex.

Sardine Dip
Each serving provides: 3 Pro. Ex, ½ Veg. Ex, 3 Fat Ex, 10 Cal. Opt. Ex.

Zippy Parsley Dip
Each serving provides: ½ Pro. Ex, ½ Veg. Ex, 1 Fat Ex, 5 Cal. Opt. Ex.

Smoked Salmon Pate
Each serving provides: 1½ Pro. Ex, 1½ Veg. Ex, ¼ Milk Ex, 1½ Brd. Ex.

Asparagus Vinaigrette
Each serving provides: 2 Veg. Ex, 1½ Fat Ex.

Mixed Green Salad with Dressing
For 6 servings – Each serving provides: 2 Veg. Ex, 2 Fat Ex.
For 8 servings – Each serving provides: 1½ Veg. Ex, 1½ Fat Ex.

Melon and Strawberry Salad
Each serving provides: 1 Fat Ex, 1½ Fruit Ex.

Fruited Coleslaw
Each serving provides: 1 Veg. Ex, 1 Fat Ex, 2 Fruit Ex, 20 Cal. Opt. Ex.

Oriental Ginger Slaw
Each serving provides: 1 Veg. Ex,
1½ Fat Ex, 20 Cal. Opt. Ex.

Jellied Beetroot Salad
Each serving provides: 1 Veg. Ex,
65 Cal. Opt. Ex.

Macaroni-Cheddar Salad
Each serving provides: 1 Pro. Ex, 1
Veg. Ex, 1½ Fat Ex, 1½ Brd. Ex, 20
Cal. Opt. Ex.

**Tomato/Cucumber Salad with
Parsley Dressing**
Each serving provides: 2 Veg. Ex,
1 Fat Ex.

Tabbouleh
Each serving provides: 2 Veg. Ex,
1½ Fat Ex, 1 Brd. Ex.

Spiced Orange Salad
Each serving provides: ½ Veg. Ex,
1½ Fat Ex, 1 Fruit Ex, 10 Cal. Opt.
Ex.

Honeyed Fruit and Carrot Salad
Each serving provides: 1½ Veg.
Ex, 1 Fruit Ex, 15 Cal. Opt. Ex.

Oriental Salad
Each serving provides: 3 Pro. Ex, 1
Veg. Ex, 2 Fat Ex, 1 Brd. Ex, 20 Cal.
Opt. Ex.

Mushroom Salad
Each serving provides: 1½ Veg.
Ex, 1½ Fat Ex.

Salad Nicoise
Each serving provides: 3 Pro. Ex, 1
Veg Ex, 1½ Fat Ex, 15 Cal. Opt. Ex.

Liver Sausage Open Sandwich
Each serving provides: 3 Pro. Ex, 2
Veg. Ex, 1 Fat Ex, 1 Brd. Ex.

Cottage Tomato
Each serving provides: 3 Pro. Ex, 2
Veg. Ex, 3 Fat Ex.

Ploughman's Lunch
Each serving provides: 2 Pro. Ex, 2
Veg. Ex, 2 Fat Ex, 2 Brd. Ex, 150
Cal. Opt. Ex.

**Lamb and Bean Salad with
Vinaigrette Dressing**
Each serving provides: 3 Pro. Ex,
½ Veg. Ex, 1 Fat Ex.

Salmon Pate
Each serving provides: 3 Pro. Ex,
1½ Fat Ex, ½ Brd. Ex.

Banana and Soft Cheese Quickie
Each serving provides: 2 Pro. Ex, 1
Fat Ex, 1 Brd. Ex, 1 Fruit Ex, 30 Cal.
Opt. Ex.

Beef and Tomato Special
Each serving provides: 4 Pro. Ex,
1½ Veg. Ex.

**Cheese Salad with 'Creamy'
Dressing**
Each serving provides: 2 Pro. Ex, 3
Veg. Ex, 1½ Fat Ex, 2 Fruit Ex, 10
Cal. Opt. Ex.

Blackcurrant Cheesecake
Each serving provides: 1 Pro. Ex, 1
Fat Ex, 1 Brd. Ex, ½ Fruit Ex, 100
Cal. Opt. Ex.

Calypso 'Cream'
Each serving provides: 1 Milk Ex, 1
Fruit Ex, 50 Cal. Opt. Ex.

Chocolate Truffles
Each serving provides: ½ Fat Ex,
½ Fruit Ex, 40 Cal. Opt. Ex.

Peanut Butter Bonbons
Each serving provides: 1½ Pro.
Ex, 1½ Fat Ex, ½ Brd. Ex, ½ Fruit
Ex, 5 Cal. Opt. Ex.

Ginger Ice Cream
Each serving provides: 100 Cal.
Opt. Ex.

Mixed Fruit Ambrosia
Each serving provides: 1 Fruit Ex,
20 Cal. Opt. Ex.

Peach Cheesecake
Each serving provides: 1 Fat Ex, 1
Brd. Ex, ¼ Fruit Ex, 75 Cal. Opt.
Ex.

Peanut Fudge Sundae
Each serving provides: 1½ Pro.
Ex, 1½ Fat Ex, ¾ Fruit Ex, 130 Cal.
Opt. Ex.

Cranberry-Orange Relish
Each serving provides: ½ Fruit Ex,
20 Cal. Opt. Ex.

Anchovy-Garlic Dressing
Each serving provides: 1 Pro. Ex, 2
Fat Ex.

Buttermilk-Herb Dressing
Each serving provides: 1½ Fat Ex,
¼ Milk Ex, 20 Cal. Opt. Ex.

**Sweet Herb Vinaigrette
Dressing**
Each serving provides: 1½ Fat Ex,
5 Cal. Opt. Ex.

Spicy Blue Cheese Dressing
Each serving provides: 1 Pro. Ex,
10 Cal. Opt. Ex.

Fruit Flip
Each serving provides: 1 Milk Ex,
¾ Fruit Ex.

Fruity Milk Shake
Each serving provides: ¼ Milk Ex,
1 Fruit Ex, 40 Cal. Opt. Ex.

Strawberry Fizz
Each serving provides: ½ Fruit Ex,
140 Cal. Opt. Ex.

Strawberry Milk Shake
Each serving provides: ½ Milk Ex,
2 Brd. Ex, ½ Fruit Ex, 70 Cal. Opt.
Ex.

READY AND PREPARED

Savoury Cheese on Toast
Each serving provides: 1 Pro. Ex, 1
Veg. Ex, 1 Fat Ex, 1 Brd. Ex.

**Toasted Cheese and Apple
Sandwich**
Each serving provides: 1 Pro. Ex, 2
Fat Ex, 2 Brd. Ex, ½ Fruit Ex.

Bacon Omelette
Each serving provides: 1 Pro. Ex, 2
Fat Ex, 1 Brd. Ex, 100 Cal. Opt. Ex.

Carrot 'Pomerance'
Each serving provides: 2 Veg. Ex,
1 Fruit Ex.

Carrot and Tomato Soup
Each serving provides: 1 Veg. Ex,
½ Fruit Ex.

Cheese and Potato Bake
Each serving provides: 1 Pro. Ex, 1
Brd. Ex, 50 Cal. Opt. Ex.

Mushrooms with Wine
Each serving provides: 1 Veg. Ex,
1 Fat Ex, 1 Brd. Ex, 10 Cal. Opt. Ex.

Minty Cucumber Soup
Each serving provides: 1 Veg. Ex,
½ Milk Ex, 10 Cal. Opt. Ex.

Curried Cauliflower Soup
Each serving provides: 2 Veg. Ex,
2 Brd. Ex.

Cheese-Filled Pears
Each serving provides: 1 Pro. Ex,
1½ Fat Ex, 1 Fruit Ex, 10 Cal. Opt.
Ex.

Piquant Stir-Fried Mushrooms
Each serving provides: 2 Veg. Ex,
1½ Fat Ex, 15 Cal. Opt. Ex.

Italian Tomato-Cheese Salad
Each serving provides: ½ Pro. Ex,
1 Veg. Ex, ½ Fat Ex, 10 Cal. Opt.
Ex.

Courgette and Pepper Salad
Each serving provides: 1 Veg. Ex.

Confetti Rice Salad
Each serving provides: 1 Veg. Ex,
½ Fat Ex, 1 Brd. Ex.

Hot Potato and Pepper Salad
Each serving provides: 1 Veg. Ex,
1 Fat Ex, 1½ Brd. Ex.

Vegetable-Cheddar Salad
Each serving provides: 1 Pro. Ex,
1½ Veg. Ex, 1½ Fat Ex, 20 Cal.
Opt. Ex.

Macaroni Salad
Each serving provides: 1 Veg. Ex,
1½ Fat Ex, 1 Brd. Ex, 25 Cal. Opt.
Ex.

**Baked Vegetable, Cheese and
Egg Pie**
Each serving provides: 2 Pro. Ex,
3½ Veg. Ex, 1 Brd. Ex.

Devilled Lamb
Each serving provides: 4 Pro. Ex,
1½ Fat Ex, 20 Cal. Opt. Ex.

Beef Spread
Each serving provides: 4 Pro. Ex, 1
Veg. Ex, 1 Fat Ex, 1 Brd. Ex.

Tuna Macaroni Salad
Each serving provides: 3 Pro. Ex, 2
Veg. Ex, 1 Brd. Ex, 10 Cal. Opt. Ex.

Sunny Fish Pie
Each serving provides: 4 Pro. Ex,
1½ Veg. Ex, 1 Brd. Ex.

Turkey Pilaf
Each serving provides: 4 Pro. Ex, 2
Veg. Ex, 1 Brd. Ex, ½ Fruit Ex.

Cheesy Danish Mushrooms
Each serving provides: 2 Pro. Ex, 1
Veg. Ex, 1 Brd. Ex.

Egg and Potato Cakes
Each serving provides: 2 Pro. Ex, 2
Veg. Ex, 3 Fat Ex, 2 Brd. Ex, 30 Cal.
Opt. Ex.

Corned Beef Cottage Pie
Each serving provides: 3 Pro. Ex, 1
Veg. Ex, 2 Fat Ex, 2 Brd. Ex.

Hot Asparagus Sandwich
Each serving provides: 2 Pro. Ex, 1
Veg. Ex, 1 Fat Ex, 2 Brd. Ex, 20 Cal.
Opt. Ex.

**Grilled Mackerel and Cheese
Open Sandwich**
Each serving provides: 3 Pro. Ex, 1
Veg. Ex, 1 Brd. Ex.

Curried Rice Salad
Each serving provides: 4 Pro. Ex,
1½ Veg. Ex, 1½ Fat Ex, 1 Brd. Ex,
50 Cal. Opt. Ex.

Liver Sausage Pate
Each serving provides: 1½ Pro.
Ex, 1 Fat Ex, 1 Brd. Ex, 10 Cal. Opt.
Ex.

Spaghetti Carbonara
Each serving provides: 3 Pro. Ex,
½ Veg. Ex, 1 Fat Ex, 1½ Brd. Ex,
40 Cal. Opt. Ex.

Frankfurter-Vegetable Stir Fry
Each serving provides: 3 Pro. Ex, 2
Veg. Ex, 1 Fat Ex, 5 Cal. Opt. Ex.

Mexican Stir Fry
Each serving provides: 2½ Pro.
Ex, 2 Veg. Ex, 1½ Fat Ex, 1 Brd. Ex,
20 Cal. Opt. Ex.

**Turkey with Sweet-and-Sour
Sauce**
Each serving provides: 4 Pro. Ex,
2½ Veg. Ex, 30 Cal. Opt. Ex.

Seasoned Bean and Egg Salad
Each serving provides: 2 Pro. Ex, 2
Veg. Ex, ½ Fat Ex, 10 Cal. Opt. Ex.

Smoked Sausage Savoury
Each serving provides: 4 Pro. Ex,
½ Veg. Ex, 1 Fat Ex, 2 Brd. Ex, 20
Cal. Opt. Ex.

Pilchard Pie
Each serving provides: 4 Pro. Ex, 1
Veg. Ex, 3 Fat Ex, 2 Brd. Ex, 20 Cal.
Opt. Ex.

Pasta Salad
Each serving provides: 3 Pro. Ex, 2
Veg. Ex, 1½ Fat Ex, ½ Brd. Ex.

Oven Cheese Sandwich
Each serving provides: 2 Pro. Ex,
½ Milk Ex, 1 Brd. Ex.

Mackerel Crispies
Each serving provides: 3 Pro. Ex, 2
Veg. Ex, 3 Fat Ex, 1 Brd. Ex, 10 Cal.
Opt. Ex.

**Sweet and Sour Cabbage and
Ham Saute**
Each serving provides: 3 Pro. Ex, 3
Veg. Ex, 1 Fat Ex, 20 Cal. Opt. Ex.

**Rice or Pasta with Quick Meat
Sauce**
Each serving provides: 4 Pro. Ex, 2
Brd. Ex, ¾ Fruit Ex, 20 Cal. Opt.
Ex.

**Savoury Bean and Corned Beef
Bake**
Each serving provides: 5 Pro. Ex, 1
Veg. Ex, 1½ Fat Ex, 1 Brd. Ex.

Chicken Fricassee
Each serving provides: 3 Pro. Ex, 1 Veg. Ex, ½ Milk Ex, 1 Brd. Ex.

Lemon Curd Cheese Mousse
Each serving provides: 1 Pro. Ex, ¼ Milk Ex, 60 Cal. Opt. Ex.

Nutty Chocolate Dream
Each serving provides: 1 Pro. Ex, 1 Fat Ex, ½ Milk Ex, 150 Cal. Opt. Ex.

Fluffy Strawberry Cheesecake
Each serving provides: 1½ Pro. Ex, 2 Fat Ex, 2 Brd. Ex, ¼ Fruit Ex, 25 Cal. Opt. Ex.

COOKING FOR THE FREEZER

Freezer French Toast
Each serving provides: 1 Pro. Ex, ½ Fat Ex, 1 Brd. Ex, 25 Cal. Opt. Ex.
With jam: add 12 Cal. Opt. Ex.
With syrup: add 20 Cal Opt. Ex.

Basic Pancakes
Each serving provides: ½ Pro. Ex, 1 Brd. Ex, 20 Cal. Opt. Ex.

Basic Pastry
Each serving provides: 2 Fat Ex, 1 Brd. Ex, 10 Cal. Opt. Ex.
With cheese: add ½ Pro. Ex.

Basic Pastry Shell
For 4 servings – Each serving provides: 2 Fat Ex, 2/3 Brd. Ex, 10 Cal. Opt. Ex.
For 8 servings – Each serving provides: 1 Fat Ex, 65 Cal. Opt. Ex.

Broccoli Soup
Each serving provides: 1½ Veg. Ex, 20 Cal. Opt. Ex.

'Cream' of Spinach Soup
Each serving provides: 1½ Veg. Ex, ¼ Milk Ex.

Celeriac and Fennel Soup
Each serving provides: 2 Veg. Ex, 1 Fat Ex, 20 Cal. Opt. Ex.

Vegetable Soup
Each serving provides: 2 Veg. Ex, 2 Fat Ex, 15 Cal. Opt. Ex.

Courgette Soup
Each serving provides: 2 Veg. Ex, ¼ Milk Ex.

Leek and Cauliflower Soup
Each serving provides: 1 Veg. Ex, ½ Milk Ex.

Fresh Mushroom Soup
Each serving provides: 1 Veg. Ex, 1 Fat Ex, ¼ Milk Ex, 15 Cal. Opt. Ex.

'Creamed' Tomato Soup
Each serving provides: 1½ Veg. Ex, ½ Fat Ex, ¼ Milk Ex.

Tomato, Onion and Potato Soup
Each serving provides: 5 Veg. Ex, 1 Brd. Ex, 10 Cal. Opt. Ex.

Sweet and Sour Red Cabbage
Each serving provides: 2 Veg. Ex, 1 Fat Ex, 1 Fruit Ex, 30 Cal. Opt. Ex.

Asparagus Quiche
Each serving provides: 1 Pro. Ex, 1½ Veg. Ex, ¾ Milk Ex.

Turkey Pie
Each serving provides: 4 Pro. Ex, 1½ Veg. Ex, 10 Cal. Opt. Ex.

Chicken and Mushroom Pancake Filling
Each serving provides: 3 Pro. Ex, 1 Veg. Ex, 1 Fat Ex, 15 Cal. Opt. Ex.

Seafood Pancake Filling
Each serving provides: 3 Pro. Ex, 1 Veg. Ex, 1 Fat Ex, 5 Cal. Opt. Ex.

Ham and Cabbage Pancake Filling
Each serving provides: 2½ Pro. Ex, 2 Veg. Ex, 1 Fat Ex.

Chilli Veal Pie
Each serving provides: 4½ Pro. Ex, 2 Veg. Ex, ½ Fat Ex, ½ Fruit Ex, 5 Cal. Opt. Ex.

Lambs' Kidneys in Mustard Sauce
Each serving provides: 3 Pro. Ex, ½ Veg. Ex, ¾ Fat Ex.

Beef and Vegetable Pie
Each serving provides: 3 Pro. Ex, 2 Veg. Ex, ½ Fat Ex, 15 Cal. Opt. Ex.

Cornish Style Pasties
Each serving provides: 2 Pro. Ex,
½ Veg. Ex, ½ Brd. Ex.

Homemade Beefburgers
Each serving provides: 4 Pro. Ex,
½ Veg. Ex, ½ Brd. Ex, 20 Cal. Opt.
Ex.

Veal Escalopes with Cheese and Ham
Each serving provides: 4 Pro. Ex, 1
Fat Ex, ½ Brd. Ex, 45 Cal. Opt. Ex.

Veal Balls with Fresh Tomato Sauce
Each serving provides: 4 Pro. Ex,
¼ Veg. Ex, 2 Fat Ex, ½ Brd. Ex, 15
Cal. Opt. Ex.

Tomato Beef Stew
Each serving provides: 4 Pro. Ex,
1½ Veg. Ex, 1½ Fat Ex, ½ Fruit Ex,
15 Cal. Opt. Ex.

Sweet-Sour Meat Balls
Each serving provides: 2 Pro. Ex,
½ Veg. Ex, 15 Cal. Opt. Ex.

Egg, Onion and Fish Pie
Each serving provides: 2½ Pro.
Ex, 1 Veg. Ex, 1 Fat Ex, ¼ Milk Ex,
10 Cal. Opt. Ex.

Parsley Fish Cakes
Each serving provides: 4 Pro. Ex,
1½ Fat Ex, 1½ Brd. Ex.

Fisherman's Pie
Each serving provides: 3 Pro. Ex, 1
Brd. Ex, 95 Cal. Opt. Ex.

Orange Lamb with Rosemary
Each serving provides: 4 Pro. Ex,
½ Veg. Ex, 1 Fat Ex, 1 Brd. Ex, 1
Fruit Ex.

Middle Eastern Lamb
Each serving provides: 4 Pro. Ex,
1½ Veg. Ex, ½ Fruit Ex.

Lamb and Jam
Each serving provides: 3 Pro. Ex, 1
Veg. Ex, 1½ Fat Ex, 40 Cal. Opt.
Ex.

Lamb Curry
Each serving provides: 4 Pro. Ex,
½ Veg. Ex, 1 Fat Ex, 1 Fruit Ex, 10
Cal. Opt. Ex.

Steak Braised in Beer
Each serving provides: 4 Pro. Ex,
½ Veg. Ex, 1 Fat Ex, 25 Cal. Opt.
Ex.

Tuna Mushroom Pie
Each serving provides: 3½ Pro.
Ex, 1 Veg. Ex, ½ Fat Ex, ¼ Milk Ex,
45 Cal. Opt. Ex.

Chicken in Wine
Each serving provides: 5 Pro. Ex, 1
Veg Ex, 2 Fat Ex, 150 Cal. Opt. Ex.

Rose Chicken
Each serving provides: 5 Pro. Ex,
2½ Veg. Ex, 2 Fat Ex, 60 Cal. Opt.
Ex.

Chicken Peasant Style
Each serving provides: 4 Pro. Ex, 2
Veg. Ex, 20 Cal. Opt. Ex.

Hot Chicken and Tomato Bisque
Each serving provides: 2½ Veg.
Ex, ½ Fat Ex, ¼ Milk Ex, 10 Cal.
Opt. Ex.

French Bread Pizza
Each serving provides: 3 Pro. Ex,
1½ Veg. Ex, 2 Fat Ex, 3 Brd. Ex, 30
Cal. Opt. Ex.

**French Bread Four Ways –
– with onion spread**
Each serving provides: ⅛ Veg. Ex,
1 Fat Ex.

– Garlic-Herb 'Butter'
Each serving provides: 1 Fat Ex.

– Cheese Spread
Each serving provides: 1 Fat Ex, 10
Cal. Opt. Ex.

– Anchovy 'Butter'
Each serving provides: 1 Fat Ex, 5
Cal. Opt. Ex.

Fish in Wine and Tomato Sauce
Each serving provides: 4 Pro. Ex,
1½ Veg. Ex, 1½ Fat Ex, 15 Cal.
Opt. Ex.

Cod in Pepper Sauce
Each serving provides: 4 Pro. Ex, 1 Veg. Ex, 20 Cal. Opt. Ex.

Hot Tomato Sauce
Each serving provides: ½ Veg. Ex, 15 Cal. Opt. Ex.

Bechamel (White Sauce)
Each serving provides: 1½ Fat Ex, ¼ Milk Ex, 40 Cal. Opt. Ex.

Mushroom Sauce (1)
Each serving provides: ½ Veg. Ex, ½ Fat Ex, 25 Cal. Opt. Ex.

Mushroom Sauce (2)
Each serving provides: ½ Veg. Ex, 5 Cal. Opt. Ex.

Plum Sauce
Each serving provides: ¾ Fruit Ex, 15 Cal. Opt. Ex.

Paprikash Sauce
Each serving provides: 1 Veg. Ex, 5 Cal. Opt. Ex.

Strawberry Sauce
Each serving provides: 35 Cal. Opt. Ex.

Apricot and Pineapple Upside-Down Cake
Each serving provides: ½ Pro. Ex, 1 Fat Ex, 1 Brd. Ex, ½ Fruit Ex, 130 Cal. Opt. Ex.

Apricot and Orange Frozen Dessert
Each serving provides: 2 Fruit Ex, 20 Cal. Opt. Ex.

'Apple Cake'
Each serving provides: 1½ Fat Ex, ½ Brd. Ex, 1 Fruit Ex, 70 Cal. Opt. Ex.

Apricot Crunch
Each serving provides: 3 Fat Ex, 2 Brd. Ex, 1 Fruit Ex, 50 Cal. Opt. Ex.

Plum Compote
Each serving provides: 1 Fruit Ex, 15 Cal. Opt. Ex.

Gooseberry Treat
Each serving provides: 3 Fat Ex, 1½ Brd. Ex, 1 Fruit Ex, 45 Cal. Opt. Ex.

Apple Crumble
Each serving provides: ½ Fat Ex, 1 Brd. Ex, 1 Fruit Ex, 5 Cal. Opt. Ex.

Mango Sherbert
Each serving provides: ¼ Milk Ex, 1 Fruit Ex, 20 Cal. Opt. Ex.

Apricot-Yogurt Sorbet
Each serving provides: ¼ Fruit Ex, 20 Cal. Opt. Ex.

Ginger Biscuit Cones
Each serving provides: 1 Fat Ex, 65 Cal. Opt. Ex.

Vanilla Fudge Swirl
Each serving provides: 150 Cal. Opt. Ex.

Rum Raisin 'Ice Cream'
Each serving provides: ½ Fruit Ex, 100 Cal. Opt. Ex.

Coffee-Rum 'Ice Cream'
Each serving provides: 65 Cal. Opt. Ex.

Rum and Orange Sorbet
Each serving provides: ¾ Milk Ex, 50 Cal. Opt. Ex.

Tropical Muffins
Each serving provides: 1½ Fat Ex, 1 Brd. Ex, 20 Cal. Opt. Ex.

Sultana Biscuits
Each serving provides: 1 Fat Ex, 1 Brd. Ex, ¼ Fruit Ex, 20 Cal. Opt. Ex.

Peanut Butter Muffins
Each serving provides: 1 Pro. Ex, 1¼ Fat Ex, ½ Brd. Ex, 25 Cal. Opt. Ex.

GUESTS ARE COMING

Avocado Salad
Each serving provides: 1 Veg. Ex, 1½ Fat Ex, 120 Cal. Opt. Ex.

Avocado and Pink Grapefruit Starter with Creamy Cheese Sauce
Each serving provides: ½ Pro. Ex, 1 Fruit Ex, 110 Cal. Opt. Ex.

Warming Winter Soup
Each serving provides: 2 Veg. Ex,
5 Cal. Opt. Ex.

Avocado and Cheese Creams
Each serving provides: 1 Pro. Ex,
150 Cal. Opt. Ex.

Cheese, Prawn and Pear Cocktail
Each serving provides: 1½ Pro.
Ex, 1 Fruit Ex, 20 Cal. Opt. Ex.

Savoury Prawn Starter
Each serving provides: 1 Pro. Ex,
½ Veg. Ex, ¼ Milk Ex, 15 Cal. Opt.
Ex.

Stuffed Pasta Shell Starter
Each serving provides: 2 Pro. Ex,
½ Veg. Ex, ½ Fat Ex, 1 Brd. Ex, ½
Fruit Ex, 20 Cal. Opt. Ex.

Smoked Cod's Roe Pate
Each serving provides: 2 Pro. Ex, 3
Fat Ex, 1 Brd. Ex, 35 Cal. Opt. Ex.

Crab Mousse
Each serving provides: 1¼ Pro.
Ex, 15 Cal. Opt. Ex.

Salmon Mousse
Each serving provides: 1 Pro. Ex,
1½ Fat Ex, 20 Cal. Opt. Ex.

Tuna and Parsley Pate
Each serving provides: 1 Pro. Ex, 1
Brd. Ex, 35 Cal. Opt. Ex.

Cream of Pea and Asparagus Soup
Each serving provides: 2 Veg. Ex,
35 Cal. Opt. Ex.

Asparagus with Sesame 'Butter'
Each serving provides: 2 Veg. Ex,
1 Fat Ex, 10 Cal. Opt. Ex.

Tangy Broccoli Salad
Each serving provides: 2 Veg Ex,
1½ Fat Ex.

Cauliflower Provencale
Each serving provides: 4½ Veg.
Ex, 1½ Fat Ex, 20 Cal. Opt. Ex.

Apple and Sweet Potato
Each serving provides: ½ Veg. Ex,
1½ Fat Ex, 1 Brd. Ex, 1 Fruit Ex, 20
Cal. Opt. Ex.

Aubergine Provencale
Each serving provides: 2 Veg. Ex,
1½ Fat Ex.

Marinated Roasted Peppers
Each serving provides: 2 Veg. Ex,
5 Cal. Opt. Ex.

Italian Salad
Each serving provides: 2 Veg. Ex,
1½ Fat Ex, 1 Brd. Ex, 20 Cal. Opt.
Ex.

Spinach Stuffed Mushrooms
Each serving provides: 1 Pro. Ex,
2½ Veg. Ex, 1½ Fat Ex, 1 Brd. Ex.

Meat Loaf Wellington
Each serving provides: 3 Pro. Ex, 1
Veg. Ex, 1 Fat Ex, 1 Brd. Ex, 20 Cal.
Opt. Ex.

Rabbit Stew in White Wine Sauce
Each serving provides: 4 Pro. Ex,
1½ Veg. Ex, 1 Fat Ex, 30 Cal. Opt.
Ex.

Ham Rice and Orange Salad
Each serving provides: 4 Pro. Ex, 1
Veg. Ex, 3 Fat Ex, 2 Brd. Ex, ½ Fruit
Ex.

Ham and Cabbage Pancakes
See individual recipes.

Leek and Cheese Crumble
Each serving provides: 2 Pro. Ex,
1½ Veg. Ex, 1½ Fat Ex, ½ Milk Ex,
1 Brd. Ex, 25 Cal. Opt. Ex.

Chicken with Ham and Cheese
Each serving provides: 3½ Pro.
Ex, 1½ Fat Ex, 30 Cal. Opt. Ex.

Oriental Chicken Livers en Brochette
Each serving provides: 4 Pro. Ex, 2
Veg. Ex, 15 Cal. Opt. Ex.

Chicken Veronique
Each serving provides: 4 Pro. Ex, 1
Veg. Ex, 1 Fat Ex, 1 Brd. Ex, ½ Fruit
Ex, 25 Cal. Opt. Ex.

Haddock Provencale
Each serving provides: 4 Pro. Ex, 219
½ Veg. Ex, 1½ Fat Ex, 30 Cal. Opt.
Ex.

Prawn Fandango
Each serving provides: 5 Pro. Ex, 1 220
Veg. Ex, 1½ Fat Ex, 1 Brd. Ex, 35
Cal. Opt. Ex.

Yogurt-Caraway Quiche
Each serving provides: 2 Pro. Ex,
½ Veg. Ex, ½ Fat Ex, 15 Cal. Opt.
Ex.

Fiesta Chicken
Each serving provides: 4 Pro. Ex,
1½ Veg. Ex, 1 Fat Ex, 1 Brd. Ex, 10
Cal. Opt. Ex.

Crispy Cinnamon-Chicken Bake
Each serving provides: 6 Pro. Ex, 1
Fat Ex, ½ Brd. Ex, 40 Cal. Opt. Ex.

**Oven-Fried Chicken with
Orange Teriyaki Sauce**
Each serving provides: 4 Pro. Ex,
½ Veg. Ex, 1 Fat Ex, 1 Brd. Ex, ½
Fruit Ex, 20 Cal. Opt. Ex.

Chicken-Mushroom Pancakes
See individual recipes.

Curried Chicken with Melon
Each serving provides: 5 Pro. Ex,
½ Veg. Ex, 1 Fat Ex, 1 Fruit Ex, 20
Cal. Opt. Ex.

Nutty Stuffed Chicken Breasts
Each serving provides: 3½ Pro.
Ex, 1 Veg. Ex, 3 Fat Ex, 80 Cal. Opt.
Ex.

Chinese-Style Pork
Each serving provides: 3 Pro. Ex, 1
Veg. Ex, 1 Brd. Ex, 15 Cal. Opt. Ex.

**Orange-Ginger-Glazed Pork
Chops**
Each serving provides: 4 Pro. Ex,
½ Veg. Ex, 1 Fat Ex, 1 Fruit Ex, 20
Cal. Opt. Ex.

216

Seafood Pancakes
See individual recipes.

Oriental Marinated Cod
Each serving provides: 4 Pro. Ex,
10 Cal. Opt. Ex.

Salmon Kedgeree
Each serving provides: 2 Pro. Ex, 1
Fat Ex, ¼ Milk Ex, 1 Brd. Ex.

Lamb Korma
Each serving provides: 4 Pro. Ex, 1
Veg. Ex, 1½ Fat Ex, 1 Milk Ex, 1
Brd. Ex.

Tuna and Tomato Quiche
Each serving provides: 4 Pro. Ex, 1
Veg. Ex, 3 Fat Ex, ¼ Milk Ex, 2 Brd.
Ex.

**Prawns and Noodles with
Tangy Tomato Sauce**
Each serving provides: 5 Pro. Ex, 3
Veg. Ex, 1½ Fat Ex, 1 Brd. Ex, 5
Cal. Opt. Ex.

Sauteed Chilli Prawns
Each serving provides: 5 Pro. Ex, 2
Veg. Ex, 1½ Fat Ex, 20 Cal. Opt.
Ex.

Tuna Crunch
Each serving provides: 2½ Pro.
Ex, ½ Veg. Ex, ½ Fat Ex, ½ Brd.
Ex.

'Frying Pan' Broccoli Souffle
Each serving provides: 2 Pro. Ex, 1
Veg. Ex, 1 Fat Ex, 5 Cal. Opt. Ex.

Veal Patties in Parsley Sauce
Each serving provides: 3½ Pro.
Ex, ½ Veg. Ex, 1½ Fat Ex, ½ Milk
Ex, ½ Brd. Ex, 5 Cal. Opt. Ex.

**Fish Salad with Chilli
Mayonnaise**
Each serving provides: 4 Pro. Ex,
2½ Veg. Ex, 1½ Fat Ex, 15 Cal.
Opt. Ex.

Rolled, Stuffed Plaice Fillets
Each serving provides: 4 Pro. Ex, 1
Veg. Ex, 1½ Fat Ex, 10 Cal. Opt.
Ex.

Carrot Cake
Each serving provides: ¼ Pro. Ex,
1 Veg. Ex, ½ Brd. Ex, ½ Fruit Ex,
30 Cal. Opt. Ex.

Festive Melon Baskets
Each serving provides: 2 Fruit Ex,
30 Cal. Opt. Ex.

Wine-Poached Pears
Each serving provides: 1 Fruit Ex,
100 Cal. Opt. Ex.

Pineapple Cheesecake
Each serving provides: 1 Pro. Ex,
1½ Fat Ex, 1½ Brd. Ex, ½ Fruit Ex,
80 Cal. Opt. Ex.

Mandarin Cheesecake
Each serving provides: ½ Pro. Ex,
1 Fat Ex, 1 Brd. Ex, ¼ Fruit Ex, 15
Cal. Opt. Ex.

Glazed Apricot Dessert
Each serving provides: 1 Fat Ex, 1
Brd. Ex, 1½ Fruit Ex, 5 Cal. Opt.
Ex.

Mince Pies
Each serving provides: 1½ Fat Ex,
1 Brd. Ex, ½ Fruit Ex, 25 Cal. Opt.
Ex.

**Chocolate and Banana Crunch
Pies**
Each serving provides: 3 Fat Ex, 1
Brd. Ex, 1 Fruit Ex, 150 Cal. Opt.
Ex.

Orange 'Cream' Pancakes
Each serving provides: 1 Pro. Ex, 1
Fruit Ex, 40 Cal. Opt. Ex.

Pineapple Fizz
Each serving provides: 1 Fruit Ex,
5 Cal. Opt. Ex.

Ginger Kisses
Each serving provides: 2 Fat Ex, 1
Brd. Ex, 45 Cal. Opt. Ex.

Strawberry Chiffon
Each serving provides: ½ Fruit Ex,
105 Cal. Opt. Ex.

Fruit Flapjacks
Each serving provides: ½ Pro. Ex,
1½ Fat Ex, 1 Brd. Ex, 1 Fruit Ex, 40
Cal. Opt. Ex.

Swiss Pudding
Each serving provides: ½ Fat Ex,
¾ Milk Ex, 1 Brd. Ex, 1 Fruit Ex, 45
Cal. Opt. Ex.

Apricot-Raisin Crescents
Each serving provides: 2 Fruit Ex,
50 Cal. Opt. Ex.

Spiced Scones
Each serving provides: 3 Fat Ex, 1
Brd. Ex, ½ Fruit Ex, 35 Cal. Opt.
Ex.

Strawberry Cheesecake
Each serving provides: 1 Pro. Ex,
1½ Brd. Ex, 1 Fat Ex, 40 Cal. Opt.
Ex.

Orange Loaf
Each serving provides: ½ Pro. Ex,
1 Fat Ex, 2 Brd. Ex, ½ Fruit Ex, 40
Cal. Opt. Ex.

Fabulous Fruit Cup
Each serving provides: 3½ Fruit
Ex, 100 Cal. Opt. Ex.

Sweet Jam Biscuits
Each serving provides: 2 Fat Ex, 1
Brd. Ex, 50 Cal. Opt. Ex.

Apple-Ale Punch
Each serving provides: 15 Cal.
Opt. Ex.

Orange Tonic
Each serving provides: 1 Fruit Ex.

Banana Flip
Each serving provides: ½ Milk Ex,
1 Fruit Ex, 130 Cal. Opt. Ex.

Avocado Cocktail Canapes
Each serving provides: ½ Veg. Ex,
½ Brd. Ex, 50 Cal. Opt. Ex.

Cheddar-Beer Crackers
Each serving provides: ½ Pro. Ex,
1 Fat Ex, 1 Brd. Ex, 15 Cal. Opt. Ex.

Golden 'Eggnog'
Each serving provides: ½ Milk Ex,
145 Cal. Opt. Ex.

Ham and Cheese Buffet Whirls
Each serving provides: ½ Pro. Ex.

'Orange-Cream' Stuffed Prunes
Each serving provides: 1½ Fruit
Ex, 10 Cal. Opt. Ex.

Tropical Wine Punch
Each serving provides: 60 Cal.
Opt. Ex.

Cocktail Toasties
Each serving provides: ½ Veg. Ex,
½ Fat Ex, 1 Brd. Ex, 10 Cal. Opt.
Ex.

Cheese Straws
Each serving provides: 3 Fat Ex, ½
Brd. Ex, 15 Cal. Opt. Ex.

'Martini'
Each serving provides: 103 Cal.
Opt. Ex.

Mimosa
Each serving provides: ¼ Fruit Ex,
45 Cal. Opt. Ex.

INDEX

269